DEVELOPING AN ONLINE CURRICULUM: TECHNOLOGIES AND TECHNIQUES

LYNNETTE R. PORTER
EMBRY-RIDDLE AERONAUTICAL UNIVERSITY, USA

Information Science Publishing

Hershey • London • Melbourne • Singapore

Acquisition Editor:	Mehdi Khosrow-Pour
Senior Managing Editor:	Jan Travers
Managing Editor:	Amanda Appicello
Development Editor:	Michele Rossi
Copy Editor:	Michelle Wilgenburg
Typesetter:	Amanda Appicello
Cover Design:	Weston Pritts
Printed at:	Integrated Book Technology

Published in the United States of America by
> Information Science Publishing (an imprint of Idea Group Inc.)
> 701 E. Chocolate Avenue, Suite 200
> Hershey PA 17033-1240
> Tel: 717-533-8845
> Fax: 717-533-8661
> E-mail: cust@idea-group.com
> Web site: http://www.idea-group.com

and in the United Kingdom by
> Information Science Publishing (an imprint of Idea Group Inc.)
> 3 Henrietta Street
> Covent Garden
> London WC2E 8LU
> Tel: 44 20 7240 0856
> Fax: 44 20 7379 3313
> Web site: http://www.eurospan.co.uk

Library of Congress Cataloging-in-Publication Data

Porter, Lynnette R., 1957-
  Developing an online curriculum : technologies and
techniques / Lynnette R. Porter.
      p. cm.
Includes bibliographical references (p.) and index.
  ISBN 1-59140-136-4 (hardcover) -- ISBN 1-59140-137-2 (ebook)
  1. Instructional systems--Design. 2. Internet in higher education.
3. Education, Higher--Effect of technological innovations on. I.
Title.
  LB1028.38.P67 2003
  378.1'734--dc21
                                                           2003008876

Paperback ISBN 1-59140-226-3 √

British Cataloguing in Publication Data
A Cataloguing in Publication record for this book is available from the British Library.

All work contributed to this book is new, previously-unpublished material. The views expressed in this book are those of the authors, but not necessarily of the publisher.

NEW Titles
from Information Science Publishing

- **Instructional Design in the Real World: A View from the Trenches**
  Anne-Marie Armstrong
  ISBN: 1-59140-150-X: eISBN 1-59140-151-8, © 2004
- **Personal Web Usage in the Workplace: A Guide to Effective Human Resources Management**
  Murugan Anandarajan & Claire Simmers
  ISBN: 1-59140-148-8; eISBN 1-59140-149-6, © 2004
- **Social, Ethical and Policy Implications of Information Technology**
  Linda L. Brennan & Victoria Johnson
  ISBN: 1-59140-168-2; eISBN 1-59140-169-0, © 2004
- **Readings in Virtual Research Ethics: Issues and Controversies**
  Elizabeth A. Buchanan
  ISBN: 1-59140-152-6; eISBN 1-59140-153-4, © 2004
- **E-ffective Writing for e-Learning Environments**
  Katy Campbell
  ISBN: 1-59140-124-0; eISBN 1-59140-125-9, © 2004
- **Development and Management of Virtual Schools: Issues and Trends**
  Catherine Cavanaugh
  ISBN: 1-59140-154-2; eISBN 1-59140-155-0, © 2004
- **The Distance Education Evolution: Case Studies**
  Dominique Monolescu, Catherine Schifter & Linda Greenwood
  ISBN: 1-59140-120-8; eISBN 1-59140-121-6, © 2004
- **Distance Learning and University Effectiveness: Changing Educational Paradigms for Online Learning**
  Caroline Howard, Karen Schenk & Richard Discenza
  ISBN: 1-59140-178-X; eISBN 1-59140-179-8, © 2004
- **Managing Psychological Factors in Information Systems Work: An Orientation to Emotional Intelligence**
  Eugene Kaluzniacky
  ISBN: 1-59140-198-4; eISBN 1-59140-199-2, © 2004
- **Developing an Online Curriculum: Technologies and Techniques**
  Lynnette R. Porter
  ISBN: 1-59140-136-4; eISBN 1-59140-137-2, © 2004
- **Online Collaborative Learning: Theory and Practice**
  Tim S. Roberts
  ISBN: 1-59140-174-7; eISBN 1-59140-175-5, © 2004

Excellent additions to your institution's library! Recommend these titles to your librarian!

To receive a copy of the Idea Group Inc. catalog, please contact
1/717-533-8845, fax 1/717-533-8661,or visit the IGI Online Bookstore at:
http://www.idea-group.com!

Note: All IGI books are also available as ebooks on netlibrary.com as well as other ebook sources. Contact Ms. Carrie Skovrinskie at <cskovrinskie@idea-group.com> to receive a complete list of sources where you can obtain ebook information or IGP titles.

Dedication

To Heather and her generation of learners who must benefit from what we create online.

Developing an Online Curriculum: Technologies and Techniques

Table of Contents

Preface

The information in the following chapters has been designed for university or college teachers who are or will become involved with online education. The emphasis is on teachers, because they are working in the front lines of online education. *You* throughout the text refers to *teachers.* However, administrators, course designers, technical specialists, and other institutional personnel should find the book useful. In particular, administrators should read the final chapter, which covers topics relevant to current and future success with an institution's online curricula.

Curriculum planning is an ongoing, often arduous activity, and envisioning the way that courses effectively fit together into programs within one or many disciplines is challenging. Teachers often are more likely to be involved with the planning or revision of individual courses, which will become important touchstones within the curriculum. Planning information for creating a new course or updating a course currently offered online should help teachers develop more effective materials to use with a wide variety of learners.

Once a course is in place, teachers may need additional guidance about using the tools required to access the information from a course Web site, as well as to work with learners in real time or at their own pace. Finally, keeping the online course current is as important as starting it off right, and information about working with administrators in particular is critical for getting what teachers need to advance professionally and to keep online education on track academically. Curriculum and course planning and development are both pedagogical and technological activities for universities and colleges. As the academic realm is forced to change at a rapid pace, the development and dissemination of information electronically become even more important.

Administrators, course designers, and others who work within the framework of a university, college, or other academic institution can use this information to learn how to work with teachers more effectively and to further the effectiveness of online education. Online teachers cannot work effectively if they do not have support from other faculty members and administrators. All levels of administration must work well together and share a coherent, cohesive vision for planning the direction that online activities will take, and administrators must be aware of the special pressures and concerns shared by online educators.

Although administrators and information designers may initially plan an online program, teachers are needed to develop viable ideas about what is required in a course and how the information should be structured. Teachers who work with learners daily understand the needs of their target audience and the language, graphic information, activities, and assignments that will work most effectively with these students. Teachers and administrators should gather feedback from learners to guide the development processes of individual courses and an entire curriculum. Although teachers may or may not have the technical expertise to implement an instructional design, they should be actively involved in developing course structures and materials.

As well, because online courses will be facilitated by teachers, they should help determine which tools are most effective and how practical a course site is for learners and other educators. Teachers will keep track of the glitches that occur among site users and the difficulty or ease with which learners work with the textual and graphical information provided at or linked to the course Web site. They will hear the praise or complaints about the course—not only from learners, but from colleagues. Therefore, teachers must be actively involved in the design and facilitation stages.

Many administrators began their careers in academia as teachers and gradually moved away from the daily rigors of teaching to focus on the institution's larger missions, such as recruiting learners, marketing courses and programs to generate interest in them, hiring and retaining faculty, and writing and updating a strategic plan. These activities fall within the broader scope of making the online programs within an academic institution worthy of respect. They make sure that online programs are able to achieve accreditation by recognized educational entities, as well as remain viable in the marketplace.

Simply by the nature of administration and the volume of the workload, administrators may eventually lose touch with the day-to-day practices of teaching and the needs of teachers and learners. However, teachers should at least be consulted as a curriculum or even a course is being developed or evaluated. Working with teachers to ensure high-quality academic programs that are relevant to learners is crucial for an online program's success. Making sure that teachers also have incentives and support is equally important; teachers must be given the time and assistance so that they can keep up with trends in online education and remain effective online educators. Administrators must work closely with teachers throughout the ongoing process of developing courses and curricula.

What You Should Already Know

If you are reading this book, you (or key members of your institution) should already be familiar with online education and have decided that you need a new online course or program. The basic curriculum is probably in place, but you need to decide whether it should be offered online in addition to on site, or if only certain courses need to be provided to an online audience. You understand how a new online course will supplement or modify the existing curriculum.

The focus of this book is not to help you decide *if* online education is the right choice. The emphasis is on how you can continue to improve personal performance in the online classroom and to ensure that the classes offer high-quality instruction through a variety of electronic media currently available across the Internet. It is designed to help you consider your response to the changing nature of online education and to be aware of recurring issues that affect teachers' and learners' performance and retention. If your institution already has taken the plunge and is planning to develop an online curriculum for a new program or modify an existing online set of programs or courses, the information in this book helps you go beyond the basics.

The Wide Variety of Vendors of Educational Information

Even within a traditional academic institution, the variety of course offerings and ways that learners can access educational information may be staggering. You may find that the nature of your academic setting is changing rapidly; you may teach on site one time and in a Web-enhanced classroom or purely via the Internet during the next term.

Some online institutions operate through an electronic campus with few, if any, physical buildings. Other academic institutions may be newer offshoots of the traditional campus model, where learners can visit a physical campus for on-site classes, as well as participate in online courses offered by the school. Developing an online curriculum can encompass both on-site and online courses together or online courses only, whichever is determined appropriate for that particular institution and the types and levels of instruction it offers.

However, online education is offered by other providers, too. Many businesses, companies, and individuals also develop online courses. Like any other educational offering, the quality of instruction, the cost of the education, and the quality of course materials vary among online providers. Businesses operate differently from academic institutions, which deal with issues like accreditation and tenure, and may focus more on e-learning or e-training than broader degree preparation.

For-profit companies, such as booksellers, market non-credit, personal interest classes. Entrepreneurial businesses may specialize in self-help courses ranging from filing taxes to growing an herbal garden. Individuals who want to share their knowledge about a particular subject—for a fee or free—develop online courses for the Internet public. Just about anyone today can provide information online, much of it deemed "educational." The number and types of training and academic programs increase with the popularity and growth of the Internet in general and online education specifically. For the public, *online education* may have very different definitions from those that can pertain to your institution's course offerings.

These basic differences in philosophy or purpose among creators of online courses may affect the number and type of programs that your institution offers. The spectrum of the types of online courses, their costs, projected outcomes (e.g., a degree, certification, or personal enjoyment), quality, and accessibility broadly spans many businesses and academic institutions worldwide. Part of your job is to help define what *online education* means for your institution and to decide what types of interaction are appropriate for people who come to your programs for educational experiences.

Fee structures, technology, and even the definition of what an online course is or should be point out some differences among educational programs or classes. Your institution must decide where its course offerings fit among all those offered by competitors. Not only the quality of education, but the way it has been designed and its purposes are the result of differing concepts of effective online learning. You, and members of your academic institution, must agree on what exactly will be provided and how online education fits with your particular college's or university's mission.

The technology needed to present online courses or programs also differs among vendors. Not all online classes have to use the latest gadgets or multimedia designs to be effective. Technology changes, some would say progresses, rapidly, and certainly there are higher-tech classes than those described in this book. No doubt the amount of technology and the availability of non-print-based media mean that online classes need to keep being upgraded.

However, many worthwhile programs rely primarily on e-mail and other text-only forms of information and communication. The lower-tech applications, simply because that's where many programs are and where many potential learners start out, are described in the application sections of this book, although the design and teaching principles apply both to low-tech or high-tech online classrooms.

Completely automated programs are not included in this discussion. The human touch, as provided by teachers/facilitators, administrators, staff, and mentors, is important for the success of most online curricula in academic settings. Teacher/student relationships are therefore recommended and emphasized in each chapter. Determining how much technology is needed to meet the needs of learners and the demands of a specific subject is also an important part of developing successful online programs.

How much information is truly electronic, how students interact with teachers and other learners, and how the courses are set up depend on the individual definition of *online education*. By the time you finish using this book, you should be familiar with several possible definitions and should be able to define *online education* for your institutional situation. You also should have a clearer vision of what is needed to develop an online course and to facilitate an online class—tasks that are part of the larger activities required for developing an online curriculum.

The Structure of This Book

Faculty who are interested in developing a curriculum that can be tailored to meet accreditation standards or can be designed based on educational pedagogy should find the following chapters informative and practical. Teachers building an online curriculum can use this information to design classes or entire programs for specific clientele. For example, the methods of teaching young students and the requirements for public elementary and secondary education differ from those for teaching in private institutions or post-secondary programs, but they have in common the principles of working online. Teachers from all types of institutions should be able to apply the ideas in the following chapters to their specific work environments.

The book has been organized into three sections of three chapters each. Activities associated with curriculum planning through evaluation and change fall within three primary tasks:

1. Developing the curriculum

2. Implementing the curriculum

3. Maintaining the curriculum

Each of these tasks is discussed within a separate section.

The first section explains how to *develop* the curriculum. Part 1 consists of Chapter 1. Facilitating the Online Curriculum, Chapter 2. Adding a Course to the Curriculum, and Chapter 3. Updating and Developing Course Materials. These background chapters illustrate how to add new courses to an online curriculum and are especially well suited for new online teachers or teachers who significantly need to update an online curriculum.

Part 2 covers the ways to *implement* the curriculum through teaching online courses. This section is made up of Chapter 4. The Tools of the Trade, Chapter 5. The Daily Work of Teaching, and Chapter 6. The Aesthetics of Teaching. These chapters offer practical guidance for managing online classes and facilitating learning. They explain how to put the courses in place and work with learners regularly.

Part 3 describes how to *maintain* the courses for the curriculum to be competitive and relevant, and to attract and retain learners and teachers. In addition to teachers, administrators and course planners should find this section practical. This section consists of Chapter 7. Developing Support Networks, Chapter 8. Managing Programs and Faculty Concerns, and Chapter 9. Planning for the Future. Information to keep your curriculum fresh is highlighted in this section. Issues that have an impact on teacher training and retention also are featured.

Each part is prefaced with an overview. References are listed at the end of each chapter. An index of keywords highlights major concepts across the three sections, and a glossary summarizes the concepts and explains acronyms and abbreviations used throughout the book.

Some examples and lists include URLs/URIs and other information based on a university's or a publication's Web site. All information was available in late 2002.

Call for Action in Online Education

Online teaching can be highly rewarding and enjoyable, but much needs to be done to improve the online learning community and make education more accessible to students worldwide. Educators should look forward to the day when all teachers receive the same understanding, respect, and recognition, whether they teach purely online, on site, or through a combination of the two. Online education should not be second class, in quality or respectability. Perhaps this book will encourage more academicians to continue to improve online education and to share their love of teaching with more students through the Internet.

The state of online education is changing rapidly, and some educators rightly call it a revolution. Some issues to think about in developing an online curriculum are highlighted in the book, but by no means are definitive solutions proposed. The nature of online education should continue to be debated within individual universities or colleges and across the broad spectrum of academia. Summaries of concerns and directions proposed by online educators are featured in this book, particularly in the last chapter.

In the interest of high-quality online education, and the variety of forms it currently takes, the debate must continue, and educators must respond more quickly to the challenges facing us. It is impossible to keep up with all the latest advancements, but as educators entrusted with the preparation of younger students and adult learners, we must become actively involved in the discussions about pedagogy, the nature of academic institutions, and the roles of teachers in the educational process.

Acknowledgments

I thank the many online teachers, course designers, and administrators who have talked with me, formally or informally, about distance learning and online education. I have gained a greater understanding about the scope of online education by talking with educators at conferences, via bulletin board discussions, in e-mail messages, and through online workshops and classes. In particular, I acknowledge the faculty at Embry-Riddle Aeronautical University, Daytona Beach, Florida; the faculty, staff, and administrators at Franklin University, Columbus, Ohio; and participants of conferences held by the Society for Technical Communication, Asia-Pacific Chapter of the Association for the Advancement of Computing in Education, and Australasian Society for Computers in Learning in Tertiary Education; these educators provided me with valuable insights about their work.

I also thank Amanda Story for her work as a reader during the revision process.

I could not have completed this book without editorial assistance from Bartley Porter. My thanks go to Jimmie, Nancy, Heather, and Elvis for helping out in many ways.

PART 1.

DEVELOPING THE

CURRICULUM

In Part 1, you will read about the activities and issues that are especially important in developing an effective curriculum design. Planning an online course requires the cooperation of many people and reflects many possible design scenarios. Teachers must be an important part of the development team.

As a teacher, you are actively involved with the educational process and should understand the needs and expectations of learners. You should collaborate with learners to gather their ideas about what should be included in an online course or curriculum. You should be highly familiar with the subject areas you teach and therefore realize what needs to be included for a course to be relevant. You should have a good idea where each course fits into the overall curricular plan, and what information and skills activities need to be included within a particular structure. The sequencing and structuring of individual learning units should follow a logical plan, which has been ascertained, by you and other subject experts, to be most important for learning about a specific discipline.

You also see how individual courses fit together, and when one course needs to be developed as the whole curriculum shifts toward a new direction or is expanded to meet new demands. You have a good feel for which individual courses need to be developed, as well as how the entire curriculum should be modified.

However, what you may lack is the technical know-how to put this information in place. You might also be a wonderful on-site teacher, but this is your first opportunity to develop a course or provide suggestions toward an online curriculum for students who will work with a variety of electronic tools and complete much of a course without your direct supervision. As a teacher, then, you may work with course designers, other teachers, and administrators as a member of a course- or curriculum-development team. Part 1 should help you design new online courses or update existing ones as part of a larger curriculum.

In Chapter 1. Facilitating the Online Curriculum, you will read definitions and descriptions of topics important for a basic understanding of online education. You also will read more about the special considerations that make online education both challenging and rewarding. You will need to emphasize the strengths of online education as you develop your courses or an entire curriculum for electronic media.

Chapter 2. Adding a Course to the Curriculum covers information to help you, alone or collaboratively, plan the day-to-day workings of a class. This chapter is important for all teachers to read, but it has been especially designed for those who are planning a new course or significantly changing an existing course.

In Chapter 3. Updating and Developing Course Materials, you will look at the ideas described in Chapter 2 about course materials in greater depth. The types of materials you, or you and others, will develop as part of an effective curriculum are described and illustrated in more detail. This information may help you build models for your own courses.

A special section provides ideas for teachers who will be using someone else's design, but modifying the course to make it their own. Becoming familiar with someone else's course design and online materials is important so that you either do not feel overwhelmed as you go through the course or feel tempted to put the class on autopilot as learners use the materials. Making a class your own, and knowing how to work within the technical and educational structures of someone else's course design, are important for success as an online teacher.

Planning is an important step within the successful completion of any endeavor. If you do not have a plan in mind when you develop an online curriculum or course—or facilitate one, you will find it difficult to provide all the high-quality materials you want learners to use throughout the class. You will also be overwhelmed if Murphy's Law hits you with a technical glitch here or there. Although planning cannot eliminate all gremlins from online courses, it can help establish a sound educational outline for each course and meet the needs of learners with different learning styles and preferences. Clear, timely planning, following suggestions and discussions in Part 1, should help you develop the kind of course you (or other educators) want to teach and learners want to take.

Curriculum design takes careful planning. You need to determine which online courses need to be developed to supplement the existing online curriculum and then determine how best to develop them. You need a broad view of an entire degree program, so that you can see which courses need to be added, removed, or updated.

If an entirely new curriculum is being put into place, you need to see how individual courses will help meet the learning objectives established for the entire program. Starting with the basics of online course development is an important step in developing an effective online curriculum. With a firm grasp of the concepts and practical guidelines in Part 1, you should be ready for the big step: teaching online.

Facilitating the Online Curriculum

1

What is a "traditional" classroom? Many adults may still think of a traditional classroom as a room within a building, probably on a university, college, or other educational institution's campus. It may contain computer equipment, but it may be pictured as an older, whiteboard-only classroom full of desks or tables, with a teacher lecturing students face to face. Indeed, this example is a traditional classroom for many learners today, and it is likely to remain one definition of a traditional classroom for years to come. However, as more learners grow up with computer technology, the definition of the traditional classroom becomes more diverse.

A traditional classroom might be found in the workplace or an office building, at home or at a field site, during a plane ride or at the beach. What is traditional is that there is an established place (which may be an electronic location) where learners meet with one or more teachers—or the materials they have created and set up to work interactively with students—and learning (supposedly) occurs. The *place* is not as traditional anymore as the expectation that somewhere, either electronically or in person, educational materials are made available so that students can interact with them.

Much of the work is expected to be completed by the individual learner, often working alone but sometimes with other groups of learners studying or applying the same concepts. Even the teacher is not a given, at least as a friendly face or voice, although the teacher's (or course designer's) presence may be felt through the selection of materials for learners and feedback about assignments or activities.

Although the setting and amount of teacher direction may be changing many learners' perceptions of what is "traditional" about education, setting aside a predetermined time for educational pursuits is still an ingrained part of a traditional learning experience. Although online education is predicated on the idea that learning should be directed by the individual student, meeting with other learners and teachers at the same time continues to be an expected part of most educational endeavors, whether in person or online. Most learners and teachers still set up at least a few common meeting times for group activities and required interaction. Although the interaction may be minimal, some type of human connection is still considered desirable by many adults who are used to face-to-face learning experiences.

Online education in many respects is traditional, and much has been made about if or how online courses or programs of study are superior to face-to-face degree offerings. The implication is that online courses need to be better or at least different (in a positive sense) than face-to-face classroom experiences. Simply dumping printed information on a Web site is not going to promote learning any more than handing out pages to students and watching them read during class. Interaction and socialization are keys to effective online education. The questions then center on how best to deliver the materials and provide the experiences and interactions that promote learning and how educators, including but not limited to teachers, can guide students throughout the learning process.

Variations on a Theme: Different Types of Online/ On-site Courses

Online education has the potential for being so much more than just a copy of an on-site classroom. Although technology levels worldwide vary greatly, and not all Internet-based instruction can or should be created in the same format, the possibility exists that online education can go beyond its current formats and engage learners in new, exciting ways. As institutions and nations develop their online educational infrastructure, the types of activities and methods of providing instruction will continue to change.

This book describes low-level technologies that can be accessed by just about everyone with an Internet connection. However, the issues and structures proposed for effective online education certainly go beyond the low-tech versions of online courses. As the technology changes, more interaction will be expected, and the types of interaction will evolve. Nevertheless, the principles of effective curriculum design and the issues involving faculty, administrators, and information technology (IT) specialists will still be relevant.

In the meantime, until everyone globally has equal access to high-tech types of interaction, the following "online" elements often are found in both on-site and online types of instruction:

- Face-to-face with some Web-based instruction
- Web-based instruction with some on-site requirements
- Purely Web-based instruction

Teachers in online and on-site classes use the Internet in a variety of ways. For example, the Internet is often used as a research tool to help students learn to find and evaluate the quality and appropriateness of Web-site information. In design classes, learners can test the usability of different commercial sites and then develop personal Web sites that reflect the best designs for the type of information they want to present. As a communication tool, the Internet is important by allowing e-mail communication among learners and faculty, participation in mailing lists and e-groups, and bulletin board messages about class-based activities and events. These are just a few ways the Internet can be used with on-site and online classes.

Internet activities may be asynchronous or synchronous, and effective online courses or components of courses use both. Synchronous, or real-time, activities may include online chat sessions, whiteboard drawings, in-person discussions and lectures, streaming video, and streaming audio. Asynchronous activities are completed by individuals at their own pace and outside the time frame when others complete the same activities. E-mail messages are asynchronous communication, for example, because the message is sent at one time and only later retrieved and answered. The response is not instantaneous, as it is with a chat session. Bulletin boards, online tests and simulations, downloadable video or audio segments, and Web links can be used at the learners' or teachers' convenience. Not everyone uses the same information at the same time.

In on-site classrooms, there are traditionally more synchronous activities and communication than asynchronous ones. In-class discussions, presentations, workshops, and Q&A sessions are held most often within the classroom and perhaps during study sessions or office hours with the teacher. Out-of-class asynchronous communication may take the form of written notes left in a campus mailbox, e-mail messages, voicemail, or faxed documents. In online classrooms, if the course is taught purely online, there are probably more asynchronous than synchronous activities, although both are important to a well-designed Web-based class.

Face-to-Face with Some Web-based Instruction

Even in on-site classrooms, the Web is playing a more important role in educational activities and the dissemination of course materials. For example, learners in a computerized classroom can develop documents using word processing and desktop publishing software, conduct research on the Internet, design graphics with drawing software, and build a Web site. On some days the teacher may lecture, using computerized slides or Web-site notes as a backdrop for students' note taking. On other days, learners write, edit, and design information alone or in groups through workshop activities. There may be discussions or role-playing activities, which might take place in person, through a chat room, or on an electronic bulletin board.

The syllabus, course outlines, assignment sheets, and reminders of upcoming tests or events can be posted on a course Web site; hardcopy versions might also be given to learners during a class session, whereas the online version provides a convenient backup for all course information. Learners can post assignments to their Web sites and invite feedback from the teacher and other learners.

E-mail is a popular way to send drafts of assignments back and forth. Learners can ask the teacher questions after office hours and on weekends by sending e-mail, which can be made accessible at several points on a course Web site. Learners can also use the Internet or an intranet just to send e-mail to other learners or to the teacher.

In addition, learners may be encouraged to participate in Web-based e-groups hosted by professional associations and to regularly gather information from the Web sites of professional groups affiliated with students' major areas of study. Although teachers work in person with students, more of the day-to-day work involves the Web, as well as in-person teaching, to meet learners' needs and to facilitate learning outside the traditional time blocks set aside each week.

The variety of ways in which online components can be added to face-to-face instruction continues to grow. The term *Web-enhanced courses* already may be outdated, as learners come to expect Internet-accessible components in almost every course they take, whether on a physical or a virtual campus.

Southard and Rubens (2001), for example, have further broken the "Web-based" category into finer distinctions; they use *Web-based, Web-intensive, Web-supportive,* and *Web-ephemeral* to describe variations in Web usage in a curriculum. According to this classification scheme, Web-based courses are taught completely online; Web-intensive courses rely primarily on electronic communication, but also require some in-person meetings at specified times during a course. Web-supportive classes meet more frequently, more like in-person classes, but course materials may be electronic as well as hard copy. Web-ephemeral classes are the most traditional, meeting in person on a regular schedule but also using some

Web resources to support specific course objectives, such as research. As Web usage in the most traditional of classrooms becomes more common, the distinctions between on-site and online courses will become less clear-cut.

Other teachers use the term *hybrid classes* to describe courses in which Internet use is required, often in lieu of some face-to-face class sessions, but the course is offered on campus. Meeting with a teacher and other students face to face for much of the class is still expected.

Web-based Instruction with Some On-site Requirements

Some institutions offer what they term "online" courses, but there are still a few requirements to participate in on-site activities. For example, although the course materials may be accessed through a Web site and students complete the work electronically, tests or lab activities may be required on site.

In a Web-based degree program, students may take the majority of their coursework online, but at some point they have to take at least a few courses on site. Learners may be expected to visit the physical campus once or twice a year for meetings with advisors or to complete certain activities, although the majority of their classes are taken via the Internet.

Purely Web-based Instruction

In online classes, most or all information is found on a course Web site or through the Internet. Activities are completed online; groups communicate only electronically; information is used or gathered from the course or other Web sites. Instead of using the Internet as a supplementary tool to activities and information presented in person, online classes require Internet use as the primary tool for all educational events.

The online curriculum requires learners and teachers to communicate electronically, often by print e-mail and bulletin board messages. Other formats, such as phone calls or faxes, also might be used, depending upon the course structure and types of communication required. Transcripts of chats, bulletin board examples, and written documents linked to the course Web site or shown as full-text samples are typical ways that important course content is documented online. More visual means of communication, including whiteboard drawings, sometimes combined with chat sessions, and videoconferences, allow learners who like to use different media to work with non-print messages.

Chat sessions are often required in online classes, so teachers and learners have at least some synchronous communication. Whiteboards can be used to illustrate points during a synchronous discussion, and teachers may direct learners to specific URLs/URIs during the chat. However, working in real time, whether as a whole class or smaller groups, is an important addition to the asynchronous materials found at the course Web site.

Multimedia materials are more easily accessible on a Web site. Video or audio segments, for example, can be added to the course Web site or a separate online tutorial. In a traditional classroom without computer access, using different media to present information necessitates the teacher bringing in additional equipment, like monitors and VCRs, DVD players, and CD players. Models may be large and awkward to bring into a classroom, and they take up lots of space. Simulations may be difficult to set up. Field trips outside the academic classroom, although providing real instead of virtual experience, require lots of planning and usually transportation to another site. In a Web-based class, many of these difficulties are eliminated.

Simulations, webcam, streaming audio or video, audio or video clips, animation, static graphics, and interactive texts and graphics are just some ways that multimedia can be added to a course Web site. Learners who can access the Web site also gain access to a number of different materials that can be used in creative ways to present information, test knowledge, or provide practical, hands-on experience.

Some online courses are completely automated. Students go through the course at their own pace and receive feedback electronically. A human teacher is not readily apparent, although obviously some educators along the line were responsible for designing the course system and creating the materials and experiences that are accessed online. In this book, however, automated courses are not described, and a human teacher is an important part of the educational process.

Pedagogical Concerns—Approaches to Course Design and Constructivism and Behaviorism

Teaching methods and strategies have been categorized in many ways, both for teaching and course development. In regard to course development, researchers often argue for a user-centered design, which is based on the ways computer users work with technology. In fact, an online course itself is a system and a technology with which users (teachers and students) must learn to work (Blythe, 2001).

If a user-centered focus is the basis for an online course design, then the users must become involved in the design process (Johnson, 1998). If your institution favors a user-centered approach, prospective and current students must be brought into the design process. This step requires a great deal of planning to ensure that the design works well with a variety of users and that their input is continually valued and sought to assist in course maintenance and revision, once the course is in place in the curriculum.

If a designer-centered approach is used by the institution, teachers should be actively involved in the process. Some universities and colleges now rely on outside vendors to supply course materials or structures, which may or may not be appropriate for all courses in the curriculum. In a designer-centered approach, whoever is the course designer determines how the course site will operate and what will be included in the electronic materials (Blythe, 2001). In addition, the amount and types of interactivity with the system and with other learners and the teacher/facilitator also have to be determined. If the course-development process will be designer-centered, teachers should work closely with technical specialists to create a usable, appropriate structure and content for each course.

Instead of *user-centered* or *designer-centered* as terms describing the design process, other researchers use *teacher-centered approach* and *learner-centered approach*. If a design is centered around the teacher's preferences in materials and activities, the design is teacher-centered, whereas if students' preferences are the determining factors in the design, the plan is said to be learner-centered.

Cooney and Stephenson (2001) noted that teachers often recreate the educational stance that is most familiar or comfortable for them. However, for online education to be effective, learners must work with a wide variety of materials and resources. Much of online education needs to be learner directed, and course developers need to consider students first in course and curriculum design.

As a course is being planned, designers need to determine how many and what types of materials will be included at the course site and how much and what types of activities will engage learners with these materials. Designers need to determine how much of a constructivist approach or a behaviorist approach, or a combination, will be used to frame the design.

In a constructivist approach, real-world work experiences and social contexts in which knowledge and skills are typically used are emphasized (Mayes, 2001). For example, online activities may mimic those tasks required in a workplace. Problem solving, simulation, and team building may help create that real-world environment. In a constructivist approach, students add to what they already know and apply what they are learning. Course projects are often used in a constructivist approach (Makkonen, 2002). Dialogue among learners, the teacher, and other subject matter experts, as well as group activities that foster learning partnerships, help students construct knowledge (McDonald & Reushle, 2002). Group activities, social interaction, and application of concepts are often used online as part of a constructivist approach.

A behaviorist approach provides students with materials through which learners gather the important concepts. This approach is often pictured as the teacher imparting information through lectures or notes and is generally more passive for learners than a constructivist approach. With a behaviorist teaching approach, learners are given links to other Web sites, notes, lectures—whether in print or multimedia—and other materials as a framework of knowledge necessary to understand a subject (Makkonen, 2002).

A balance between constructivism and behaviorism is often found in online classes. Students are "lectured" in some format for part of the course, but practical applications and the making of meaning through learners' activities are also emphasized.

The levels of interaction with materials and activities also are important to consider in course design. Rote memorization and repetitive tasks are lower-level cognitive activities. Recall or identification of information is the lowest level (Knowledge) in Bloom's taxonomy of cognitive levels, with the highest level at Evaluation. The mental processes become increasingly complex from the lowest to highest levels (Bloom, 1964).

Within the curriculum, early (lower-level) courses may involve less complex thinking, but as mastery of knowledge and skills increase, students should demonstrate higher levels of thinking, such as synthesizing information and applying concepts. Throughout the online curriculum, as students progress within a course and from course to course, a variety of experiences must be provided to stimulate students' higher-order mental processes (Aguilera, Fernandez, & Fitz-Gerald, 2002).

As Aguilera, Fernandez, and Fitz-Gerald (2002) noted, there may be gaps in what students know, or wide variation among learners in a class as to what they know. A blend of behaviorist and constructivist approaches should be used to prepare students to complete an activity appropriately, but not to reveal the point of the activity. Learners should be able to explore materials and come up with their own answers, but they must be guided along this process so they have a starting point to approach an exercise. In your planning, you should anticipate the range of experiences and knowledge that students have when they enter a course or begin their work in a degree program.

As you plan a single course or an entire curriculum, you and the team working with you must determine what types of interaction are appropriate for the level and subject matter of the course. Students in an online academic environment must be able to think critically, not merely memorize information, and apply their knowledge to new situations. The way you design courses and plan the curriculum should reflect students' progression through a series of carefully created and monitored learning experiences.

Benefits of Online Education

A balance between constructivist and behaviorist objectives and methods probably needs to be determined for your institution's programs. Educators certainly must be actively involved in determining the appropriate pedagogical approaches for their market of students and the types of courses that they teach. Providing an effective learning environment to more students worldwide certainly is an altruistic objective, one that can promote educational ideals—that in itself is at least a theoretical benefit to online education.

Practical benefits, particularly convenience, also attract students to online programs. Learners who work well on their own, are computer literate (or can quickly develop the required computer skills), and have access to the Web are likely to be interested in online education. Because these learners can take classes anywhere, at almost any time, the convenience factor attracts new students who want to try online courses (Demirdjian, 2002).

For their educational pursuits to be successful, however, learners must be prepared to work online. Helping learners to use the technologies and structures found in online courses and socializing students to work with others through the Internet are necessary components to success. Effective online curricula include classes or at least modules that help students become acclimated to electronic education.

Another benefit to online education is the possibility of working with more learners, teachers, and subject matter experts outside a student's limited geographic area. Collaborating with people from different cultures and levels of experience is a potential benefit that can enhance the learning environment and provide learners with a wider network of contacts.

Online classes may offer special benefits to learners who are shy, have difficulty keeping pace with other students during a face-to-face class, or need time to express themselves effectively. Learners may feel more confident in an online class, even during a real-time chat session, because they perceive that the online venue creates an equal playing field. Learners who look or dress differently from others are treated equally online, because other students cannot see their peers in a text-based course. Learners who may need more time to express themselves can take that time before they post a bulletin board message or send e-mail. The quality of the work, not the appearance of the learner, is what is evaluated.

Online courses can increase participation among all learners. During a chat, for example, all students are encouraged, if not required, to participate. Everyone has a chance to be heard; it is difficult to hide at the back of the classroom.

Students have noted that the feedback they receive online is more often positive and supportive. Comments like "good point," "I never would've thought of that," or "great idea" are often more common online. Even if learners in a traditional classroom agree with a speaker, chances are that they will not speak up to make a positive comment. A nod here or there is more likely to be the only positive reinforcement given to in-class speakers. Seeing several written positive comments gives online learners a boost in morale (Porter, 2001a,b).

Some learners feel uncomfortable speaking up in a traditional classroom because other learners give negative nonverbal cues, like frowning, rolling their eyes, sighing loudly, crossing their arms, or shaking their head. Online, even if other learners feel negatively about a statement, the learner writing the comment gets to complete the thought before someone else posts a reply. Plus, learners—at least in a print-based chat session—do not get the chance to see or hear each other during a chat. The impact of negative body language or censuring tone is missing from an online written chat.

For learners to reap these benefits, however, teachers must create a supportive, professional, yet personal atmosphere in the online classroom. Having access to a variety of materials and being able to communicate with people internationally through e-mail and chat are wonderful benefits provided by Web-enhanced courses. However, these benefits are only realized if learners feel comfortable using the tools and working together to build an online community of learners.

Teachers can only create a supportive, creative environment if they are given the tools and time to develop meaningful materials and activities, as well as learn how to teach online. Administrators and technical specialists must provide this support, which requires a high-level institutional commitment not only to the infrastructure of online programs, but to faculty training and development. Many teachers are concerned that they may not have this support, because course development, facilitation, and maintenance are time-consuming activities that involve a team of technical and pedagogical specialists. Making sure that teachers develop course materials and are "actively engaged" (Charp, 2001) in creating programs is imperative for successful, beneficial online programs.

In addition to these loftier benefits, cost factors may also be beneficial. Students' educational costs may be lower, if they already have access to computer technology required for their online courses. Activity fees, on-campus or nearby housing, parking, and other costs associated with attending classes on a physical campus may not apply to online learners (Demirdjian, 2002). The fee structure can be a benefit to some online learners.

Economics is an important element in the success of online programs and the reason why many institutions first decide to jump into online education. However, if online courses do not attract students or make enough money, the university or college is likely to drop them. The costs associated with maintaining the technology and keeping up the level of innovation may be higher than the institution is willing to invest. However, at least theoretically, online classes can attract students around the world, opening the institution's programs to a wider market. As well, depending on the amount of interaction required for an effective learning situation, some highly automated classes may be able to accommodate many more students in one session than could possibly fit into an on-site classroom guided by one teacher (Demirdjian, 2002). Making online programs fiscally viable without sacrificing quality is a challenge, but online courses can bring new monies to the institution.

There are many "ifs" involved in creating a successful online course, much less an entire curriculum. However, if the entire institution is devoted to high-quality online education, learners, teachers, and the institution as a whole can reap benefits.

Establishing a Curriculum

The question in developing an online curriculum is this: How much and what type(s) of interaction are optimal for an effective learning environment? If you are going to develop a curriculum and teach online courses, you need a well-developed plan to make the program successful.

Each course within a curriculum must be well developed and a complete unit unto itself. Online courses must present a manageable amount of content and number of activities specifically designed to be completed online. Each course should also be similar in design to other courses offered by the institution. It must fit well with other course offerings to support a program of instruction, most likely leading to a specific degree or as general educational requirements for several possible degree programs in an academic institution. The series of courses must lead students from introductory skills and knowledge to higher-order activities and ideas.

Course materials should be designed for students with different abilities and learning styles. They should invite interaction and offer more than rote memorization or repetitive activities. They should be creative and innovative (as should all course materials, regardless of the venue).

The structure of online courses across a program of instruction (such as those leading to a particular degree) should be similar and use similar technologies. Learners who take one online course and find the online experience pleasant and valuable may decide to take another course or two, or they may enroll with the idea of taking all courses online. The online tools and overall design should be similar among all courses offered by the same institution, so that learners can transfer the skills they learned in one online class to another.

As well, learners in online classes may be expected to interact with the teacher and other learners through asynchronous and synchronous activities, as well as work on their own. Creating an online community of learners is an important part of most online classes. Socialization is part of a successful course, and socializing activities should be included throughout the curriculum.

In education today, the need for an effective curriculum is imperative for successful online programs. It is no longer enough just to determine whether your institution should offer online education; the structure and design must be sound if you decide that online education is a worthy undertaking. Learners expect a complete, well-designed, cohesive curriculum. They also are more likely to demand that the curriculum be innovative and interactive—or they are likely to go to another vendor whose curriculum meets these criteria.

Online educators' aims are to provide learners with a knowledge base about a variety of subjects and to help learners develop subject matter expertise in at least one specialized area. In addition, learners should be able critically to evaluate information and analyze and synthesize data. They should clearly express themselves in person, print, and presentation. A well-rounded educational curriculum does encourage learners to practice skills, but it also provides ways for learners to develop an understanding of subjects and to express their ideas effectively. Individual courses within the online curriculum should then be building blocks toward this intellectual development.

Teaching Online

Teaching adults online is just as, if not more, time-consuming and involving than teaching on site. The teaching experience is just as rewarding and the need for high-quality instruction just as important. When you look at online education that way, maybe there are not as many differences from teaching on site as you would first suspect. Although the materials and teaching methods should be designed for either the in-person or electronic version of a course, the educational philosophy and desire for learners having an effective educational experience are unifying principles for both online and on-site courses.

Teachers planning to facilitate their first online class sometimes focus on the differences between teaching online and in a traditional classroom. Although there are some obvious differences, such as a lack of regular face-to-face encounters with learners in an electronic classroom (unless multimedia are frequently used), distance and in-person classes both require a personable guide who can facilitate the learning experiences. Table 1-1 compares online courses to on-site courses.

Table 1-1. Online and On-site Curriculum Implementation

	Online	On-site
Teachers/Facilitators	Professionals in other fields (not professional educators) Vendors/corporations Automation Part-time educators (adjunct faculty) Full-time educators (probably tenure track)	Visiting professionals from another field or within education Part-time educators (adjunct faculty) Full-time educators (probably tenure track)
Delivery (Communication or Presentation) Technologies	Course Web site CD E-mail Bulletin board Whiteboard Teleconference Chat	Course Web site CD E-mail Bulletin board Whiteboard Teleconference Non-computerized classroom technologies: overheads, handouts, etc. Chat Face-to-face lecture or discussion
Human Touch in Delivery/Presentation	Teacher (e.g., through chat, e-mail, teleconference) Other students (e.g., groups, communities, individuals) Subject matter experts	Teacher (e.g., through face-to-face interaction, chat, e-mail) Other students (e.g., groups, communities, individuals) Subject matter experts
Type of Communication	Mostly asynchronous	Mostly synchronous
Type of Classroom/Places to Go	Web site Other Web sites/Internet links "Field trips" at individual's discretion	Campus classroom, lab, etc. Web site Other Web sites/Internet links Field trips
Time Commitment for Students	Time intensive—individual work, plus electronic response time	Increases with more online requirements—may or may not be as time intensive outside of face-to-face class sessions
Time Commitment for Teachers/Developers	Time intensive to develop materials Time intensive to respond electronically to e-mail, grade assignments and post feedback, etc. Less face-to-face interaction	Time intensive to develop materials Less electronic response time More face-to-face interaction

Tasks for Online Teachers

Although online teaching can and should be as high-quality and effective as on-site education/training, some professionals are better suited than others to working online. Online educators need to facilitate individuals' learning; bring together students with diverse interests, skills, and needs to form learning communities; clearly state expectations and maintain high standards; be adaptable in regards to learners' needs; communicate clearly and effectively; and enjoy working with the Internet.

Facilitate Individuals' Learning

Teaching online is sometimes like being a coach or a cheerleader. You need to help learners develop strategies for working efficiently on their own and gaining the information and skills they need to complete the course (and, you hope, apply the information to their lives or careers). In academic settings, new online learners may need you to be part of their educational support network, to provide encouragement as they return to school after a long absence and work with a newer medium.

Facilitating individuals' learning also means that you continue to develop teaching materials and find ways to help learners find information in a format to meet their learning preferences and learning or personality styles. Although you might not be able to meet every student's preference with every activity, across the course and the curriculum there are a number of different activities designed to help people who best learn with differing methods.

Individual needs also may include learners who are widely separated geographically from other learners and need assistance in connecting with other people going through the same program. You may encounter communication problems, because learners are in different time zones, and their work or travel schedules may preclude finding convenient times for synchronous communication. Learners also may vary in their skill levels and physical abilities, which require innovative teaching or training approaches to provide information and activities in usable formats.

Instead of being the source of information for learners, you are the guide who directs learners to resources, oversees progress, and initiates groups and activities to help people learn.

Form Learning Communities

You also need to make learners feel a part of a larger group and develop activities to bring learners together in meaningful ways. Learning communities, small and large, are an important component of successful online education. By socializing learners to the online environment, you help them connect with others to discuss ideas and share information.

State Expectations and Maintain Standards

Online learners are very focused on their educational needs and want clear statements of what is expected from them in the course. They prefer standards be outlined at the beginning of the course, so they can measure their progress and understand how their performance will be evaluated. Clear expectations and the consistent application of standards are important to online learners, and you must consistently stand up for the stated objectives, expectations, and outcomes for the course.

In an academic course, learners also should be expected to be critical thinkers who discuss information with other learners and the teacher, develop interests that may not have a direct bearing on their careers, and learn to find and evaluate additional sources of information that can help them continue their education on their own. These types of objectives should be explained and encouraged by the teacher; they may be part of the stated course objectives, but they are far more difficult to measure. As the facilitator/guide, you must ensure that discussion, debate, and critical thinking are parts of an effective online academic course.

Be Adaptable

Because you work with technology, you must be able to learn to use a course Web site, update materials, troubleshoot basic problems, and feel comfortable learning new computer skills quickly. Technology changes rapidly, and you must feel comfortable working with new tools and information designs. As well, you need to be adaptable to learners' needs, so that you can explain assignments or activities in different terms, possibly for international audiences, and help individuals succeed in the course. Flexibility and adaptability are important traits for any online teacher.

Communicate Clearly and Effectively

Although more multimedia are becoming available for online courses, most online communication with learners in academic programs will be written. You may occasionally use videoconferencing or audio files to present information or discuss topics with learners, but primarily you are going to be sending lots of e-mail, posting bulletin board messages, keyboarding comments in a printed chat session, and drawing or writing on a whiteboard.

It is imperative for you to communicate quickly, clearly, cleanly, and correctly to everyone, but you should especially be careful to craft information for international audiences. You need to be sensitive to the nuances of language, as well as different cultural expectations for different types of messages.

Your written communication must be a model for your learners' written work. Because written communication may be studied and interpreted long after you send it, your communication must be able to stand up to scrutiny by a variety of readers.

When you use multimedia, you need effective presentation skills. You should be interesting for learners to hear, as well as precise and clear with your message. Your speaking rate, word choice, and enunciation are crucial to learners' understanding. You also need the ability to think on your feet as you respond spontaneously to questions and comments.

Enjoy Working with the Internet

You must enjoy using the Internet. Learners use it often, and you should keep up with trends in design and information. You should feel comfortable browsing the Web for new information for your courses, and you need the skills quickly to find information stored in potentially millions of sites and databases. You need to be familiar with a variety of search engines and be able to help learners differentiate among appropriate search engines for their work. You have to be an efficient online researcher and, ideally, a competent information designer who keeps up with usable educational interfaces and technologies. If you are going to work online, you have to enjoy your working environment and be able to discuss Internet news with learners.

The following checklist of statements may help you assess your competence in each area. Ideally, you should be able to check each box. Of course, every teacher identifies strengths and weaknesses within such a checklist. You want to evaluate your overall suitability for facilitating an online curriculum. By using this checklist each time you work with an online course, you can continue to monitor your progress as an online teacher or trainer and point out areas of excellence, as well as skills that need improvement.

Figure 1-1. Checklist for Facilitating the Online Curriculum

Facilitate Individuals' Learning

☐ I develop information to meet the needs of learners with different learning styles.

☐ I develop information that is accessible to learners with different abilities.

☐ I follow guidelines, such as those set by the W3 Consortium or my institution for making course materials accessible in different formats on the Internet.

☐ I consider learners' work schedules, time zones, and geographic locations when I set up times for required synchronous activities.

☐ I provide a variety of dates and times for required synchronous activities.

☐ I consider learners' level of technical expertise when I develop assignments and activities.

☐ I provide a variety of group and individual activities.

☐ I consider the availability of computer technology and learners' access to the Internet as I develop assignments and activities.

☐ I help learners locate information on the Internet.

☐ I help learners locate information on the course site.

☐ I explain assignments, activities, and course information in terms that all learners can understand.

☐ I provide (an appropriate amount of) special assistance or additional individual guidance to learners who are having difficulty with the course.

☐ I provide additional information or support to learners who want to do more than what is required for the course.

Figure 1-1. Checklist for Facilitating the Online Curriculum (continued)

Form Learning Communities

☐ I participate in professional (external/outside the institution, business, or course) learning communities for teachers.

☐ I participate in learning communities within each class I facilitate.

☐ I require group activities.

☐ I monitor group activities.

☐ I facilitate the development of learning communities that are not required for a group project.

☐ I communicate with all learners in a course at least once a week.

☐ I assist learners in communicating with each other.

☐ I create bulletin board, e-mail, and other print communication that can serve as models of effective, positive, and grammatically correct business communication.

☐ I create a positive, professional persona for synchronous communication, through chat sessions, phone calls, videoconferences, or other "in-person" communication.

State Expectations and Maintain Standards

☐ I state course objectives at the course site.

☐ I provide on the course site a schedule of deadlines and due dates for assignments and activities.

☐ I explain on the course site the grading or evaluation criteria for the course and individual assignments or activities.

☐ I state at the course site all expectations for performance and achievement.

Figure 1-1. Checklist for Facilitating the Online Curriculum (continued)

☐ I maintain the stated standards throughout the course.

☐ I serve as a role model who meets deadlines and consistently adheres to course standards and expectations.

☐ I encourage learners to discuss their course performance and achievements with me.

☐ I work with learners individually and as a class to help them succeed in the course.

☐ I encourage questions from learners.

☐ I provide suggestions for improving assignments or completing activities.

☐ I am available several times a week for consultation.

☐ I post grades or complete performance evaluations quickly.

☐ I quickly provide feedback about learners' assignments, activities, and overall performance.

Be Adaptable

☐ I work with learners individually to help them meet deadlines and complete assignments.

☐ I work with learners to help them schedule activities within their course, work, and life schedules.

☐ I can adapt the schedule within the standards established for the course.

☐ I can provide learners with additional materials or explanations to help them modify assignments and activities appropriately for their career or professional needs.

☐ I can direct learners to other professionals within the institution who may help with specific problems or needs.

Figure 1-1. Checklist for Facilitating the Online Curriculum (continued)

Communicate Clearly and Effectively

☐ I write grammatically correct, clear, and well-organized messages and documents.

☐ I analyze the recipient(s) of my communication so that I meet their information needs.

☐ I vary my communication style to fit the situation.

☐ I speak clearly and precisely in audio/visual communication.

☐ I speak at an understandable rate in audio/visual communication.

☐ I am enthusiastic and positive in my communication.

☐ I am professional in my communication.

☐ I maintain a professional but friendly persona through my communication.

Enjoy Working with the Internet

☐ I feel comfortable using a variety of search engines on the Web.

☐ I send e-mail frequently and efficiently.

☐ I post bulletin board messages frequently and efficiently.

☐ I use the whiteboard in lectures and other course activities.

☐ I direct discussions in chat rooms.

☐ I post grades to an online gradebook or complete performance evaluations online.

☐ I participate in videoconferences or conference phone calls.

☐ I participate in online groups, through newsgroups, mailing lists, and chats.

Figure 1-1. Checklist for Facilitating the Online Curriculum (continued)

☐ I upload and download information easily.

☐ I locate electronic materials for my courses.

☐ I design or assist in designing course materials.

☐ I design Web pages.

☐ I maintain the course site or another Web site.

☐ I learn to use new software as it becomes available for learners and teachers.

☐ I keep up with Internet-related news, such as virus warnings, announcements of new services, and trends in technology.

☐ I participate in Internet-related workshops.

☐ I share Internet-related information with colleagues.

☐ I like working online.

☐ I encourage learners to take online courses because I believe in the benefits of online education and training.

Summary

Whether you teach purely online or in an on-site classroom, the curriculum and individual courses must be designed for that venue. No matter where you work as a teacher, you will probably use the Web, Internet, and intranet materials to supplement textbooks and class discussion. As technology makes it easier for you to work with multimedia, you will provide more information in different formats. Through it all, you will need to communicate with learners, whether they see you in a brick building every Monday afternoon or send you e-mail while they are on a business trip.

Being able to work with new technology and design information in the best format for learners is an important part of education anywhere. You have to be able to involve learners with each other and the course materials, and you need to have good communication skills to facilitate learning.

Online education requires careful planning, and the resulting course design should be innovative and allow learners to interact with each other and the materials. A blend of constructivist and behaviorist approaches may be useful for your course's design.

Each carefully designed individual course must fit into the larger electronic curriculum so that there is consistency in design among units, but also a way for students to progress from low-level tasks and cognitive functions to higher-order thinking and application of concepts.

Once an effective curriculum has been designed, the way you facilitate each class often determines the way students perceive the institution and the subject matter. Your facilitation skills and style are an important element in successfully implementing an online curriculum.

References

Aguilera, N., Fernandez, G., & Fitz-Gerald, G. (2002). Addressing different cognitive levels for on-line learning. In A. Williamson, C. Gunn, A. Young, & T. Clear (Eds.), *Winds of change in the sea of learning: Proceedings of the 19th annual conference of the Australasian Society for Computers in Learning in Tertiary Education* (pp. 39-46). Auckland, NZ: UNITEC Institute of Technology.

Bloom, B. S. (1964). *Taxonomy of educational objectives.* New York: David McKay Company, Inc.

Blythe, S. (2001). Designing online courses: User-centered practices. *Computers and Composition, 18*(4), 329-346.

Charp, S. (2001). Editorial: E-learning. *T.H.E. Journal.* Retrieved August 18, 2002, from the ProQuest database.

Cooney, M., & Stephenson, J. (2001). Online learning: It is all about dialogue, involvement, support, and control—According to the research. In J. Stephenson (Ed.), *Teaching and learning online: Pedagogies for new technologies* (pp. 37-52). London: Kogan Page Ltd.

Demirdjian, Z. S. (2002). The virtual university: Is it a panacea or a Pandora's box? *Journal of American Academy of Business, Cambridge.* Retrieved August 12, 2002, from the ProQuest database.

Johnson, R. R. (1998). *User-centered technology: A rhetorical theory for computers and other mundane artifacts.* Albany: State University of New York Press.

Makkonen, P. (2002). Who benefits from WWW presentations in the basics of informatics? In M. Khosrow-Pour (Ed.), *Web-based instructional learning* (pp. 252-263). Hershey, PA: IRM Press.

Mayes, T. (2001). Learning technology and learning relationships. In J. Stephenson (Ed.), *Teaching and learning online: Pedagogies for new technologies* (pp. 16-26). London: Kogan Page Ltd.

McDonald, J., & Reushle, S. (2002). Charting the role of the online teacher in higher education: Winds of change. In A. Williamson, C. Gunn, A. Young, & T. Clear (Eds.), *Winds of change in the sea of learning: Proceedings of the 19th annual conference of the Australasian Society for Computers in Learning in Tertiary Education* (pp. 431-440). Auckland, NZ: UNITEC Institute of Technology.

Porter, L. R. (2001a). *Instantaneous, empowering, and invisible: The world of online writing communities*. Presentation before the Popular Culture of the South Conference, Jacksonville, FL.

Porter, L. R. (2001b). Planning a community: The value of online learning communities in technical communication. *Proceedings of STC's [Society for Technical Communication's] 48th annual conference* (p. 52). Arlington, VA: Society for Technical Communication.

Southard, S., & Rubens, P. (2001). Students' technological difficulties in using web-based learning environments. *Proceedings of STC's [Society for Technical Communication's] 48th annual conference* (p. 83). Arlington, VA: Society for Technical Communication.

Adding a Course to the Curriculum

An academic curriculum is a series of courses related by themes and skills development. The individual courses within the curriculum help learners progress from basic, introductory levels of knowledge and skills to higher-level objectives for critical thinking, mastery of skills, and demonstration of knowledge common to a discipline. Completing specified courses within a curriculum leads to a degree, and the degree program may involve courses in several different departments or disciplines.

An online curriculum forms the basis for a program of study. For a curriculum to be successful, administrators must support online programs and keep in place an infrastructure that appropriately supports and encourages course development. The institution must have an ongoing commitment to online education and provide resources to create, implement, and modify course designs according to the subject experts' specifications.

Administrators must approve a unified framework and design (perhaps through the selection and support of courseware, such as WebCT or Blackboard) that will give the curriculum a unified appearance and structure. If courseware is not used, administrative policies concerning individual course designs and the use of technology to implement them must be put in place. All persons working with course design must understand the institution's design parameters and the process for creating course sites.

The institution also must plan for the costs of maintaining high-quality programs and delivering appropriate levels of technology. Whether the technology is low- or high-tech, all courses within a program should offer the same type of online access to and use of tools appropriate for the study of a specific discipline.

Of course, when an entirely new curriculum is being designed, the personnel who will create, teach, support technical needs, work with students in the business areas of online education, update courses, market programs, and so on, also must be hired or reassigned to these new tasks. These personnel must be trained and retained, too. As the curriculum or curricula expand, additional personnel must be prepared to assist those people who continue to work with the system. The "first wave" of personnel cannot simply take on more tasks as programs grow; the hiring and training of new faculty and staff are necessary throughout the life of the program. As well, current personnel need to participate in additional training as a course or the whole curriculum is modified and different technologies are put in place.

Completely virtual universities or colleges may have several curricula; an institution's business is to provide a variety of online offerings leading to specific degrees. However, traditional campus-based institutions may decide only to create a few online degree programs, with the majority of courses and degree programs presented on site. Some institutions may find it appropriate to offer highly popular courses in both online and on-site formats, although the entire curriculum is not offered online. The range of course offerings, and their status within an entire curriculum, often varies among institutions.

What's appropriate for your institution? Are online degree programs necessary to meet the needs of your target market of learners? Are similar curricula offered by competing institutions, or will your programs be unique? Is an online curriculum appropriate to the discipline, and will online courses that make up that curriculum be able to be structured to provide learners with appropriate course materials and learning experiences? These types of questions are crucial to not only the administration's understanding of what is required to develop and support an online curriculum, but also for the faculty and staff to support online programs and be willing to spend considerable amounts of time preparing and teaching a wide range of online courses. Information technology personnel must have resources available to them to maintain the level of technology required in courses and for administrative services for learners and faculty. As technology in general becomes more sophisticated, learners will expect more online services provided by the university or college and a wider variety of multimedia experiences in classes. Institutional planners, especially at the highest levels, must commit themselves to providing the resources needed to support a complete online curriculum for each program they want to market as part of their virtual university.

Not only must there be an institutional commitment to excellence with online programs, but the faculty and staff must be motivated and encouraged to meet the challenge. The type of learners who want to take a purely online degree program of study differs from adults who may dabble in online education by taking a class or two, perhaps a non-credit course for personal development or a for-credit course toward a traditionally offered degree. Adults interested in earning a degree through a series of online courses, however, become committed to a program and the institution offering it. Most learners who want online degree programs live far away from the physical campus. Their peace of mind and career planning depend on the institution having a well-designed curriculum that will be around for a long time (Fuller, McBride, & Gillam, 2002).

Careful planning is essential for a successful curriculum, much less several curricula leading to many possible degrees. In addition to the previously mentioned considerations, learner and faculty services also must be planned and implemented smoothly. Course registration, billing and payments, fee assessments, career counseling, assessment of transfer credit, and testing and placement in courses are some functions that need to be offered online but backed up with a human connection. Assigning teachers to staff courses, making teachers aware of student enrollment, preparing and maintaining class rosters, maintaining records of learners taking courses toward specific degrees, paying teachers, providing benefits and the services associated with them, et cetera, are crucial to enrolling, tracking, and awarding degrees to learners and working with faculty throughout this process. Faculty courseloads, payment schedules, student advising, training, scheduling, tax records, and other business actions that connect faculty with the institution and with learners in their classes also should be part of the master plan. This process needs to be available at all times, especially when many, if not all, faculty members who teach online live away from a physical campus (if indeed there is one) or are linked only electronically with the institution.

In addition, technology support and real people providing a human touch must be available for learners and teachers. Support staff must be knowledgeable and efficient in all their dealings with faculty and learners at all times of the academic year and throughout the 24-hour online academic day.

Academic socialization is another area that requires planning. Ways for learners, faculty, and staff to learn about the institution's policies and methods and to develop learning communities and friendships should be part of the plan. Bulletin boards, chat rooms, virtual coffee houses or lounges, informal telemeetings, or any combination of electronic ways and places for people to meet and exchange information help make faculty, students, and staff feel that they belong to a real institution. Although online course sites should provide educational resources for use directly from the Web site, additional research facilities must be provided to learners and teachers. Not only the vast Internet/Web, but also specific electronic resources must be available through the institution's library and laboratories.

Even this brief overview of concerns about curriculum development should alert everyone considering the creation of online programs that the issues are complex. Planning, much less implementing, a curriculum requires a huge commitment of time, personnel, and money. Maintaining and expanding programs necessitates further resources.

Fuller, McBride, and Gillam (2002) aptly described the process as complex as building the first railroad across the U.S. They likened teaching an online course to traveling west in a Conestoga wagon. Both activities were fraught with dangers, but railroad building was certainly a more demanding, intricate process. Developing an online curriculum is certainly possible; many institutions have done so quite well. However, the process requires the participation and support of everyone, at all levels of the institutional hierarchy.

A curriculum is only as strong as the individual courses that make up the program of study. Throughout the rest of this chapter, course development is emphasized. As each course is planned within the structure of the larger curriculum, its structure and the types of course materials should be similar to those of other courses offered within the same curriculum. Learners and teachers who participate in all courses within the program should be able to transfer skills and knowledge about the technology and interface from class to class. The tools, system requirements, and methods of interacting with the course site should be similar, and all courses within the curriculum should be updated according to a regular schedule so that there are no broad differences in the appearance or structure among courses.

Who Plans the Curriculum?

The people responsible for planning a new course or an entire program may represent very different groups, with different areas of expertise. In some institutions, in-house course designers, fluent in technology-speak and experienced with curriculum development and instructional design, are the ones who create and update courses. They may work with teachers who have taught online or with teachers of the on-site version of the course; they also may solicit feedback and suggestions from the institution's students. A close collaboration among teachers and designers helps troubleshoot instructional problems and ensure that the design is peda-gogically sound. If a course is offered as part of an across-the-curriculum or interdepartmental degree program, teachers from different disciplines may need to work together to develop or teach a course.

As a degree program is planned, the initial impetus for creating a series of courses that fit together as a unified program of study may come from a departmental chair or teachers who see the need for a broader series of courses that develop skills and knowledge and lead to mastery of a specific discipline. These teachers may first develop and get approval for an entire curriculum, but they need a great deal of assistance from the institution for developing and delivering that curriculum online.

At the other end of the scale, administrators who strategically plan the direction that the institution will take in the future may see the need for a new degree program, or for transferring to the Web courses that were previously aligned with an on-site program. The administration then identifies the need for an online curriculum and enlists faculty and staff in many departments to develop the appropriate courses (and materials) that will be offered as part of this curriculum.

In other institutions, course designers have the sole responsibility for planning and implementing new courses, as well as updating them. Administrators or faculty may have established the need for a series of online courses. The administration then assigns to designers the task of designing and implementing the courses so that the interfaces and types of interaction are compatible and similar among all courses in the curriculum. The planning, development, implementation, and updates usually are scheduled, so that, ideally, the curriculum is balanced with relevant, fresh, technically current courses. Faculty and staff specially trained and/or with a degree in a distance education-related subject area take charge of the institution's online education needs, procedures, and policies.

Whether your institution is developing a new online curriculum, supplementing on-site instruction with online versions of on-site courses, or updating the online curriculum with redesigned or additional courses, planning is the key. The planning process should involve everyone at the institution and requires the administration's ongoing commitment to high-quality online instruction and the infrastructure that supports it.

Developing an Individual Course

Sometimes, especially in colleges or universities new to online education, teachers have the responsibility of turning on-site courses into their online counterparts. This process may be the institution's (and teacher's) first foray into online education. Teachers may determine that a new course would be well suited to the online format and would be an important addition to the curriculum. The administration agrees, and the mechanism for offering such a course (or courses) is put into place. However, the teachers may bear the weight of planning and developing course materials and later working with technical experts to implement the course online.

If courseware selected by the university or college is used, the teacher may be responsible for uploading course materials and learning to use the courseware. In a similar way, teachers (who observe firsthand how a course should operate and how well learners understand and use materials) initiate updates. They may be responsible for uploading new information within a courseware structure, or providing materials or descriptions of activities for learners (such as streaming media) that then have to be implemented by information technology experts. If teachers update courses as they see a need for change, this situation may result in a less structured, sporadic series of course changes. Not all teachers may feel that periodic updates are necessary, or they simply may not have the time needed to update courses as often as they would like.

Administrators may determine that a new course is needed and then ask/invite/require teachers to develop materials suitable for online classes. Department chairs, deans, university presidents, or other administrators are then responsible for managing curriculum development and responding to market needs for online education. They may supervise everything—curriculum development, strategic planning, teacher training, marketing, scheduling, and other educational and business decisions.

Designing and developing online courses may be the responsibility of any number of people, who have different interests in and experiences with distance education. The amount of time for course development, schedule for implementing and updating courses, and degree of interaction among teachers, designers, and technical specialists can vary widely among academic institutions and businesses. You need to understand the infrastructure, development policies, and implementation procedures for your university or college.

If you have come up with the idea for an online course, you might do most of the planning before you propose a course to an institution's administration. If you have visited course sites similar to the one you want to develop and if you understand the institution's or corporate vendor's range of course offerings, your plan should illustrate how a new course would fit into the current series of courses. If you are familiar with online education, you may have designed a course on your own and now want to offer it to an institution already familiar with online education. In this situation, you will probably have to revise some of your plan to meet the institution's needs or overall objectives for and structure of online courses.

Perhaps your university or college is just beginning to offer online courses, and you have been asked to develop a new course, or to turn an on-site course into a compatible, effective online version. Your planning may stem from a committee's ideas about what should be in an online course, or the institution may have already developed a model or guidelines so that all courses will look alike.

Whether you are updating an older course or creating something brand new, you first must make sure that the purpose for the online course is apparent. Savenye, Olina, and Niemczyk (2001) suggested that teachers initially should select courses that they have successfully taught on site as those that are later offered online. In this situation, the need for the course has been established, the course approved and in place on campus, and some parameters for course content, prerequisites, and support already determined. In other words, you are not just creating online courses to be trendy or to prove that you can, and much of the preliminary justification or rationale for the course has been completed.

Before your course planning gets into specifics, you and others involved with program development must be confident that learners need the course, the information does not duplicate that provided in other courses, the course fits into the planned or existing curriculum, and the subject matter can be well presented online. The course must be necessary and marketable. Without meeting these criteria, a new course should not be developed.

If you are sure that a new or an updated course is warranted, no matter what your specific situation, you will need to plan the course carefully. Some administrators and teachers are surprised that this part of the process requires a good deal of time. However, you should keep in mind that even if you have taught an on-site version of a course that is about to go online, the electronic medium differs from the on-site classroom. Both venues have similar objectives for learning, but you must ensure that the online classes are interactive and have a seamless, interesting interface. Although you may have a head start on finding materials or a model to follow, you still have a great deal of planning to do to create an effective online course. Course designers must ensure that the educational structure is sound and meets students', teachers', and the institution's needs (especially in the development of degree programs and in light of accreditation).

Preliminary Considerations

Downey (2001) stressed the importance of strategic planning. Whether you are one of the team members responsible for this planning or working on your own, you need a clear map and an effective vision of where you are headed. Downey suggested that the strategic planning team consist of technologists, administrators, content delivery experts, end users, and external representatives, such as members of the community or business leaders.

Although you may not officially be able to assemble such a team, you should consult experts in each of these areas during the early planning stages. Bringing learners (end users) and other teachers (also end users) into the discussions improves the likelihood of a successful beta test later on. These groups also have insight into what makes a useful, interesting curriculum and courses and provide a different perspective from that of administrators, institutional designers, and technical experts. External team members, such as businesspeople familiar with trends in online education or specific subject matter, may also be able to suggest improvements to make the curriculum, as well as individual courses, more marketable.

However, just because your strategic planning committee may not include so many people, you can still come up with an innovative, manageable course design. Shank (2001) explained that creativity should be a key element in course design, and you can come up with innovative materials and interesting presentations. Going beyond the same old design is important for keeping online courses fun, educational, and interactive. Learners should enjoy the learning process. Instructional designs that make students look forward to learning and guide them toward self-education in an accessible, stress-free environment, are the ideal.

Planning an online curriculum or a single course that fits into the curriculum may require you to do more research. You may have to collaborate with or get advice and ideas from different groups of subject matter experts, designers, technical specialists, administrators, and learn-ers. You may need to approach course and materials planning from a different direction and rethink what you know about designing on-site classes.

In the on-site classroom, you know that different learners respond well to different media and forms of interaction with materials, the teacher, and other learners. However, the computer is also an important part of the mix, an element that may be found in on-site or hybrid classes (taught partly with the Web and partly in person) but is an integral part of online education. Serdiukov (2001) described the interaction as a "triad." The three members or sides are the computer, the teacher, and the student. The machine is an equal part of this model. Its software, links to the course site and other educational materials, and access to the Internet at large make it as important as the teacher or student. Only by smooth interaction among all three will the learning environment work successfully.

No matter which types of instruction you choose, whether primarily a constructivist or a behaviorist approach, you must consider how the course materials and assignments will come across via a computer screen. Learners will interact with the computer interface more often than they will with you or each other. Personalizing instruction, offering different types of collaborative and hands-on activities as well as individual assignments, and minimizing learners' frustration with the technology are important tasks that shape your course planning.

As well, on-site teachers usually can tell from the quizzical expressions on learners' faces when they do not understand a topic, or educators see learners' enthusiasm for a particular assignment or activity. By reading body language, hearing vocal cues, and observing interactions in the classroom, teachers learn the effectiveness of the course materials and methods with a particular group of learners. Any modifications that need to be made to instructions for an assignment, the format(s) in which materials are presented, and the pace of the instruction can be modified during the course, if necessary.

Although you do not have the benefit of watching learners as they work together online or tackle an assignment, you should consider how learners will be socialized in your course. The human element must be carefully constructed in online classes so that learners can solve problems quickly and without too much pain; the tone and "personality" of written and visual information at the course site should help learners find the information they are looking for and work with Web site tools easily. Instructions for navigating the course site should be clear; testing materials with real learners before a course site is launched is a good way to troubleshoot the grimace-inducing problems that you will not be able to see when learners use the course site.

You quickly learn, by talking with learners and observing them, which people prefer a lecture format, which ones gravitate toward hands-on activities, and which ones like to talk through their ideas in a discussion, for example. If you have taught online classes, you understand firsthand learners' joys and anxieties about taking online classes. As an educator, you also understand the wide variety of learners' needs that are evident in a face-to-face class; you should keep these experiences in mind as you design courses for learners who will be facing a screen instead of a person and gathering information electronically, often through asynchronous forms of communication. Effective teachers are flexible enough to structure (or restructure) course materials so that ideally everyone in the class finds favorite activities at least part of the time. A variety of teaching methods and media help ensure that all learners' needs are being met.

Williams, Paprock, and Covington (2000) noted the difference in the teacher's ability to troubleshoot problems when learners use materials in on-site classrooms and when learners work with online materials on their own. Teachers who want to change the day's lecture notes or add a new transparency, PowerPoint slide, or handout can easily integrate these materials into that day's lesson plan. Last-minute changes are possible. Teachers also can explain any problems that arise as students work in a lab or collaborate on an assignment in class.

Online teachers must develop materials well in advance of the time when learners will use them and must anticipate learners' possible difficulties with the materials. The information must be self-explanatory, because no one may be immediately available to explain the assignment to online students. Williams, Paprock, and Covington (2000) admitted that developing high-quality materials for distance learners is therefore time-consuming and requires much planning; the materials must be educationally sound, as well as diverse and innovative. In addition, they must fit into the structure of the institution's other online courses, plus respond to the interests and expectations of increasingly sophisticated online learners.

On-site learners may practice skills or conduct experiments during workshops, listen to lectures, watch videos, attend performances, write papers, and have other multimedia, multisensory educational experiences. They may work alone or within groups, inside or outside the classroom. They may have as much or as little interaction with the teacher as they want or need, or as much as you build into the initial course design and encourage through e-mail messages, chat sessions, or bulletin board discussions, for example.

In general, teachers usually have many responsibilities if they are in charge of developing course materials. They control the amount of material covered in a learning module. They determine the sequence of activities, pace of instruction, organization and scheduling of learning units, as well as the forms of information delivery. Although some learners may work faster or slower than the group norm, the majority are kept moving through the course at the same pace. Any questions or problems in completing activities or comprehending information can be taken care of in the classroom. If you plan to develop an online course, you must be able to plan and complete all these tasks.

As described in Chapter 1, there are more similarities between effective on-site and online classes than you might have imagined. However, in an online environment, you have to emphasize an intuitive user interface, develop experiences that surpass (not just mimic) in-person activities, and work with the institution's technical or budgetary constraints. You have to be a perceptive guide and presenter in either an online or an on-site format, and you should be an innovative thinker in both teaching environments. When you facilitate an online curriculum, however, you have to anticipate learners' needs and solicit feedback in different ways.

When you plan an online course, you have to research what learners will need and how they can best master skills or gain knowledge. Not only must the curriculum be sound, but different types of learning experiences must be offered throughout all courses in that curriculum to accommodate different learners' needs. In addition, the course design must be flexible enough that learners can progress at their own pace and even, perhaps, complete units out of sequence, as long as they meet course objectives by specified deadlines. All instructions, explanations, descriptions, et cetera, must be clearly worded so that learners understand all information easily and interpret materials the same way.

Because people working with an online curriculum most often will be working on their own, the course materials must be self-explanatory and suitable for a wide variety of learners. Instead of the teacher directing the educational activities, the teacher/designer plans the educational structure and, during the course, facilitates educational activities and acts as a coach. Learners either can follow the organizational structure as presented in learning modules or create their own sequence of activities and depth of experiences within the established framework.

You need to make sure you understand the course's purpose and how you plan to meet that purpose. Then you can plan the specifics of the course, such as the readings you want to include, the textbook selection (if there is one), the numbers and types of assignments, and the media to be used in the course.

The following list of questions can be useful in helping you determine exactly what a course should entail, and why the stated learning objectives are necessary. The parameters for each course should be clear before the internal framework is designed. Without a clear map of the overall purpose and design of a course, the internal design of modules, sequencing, content, and activities will be weak.

Figure 2-1. Preliminary Questions about Your Course

- What is the course's purpose?

- How does it fit with other courses in the curriculum?

- How is it appropriately unique?

- What are the course's objectives for learners?

- How can the learning objectives be easily met by learners taking an online course?

- What knowledge base should be increased by taking this course?

- Which skills should be developed or enhanced by taking this course?

- Which skills should be emphasized and strengthened?

- Which subject areas should be presented?

- What prerequisite knowledge or skills must learners have to begin this course?

- How effective will this course be in a year?

- How will the course fit into any planned curriculum changes over the next year?

- What proposed changes in subject matter, professional requirements (e.g., for certification within a profession, such as accounting), or academic requirements (e.g., for accreditation) will have an impact on this course?

- How will any planned changes to the budget affect this course?

- How will any planned technology upgrades affect this course?

- Who is available to teach this course, or multiple sections of this course, each time it is offered?

- What types of training will teachers need to be able to facilitate this course?

- How does this course fit with the current curriculum (e.g., a required course, an elective)?

Answers to these questions can lead to further questions about the structure of the course, as shown in the following list.

Figure 2-2. Secondary Questions about Your Course

- What is the progression of skills and knowledge throughout the duration of the course?

- What is the starting point (e.g., prerequisites, place within the structure of other courses, expectations for entry-level skills and knowledge)?

- What is the ending point (e.g., leading into another course, logical cutoff point for information or skills development)?

- How do these endpoints indicate the material should be structured?

- What are logical modules or units within this structure?

- How can assignments and activities fit into this overall plan of modules or units?

- How can the amount and types of content and activities/assignments be balanced in each module or unit?

- How do this course's amount and type of information and activities fit within the overall curriculum?

- What pre- or co-requisites are needed for successfully completing this course? (and are these pre- or co-requisites part of the program's curriculum?)

- How have constructivist principles been applied to this course?

- How have behaviorist principles been applied to this course?

- What is the time frame for completion of each activity and assignment?

- How do the deadlines fit with the overall starting and ending dates for the course?

- How often will this course be offered online?

- How many learners can take this course in the same section?

- How many sections will be needed each term?

- Will learners be able to complete degree requirements with the proposed schedule for this class?

Before you continue with the planning, your answers to these questions should be similar to the answers provided by the administrators, other teachers or designers, and the technical experts who will be working on the course. (If you need to convince these people to add a course that you are designing to an established program or series of non-credit courses, you must ensure that your course is compatibly designed to fit with others offered by the same institution.) Implementation of the design you are now planning is much easier when everyone shares the same vision of what the course will be.

Of course, your vision, as an educator knowledgeable about pedagogy and your subject area(s) of specialization, must always be influenced by the audience for the course—the learners. Their needs, interests, expectations, and concerns also must have a high priority in your planning. Each online course first must be educationally sound. However, it should also be innovative, interesting, enlightening, engaging, and usable.

Results of a study reported by Muirhead (2000) of online teachers in Alberta, Canada, illustrated the many dimensions of developing such course materials. Muirhead explained that everyone in the study reported the complexity of developing a course and its online materials. Both pedagogical and technical concerns must be addressed. You need time to design usable, enlightening materials and the institutional support to implement the design.

Types of Course Materials

Making the class meet all these criteria is challenging. As you plan a new course, you need to determine the types of course materials that will be offered to learners; the ways you'll meet different learners' needs, expectations, and learning preferences; the amount of subject matter content appropriate for the level and length of the course; and the technology required for learners to gather information, interact with the materials, communicate with you and other learners, and complete assignments. A sound educational plan in all these areas is necessary before the class goes online.

Course materials can be planned by the type of interaction learners will have with them. Course content (e.g., readings), activities and assignments, and evaluations or feedback are three types of materials you will want to make available on your Web site.

Course content usually is information that students receive more passively, through readings, multimedia files, and graphics. Core content can be linked through your course site, as an internal link to information stored on the institution's server or an external link to a site developed by someone outside the institution, such as a corporation, a non-profit group, or other learners. The information may be available in different formats, such as a printed textbook, a CD, or Web-based information, but it covers the subject matter and presents information to learners.

Activities and assignments are interactive. After learners have read or viewed subject information, they apply this knowledge to skills-building or information-sharing activities. Learners may discuss topics in a chat room, post messages to a bulletin board, go on a field trip, practice a skill, complete a simulation, write a paper, or take a test. The emphasis is activity and application.

Learners may need to synthesize information, explain their ideas, conduct research to answer questions, criticize what they have read, and compare what they have read to what they observe with all their senses. Online course materials must involve activities, as well as assignments like writing an essay. Doing is a big part of learning, especially for students who need tactile, auditory, and visual stimulation to help them learn.

Feedback is another important part of the course materials. Learners and teachers must evaluate each others' work, as well as the course as a whole. Learner, teacher, and course evaluations are an important part of the educational process for the current class. As well, evaluations help learners and educators improve the course for future learners and teachers.

The following sections highlight these three types of information (i.e., content, activities and assignments, and feedback) that you will need to plan for your course.

Course Content

You need to determine how much information should be available through the class Web site and peripherals such as textbooks, CDs, videotapes, or other materials students have to purchase or borrow for home or office use. You may want a primary textbook (or more than one) that can be kept long after the online class ends and the course site is no longer available. On the other hand, you may want to cut back on the cost of additional materials learners need to complete the course and therefore provide all or a majority of materials through the course site only. Based on your analysis of learners' needs and preferences, you choose appropriate temporary or permanent educational tools.

Wherever you offer course content, the material must be clearly organized so that learners can easily navigate the information and make appropriate connections between sources of information. Research has indicated that the way information is organized is the key to learning, not simply the use of multimedia, which in itself does not improve learners' retention of information.

Parlangeli, Marchigiani, and Bagnara (1999), for example, concluded that learners often have problems when they are unfamiliar with the way to use the system *and* with the subject matter. When students have to concentrate on how to find information and move around the course site, they cannot focus on learning the subject information at the same time. Simply plopping information onto a CD or linking Web sites to course readings will not help learners make sense of the information. Learners may have trouble using tools to find information or understand in which order topics should be covered. Clear organization of topics and prior instruction in using course tools and navigating information are as much a requirement of good content as having innovative, educational sources.

Your choice of well-organized topics may involve different media through which the information is presented. Subject matter materials to be accessed through the course site can be presented in different formats: print readings, graphics, and streaming audio or video. Most courses still rely primarily on texts that can be downloaded to disk, printed easily and quickly, or read on screen, although multimedia formats are gaining popularity. Information on the Internet can be created just for your course site, by you or someone else, or it can be found on Web sites beyond the institution. Linking the URLs/URIs of external sites may require you to get permission before you direct students away from the course site and to the

Internet at large. (Chapter 3 offers more ideas for developing and integrating course content.)

Readings

Readings are the most common information on course sites, and they most resemble the traditional texts that learners also may be required to study. The information should be short enough to be downloaded quickly and easily; a no-frames, text-only, or printer-friendly version should be available for learners to print or save to disk. Because some readers have unlimited computer time or may want to read online while they are on a break in the office, for example, texts linked to the course site should be scrollable and easily readable in a short time period. Long, dense texts should be avoided, but scrollable texts that have been "chunked" appropriately so they can be easily read online are good to use.

Keep in mind that not all learners may have unlimited online access. Students connecting to your course from another country may have to pay by the hour for online access or may have to share technology with many other users. You have to consider all learners and the amount of time they can spend on the Internet as you design readings.

Because learners should be able to access subject matter materials from the Web site, the readings should be available throughout the duration of the course. The links must be active and accurate at least for that time period, and the course Web site must be accessible from at least a week before the class begins to at least a few days after the course ends. Also, because you probably will want to use at least some readings more than one term, the links to course readings should be stable so that they will be available for months at a time.

For example, if you require learners to read current events news stories, you may need to check the URL/URI frequently. News stories found at one location when they are current may be moved to a different URL/URI, such as an archive, as more recent stories are posted. Some news stories may not be linked at all once the news is old. These articles might not be your best bet for course readings, unless you can get permission to reprint the articles in one place with a stable address.

As with other easily readable, downloadable texts, online course readings should have few pictures, or at least graphics that load quickly and take up little space. Multicolumn formats should be reproduced easily in downloadable form without causing readers to lose the organization of the original article. As you choose links to texts stored outside the course site, you should make sure that the information can be loaded easily by learners with different levels of technology and can be downloaded in print or to disk in a format that easily duplicates the original.

Good readings allow learners to understand information from different perspectives. As you choose online readings, you should select a variety representing people from different countries or locations, cultural or experiential backgrounds, and views or beliefs. If learners are going to review information critically, you need to provide a number of accurate voices that speak on behalf of different groups or provide different arguments. Helping learners develop a balanced view of a subject is an important consideration when you select content material.

You also need to represent information within an accurate time frame. If you want learners to study an event over time, the readings should reflect information about the event as it happened, as well as later, more interpretive information. If you want readers to study history, for example, you might include readings from the event's or person's own time period, but then allow learners to read what recent historians have written about the event in retrospect. Creating a balanced perspective involves not only a variety of voices, but also of times.

You hope that all learners in your class will have the same reading competency and level of literacy. However, you need to ensure that the majority of learners can understand the readings you select. You may want to run a readability test scale on the readings you want to link to your course site.

You may need some variation in the reading grade levels in the information, just to make sure that all readers can understand the subject matter. If the required reading levels are too high, learners become frustrated and abandon the readings. If the levels are too low, learners feel that the information has been watered down, or that the tone is condescending. You want to entice learners to complete all online readings. Making sure readers can understand all, or at least the majority of information, is an important part of making the information accessible and encouraging learners to take time with each required reading.

Of course, any information that you link to your Web site must be reproduced with copyright permission. If you are going to use someone else's information and expression of an idea, you need to have permission. Only include information on your Web site that has been approved for use on your site, by the institution as well as by the copyright owner of the original.

Some information may require the institution to pay fees for its use. Before you require students to read information or complete a survey, you need to make sure that the site is free, no subscription is required, or no usage fees to be paid. Also, if your course is going to be offered internationally, your institution should be able to provide you with guidelines for dealing with copyright issues that affect international distribution and fair use of materials. As Kennedy summarized in a recent *E-Learning* article (2002), the copyright law is often confusing or unclear, especially in an international forum. One reasonable solution is to develop a contract with the institution that spells out who owns course or other academic materials. A good rule of thumb is to learn your institution's policies regarding academic integrity, fair use, copyright, and trademarks before you decide which outside materials you need to use in your course.

Because of the need for copyright permission and the possible fees associated with linking some sites to your course site, for example, you may decide to create some readings yourself. You can create sample documents like those learners will have to turn in as part of their assignments, or you may want to share some of your own work with learners. However, you shouldn't be the sole creator of online texts. Even if you have the most valid points to make, your voice is still only one. Learners need to get a variety of views about a subject area.

As with other online materials, online readings should be developed first, and the technology to use them should be developed after the educational design. With that said, however, you also need to know how many readings, how many kilobytes (K), and how much bandwidth are allowed for each module and course. You have to be selective in the numbers of readings for each educational unit. Not only will learners feel overwhelmed if they face dozens of links about the same subject, but they probably will only check the first few readings in a long list.

You also need to indicate in which order the readings should take place, if there is a precise order, to make sense of the topic. Learners should be able to keep track of the readings that they have accessed. If the links do not remain marked so that readers know which links have been previously used, some other system should be devised to let learners know at a glance how much reading remains to be done or in which order they have covered the material.

De Bra (2002) suggested the use of link annotation and link hiding as two forms of adaptive navigation support that may be appropriate for online course materials. Each link on the course site can be designed to indicate a hierarchy. One type of link indicates that the material is new; another, that the information requires previous readings (prerequisites) before learners access the higher-level or later-sequenced information. Additional descriptive information about each linked item can also assist learners not only in comprehending new information, but also in understanding the relationship among linked materials.

If you want readers to check out all links about a topic, you must provide a manageable number of readings for each unit. If you want a manageable Web site, you want the readings to be easy to find, load, and use. Before you add every reading you would like learners to view, you need to discuss with technical staff how many documents or links are possible for your site, and what types of information can be supported by the system. You also need to keep in mind the level of technology to which most learners have access.

The following checklist offers some questions you need to consider as you plan course readings.

Figure 2-3. Choosing Effective Reading Materials

- Will the readings supplement a textbook or other reading material? serve as the primary course content? or both?

- How many readings should be provided about the same subject?

- How many readings should be required for each module? for the course as a whole?

- How many readings should be optional for each module? for the course as a whole?

- How will learners use the information they have read?

- How will learners show their mastery of a subject after they have completed the required readings?

- How can accuracy of the information be verified before you require students to read it?

- How recent does the reading have to be?

- What are the author's credentials for writing this information?

- How does each reading help create a balanced view of the subject?

- Which readings should be grouped together as a unit?

- Which readings should stand alone?

- When do learners need each reading?

- How long will this reading be useful (e.g., one term, indefinitely)?

These types of questions help you evaluate each reading individually for its applicability to and purpose in your course. They help determine the amount of core content learners will receive from the list of readings, and how this content matches information and experiences gained through other, primarily non-print, media.

Because readings are a key part of the information learners take away from the course, you need to make sure the amount of reading material is appropriate for the subject matter and the type of course. You also must ensure that the readings will be valuable in helping learners read about new subject areas and apply their knowledge in appropriate ways to their lives or careers.

Multimedia Files

Linked audio and video files can be important supplements to textbooks, discussions, and the print documents stored at the class Web site. The more interactive the site, the more it will meet the needs of learners with different abilities and learning preferences. Of course, you do not want the class site to require so many special media players or such a fast modem that learners with low-tech hardware or software cannot access valuable information. You should establish a balance between larger audio and video files that may require plug-ins and the plain text documents and .GIF or .JPEG/.JPG files that take up less space.

A good file is one that is usable for several classes. It is not outdated quickly, the quality of the file is high, and the information provides insights or experiences that text cannot offer. Interviews, lectures, speeches, newscasts, tours, jobs in progress, concert performances, and demonstrations are some good examples of audio or video files that may be useful to your students.

If a file requires a plug-in or player, you should make sure learners know how to download the required software and use the file. Free plug-ins or those supported and subsidized by the institution are the best way of encouraging learners to take the time to download what they need to be able to access audio/video files.

Files that can be downloaded usually are a higher quality and can be reused by several classes. They lack the immediacy of streaming audio or video, but they may be more practical for use in your classes.

Graphics Files

Some graphics may be incorporated into the readings you develop or use from another source. To make sure that everyone can access information, you probably do not want to rely too heavily on graphics, even if you are teaching a class that is heavy on visuals, such as an art appreciation or a Web design course.

All graphics should have captions and textual descriptions so that learners whose computers cannot handle the graphics can still make sense of the material. Keep in mind, too, that some learners turn off the graphics capability of their systems so they can load information more quickly. Others use text or line readers to translate the information into a format they can read, such as Braille; yet other learners use old systems that may not be able to load and display graphics quickly or at all.

Although graphics can be an important part of course content, you should also provide text alternatives to graphics. Learners who cannot view graphics in a text or as separate files will need a prose description of what they are missing, as well as the significance and background of the graphic.

In addition to using graphics that automatically come with readings or texts linked to your course site, you may want to add graphics by themselves for viewing or as additional components to text you create. For example, you may want learners to view lots of different recruitment and war bond posters as part of their study of World War II. You may provide internal course links to a series of separate graphics files, each with a different poster. If you want students to see photographs you took during an archeological expedition, you might scan the photos so that each photograph is a separate file, also linked internally to the module from which you want students to view the pictures. Static (non-moving) graphics, alone or with text, can be an important visual component of the course content.

The most common types of graphic files are .GIF and .JPG (sometimes noted as .JPEG). Graphics Interchange Format (GIF) files are best for line art and designs like logos. GIF files may not have the same quality as the higher resolution JPEGs, but they take up less space. Joint Photographic Experts Group (JPEG) files are best for photographs and other artwork that requires a higher number of colors and a finer resolution. JPEGs take up more space, but they may look better on screen, depending upon the type of image you want to show.

A third graphics file type is PNG—Portable Network Graphics. This file can be used as an alternative to GIF files, but it supports true color, which also makes it easier to use in grayscale (Napier, 2000).

Streaming Audio or Video

Streaming content is either broadcast or on demand (Strom, 2001). Broadcast audio or video is viewed as an event happens; often this type of streaming allows learners to watch or hear the event only one time. The immediacy of the event requires learners to schedule this synchronous activity into their course time, or to allow a certain amount of viewing/ listening time to an ongoing stream.

On-demand audio or video, such as previously recorded lectures, animation, and guided tours, can be accessed as learners have time to play a file. They can replay all or part of the file, pause it, and fast-forward it whenever they want. Of course, the immediacy of the event is lost in a previously taped file, but the reusability of the information is highly desirable.

Broadcast audio or video may be useful in classes where breaking news, current events, and one-time-only showings provide information for a specific group. For example, learners in a news production class may need to view a news event online; learners in a radio broadcast class may listen to streaming audio from stations around the country or world.

Although streaming audio or video of live events is more difficult to capture, its immediacy may make up for the learners' inability to view the file again and again. The quality of streaming media may be lower than some learners would like, especially if they have low-tech equipment. Nevertheless, you may want to link learners with sites that regularly offer streaming audio or video, like news and broadcast outlets, or you may provide special events online.

Your lectures during on-site classes, speeches, special presentations, and virtual tours, for example, can be videotaped first and then streamed so that learners can view them after the fact. Unlike streaming audio and video of events as they happen, on-demand information added to a course site can allow learners the benefits of watching streaming media without having to view the event as it happens. Streaming media of previously videotaped events can provide the best of asynchronous learning and multimedia technology.

Harvard University's online education programs use streaming video to allow online learners to see and hear a teacher's lectures, just as the information was presented to an on-site class. The university requires students to use technology meeting Internet, hardware, and software requirements, which are published online.

For example, in the guidelines provided in 2001, students were required to download and install RealPlayer V8 and to have a 56 kbps dial-in access link to be able to view the videos. However, a cable modem or T1 line were recommended for better viewing. The latest versions of Netscape Navigator or Internet Explorer were also suggested. The recommended PC hardware included Windows '98 or NT 4.0, a Pentium II processor, 64 or more MB of RAM, support for 256 colors, resolution of 1024 by 768, and a screen resolution of 800 by 600, at the minimum. Mac hardware requirements included, at the minimum, OS 8.6, a 400 mHz processor, 92 or more MB of RAM, and the same support for colors and resolution required for PC users (Harvard University, 2001).

If you are going to provide streaming audio or video, you need to make learners aware of the technical requirements for accessing this information. Without the minimal technology, learners can miss a great deal of course content stored in video files or available through "as it happens" streaming audio or video.

The quality of streaming media must be high enough that students avoid frustration in trying to see or hear a low-quality presentation and a lag time between frames. Strom (2001) reminded teachers that video must be viewed as a continuous feed of information. The images have to appear in the proper order, and the viewed series of images must be smooth and uninterrupted. When a file is accessed, a certain amount of information is sent to a buffer. When the file begins to play, more information is sent into the buffer. If the bandwidth for playing the media is not enough to sustain the stream of information, students see a jerky video with a staggered audio. Only a part of the clip plays, then the player pauses while more information is downloaded, and finally the next segment is played. This piecemeal presentation is difficult for learners to follow, and it takes a long time to download. Long presentations therefore become unusable, as learners become frustrated long before they play an entire file.

Even compressed multimedia files take up a lot of space (Strom, 2001). Allowing enough server space for multiple files is important when you plan to use a lot of streaming video or audio files. To save space, Belanger and Jordan (2000) suggested reducing file sizes by experimenting with different frame rates and keeping the video display small. Less color and a small soundtrack also help save space. Whatever you can do to keep files small, do it.

Figure 2-4. Analyzing Media for Your Course

- Should viewing media be a synchronous or an asynchronous activity?

- Which course objectives can be met by using streaming audio or video?

- What course topics are best suited to broadcast or on-demand multimedia files?

- How can multimedia be integrated with other course materials to cover this subject matter?

- How often should multimedia be used as a source of core content?

- How often should multimedia be used as a supplementary source of course content?

- What quality of files will be available to all learners?

- What kind of technical requirements will learners have to meet before they can play media?

- How long should each on-demand file be?

- How many links to broadcast media should be included on the course site?

- How long can an on-demand file be used in this course?

- How often will new materials need to be videotaped for on-demand viewing?

- What kind of copyright and other permissions or protections are needed for these multimedia files?

The technical realities of using streaming media may make video or audio files less realistic in your course design. As learners have more access to higher levels of computer technology, and as the institution supports multimedia applications, you probably will want to integrate more streaming content into your courses. However, just because you and your students can use multimedia more easily does not mean that you use it exclusively. As with other types of online information, you need to make sure the medium suits the type of information being presented and is useful to learners with different abilities and learning preferences.

The list of questions in Figure 2-4 can help you determine how much and when you should use media, either streaming or on demand, in your course.

Offline Peripherals

The course materials discussed thus far can be linked to your course site, either as external or internal links, depending upon where the material is stored and who creates it. Online learners should be comfortable locating and using a variety of forms of electronically generated and stored information, and they may prefer to download information to their computer or printer if they want to read offline. Online learners also prefer to do as much of the grunt work of education online. They do not like to drive to a physical campus to register for classes or buy books, for example. If they are going to take classes online, they want the rest of the academic process to be electronic, too.

If you require learners to use textbooks, CDs, or other materials they must purchase, you should at least make it easy for them to find and buy the materials. Peripherals might play a critical role in the course; they are added to what learners use online. These materials become the extras that learners must buy or receive before they can start the course.

An online bookstore, or at least a phone or fax ordering system to the institution, should be used to help learners purchase the correct book(s), disks, tapes, and so on for each class. You might also choose materials that are easily purchased from other online bookstores, such as Amazon.com, BarnesandNoble.com, et cetera. If materials are sent as part of a course packet, and paid for as part of the total course fee, the materials should be sent as soon as learners register for a course.

The benefits of requiring learners to use printed peripherals are the same benefits of using any type of hardcopy information: It is portable wherever they go. Learners do not need special equipment to access a book, although they need VCRs or CD or DVD players for other types of course materials. They do not have to worry about the server being down or lack of access to a computer. They can keep the materials once the course is over, without downloading information from the course site. Some learners also like the feel of a textbook, because that is traditionally what they think of as a repository for course information. Real classes, to some learners, require at least one textbook.

Information on CDs or even floppy disks (as long as they remain available) can provide learners with sample documents, additional software or plug-ins that will be useful to their online work, and practice exercises or simulations to help them complete an online task once they log into the course site. You or your institution may produce disks with information and examples customized especially for your course. You might want to create tutorials to help learners use the software required for the class or to practice using tools that they will find on the course site. You might have background readings that supplement the linked information found at the site. Whatever is appropriate content for your course might be added to these personalized disks.

Many printed textbooks also bundle CDs with the book. If you have selected a textbook as a peripheral for your course, you might see if additional materials, such as a CD, come with the book. This process could save you the time and expense of producing customized materials to go along with what you have designed for the course site.

However, the downside is that materials designed to go with a textbook provide standardized examples, not ones specific for the approach you are taking toward the subject matter or the assignments you have developed specifically for the people in your class. You should check the effectiveness of any supplementary materials that come with textbooks to see how much information will really be useful in your course and if you still need to provide more personalized information for class members.

If you develop peripherals on your own, disks are a good choice, because they can also be useful for storing multimedia files that may take up too much space on the server or be more difficult to access and use repeatedly from the course Web site. Of course, the problem with using disks is that learners have to use them with their computer, which may make the peripherals less portable. Adult learners on a business trip, for example, probably will not drag several CDs with them; they will use the course Web site and perhaps take a book to read when they do not have computer access.

Peripherals should offer convenience, variety, and materials that cannot be used or easily found on the course site or in another format. They should justify the extra cost or time in using them as part of the core course material. They should allow skills development or provide in-depth information not found in other sources.

If you require peripherals, choose them carefully so that they provide easily recognized benefits to students. The number of peripherals should be low; you want to encourage online learners to do much of their learning online.

Activities and Assignments

When you design course activities and assignments in conjunction with the readings and other core materials, you are planning an effective educational design. With that in place, you can work with technical specialists to design an effective format so that learners can easily access the information you want them to have. Any modifications at the technical development stage should come after you have planned a sound educational strategy for the curriculum and each course.

Just as you determine how many readings or other media used to provide core subject matter are appropriate for the course's length, academic level, and topic, you have to determine how many activities and assignments are appropriate for the course. Most classes are broken into learning modules, which may last a week or two, and are based around a theme. That theme may involve several chapters of a textbook, a time period in history, a type of experiment, and so on. Whatever themes are appropriate for your course should be integrated into the assignments and activities that reinforce what learners have read, heard, or otherwise studied in the unit. Activities and assignments also must help learners to develop skills.

In each module or unit, you need to make sure that learners have several activities that reflect different learning styles or preferences, but the number of activities and graded assignments must be manageable for adults with busy lives outside the classroom. For example, you might consider assignments from within the categories listed in Figure 2-5.

Writing assignments should be considered carefully. In an online format, especially if learners and teachers primarily communicate through written messages (e.g., e-mail, bulletin board posts, keyed or typed chats), writing is an important skills area to develop. Although the written word has always been an important form for self-expression, it is crucial in online courses requiring mostly written communication. As well, a hallmark of academic excellence traditionally has been the ability to write well.

For these reasons, as well as to meet specific writing skills requirements associated with a degree program (such as, but not limited to, linguistics, composition, rhetoric, technical writing and editing, print journalism), you may want to emphasize written assignments as you develop course activities. Of course, other types of learner-evaluation assignments should be used, but written assignments can help build learners' skills and provide an effective format for evaluating learners' understanding of course content and ability to express themselves clearly.

Through a dialogue between you and learners about a written assignment, and as you review and assist in the preparation of drafts, trust develops between you and students (Bauer & Anderson, 2000). As long as you constructively criticize learners' work and discuss students' ideas objectively, trust can be built through writing assignments. Although written assignments offer benefits by allowing you and students to get to know each other and discuss ideas, they are also a valuable feedback mechanism for learners and an evaluation tool for you.

After you have determined which activities and assignments will be included in a module, you need to figure out which assignments will be done asynchronously or synchronously. You also should create a blend of activities and assignments that allow learners to work together. Some assignments should be individually completed, but you may, for example, create a group project with some group-graded assignments and some individual responses to what the group learned.

In addition to determining how many and what types of assignments are practical to help learners meet course objectives, you also want to ensure

Figure 2-5. Assignment Categories

Writing assignments/activities

- Essays emphasizing personal reflection, restatement of ideas based on interaction or discussion with others, or shared personal experiences

- Research papers emphasizing secondary sources of information and primary sources gathered through interviews, experiments, and observations

- Bulletin board posts to foster group discussion

- Journals to help learners record thoughts, feelings, ideas, and experiences as they relate to course topics

- Text of speeches or presentations that will be made to the class

Speaking assignments/activities

- Videoconference or video file presentation to other members of the class

- Audio files, audio e-mail, or video e-mail to discuss the learner's reaction/response to a topic

- Chat sessions with multimedia capabilities

- Group discussions through conference phone calls or videoconferences

Designing assignments/activities

- PowerPoint presentations to highlight research or a topic presented in course materials

- CAD design or models to illustrate a project

- Art/drawings to illustrate ideas or share art works

- Whiteboard presentations or drawings that reflect a learner's understanding of a course topic

- Desktop publishing to create model documents, such as newsletters, brochures, or business cards

Testing activities/assignments

- Multiple choice or True-False interactive tests over course readings

- Essay tests over course readings or personal experiences

- Simulations and practical exercises to show skill mastery

that independent learning takes place. You may allow learners leeway in the choice of research topics, for example, to encourage individuals to learn more about a topic of particular interest to them. You might encourage outside field trips or activities that learners can complete in their communities. Each person can direct his or her own learning experience by, for example, deciding to visit the local museum, participating in a community event, or talking with people who live in the same area. The types of assignments and activities should be flexible, so that learners have some choice in the types of experiences they have during the course. They can also choose topics and activities that reflect their interests and educational needs.

As you schedule assignments, you need to make sure not all assignments are due at the same time, such as at the end of the course. The assignments should be structured so that they increase in complexity or show mastery of a subject matter over the duration of the course. Graded assignments should be weighted so that this mastery of a subject can be measured *by* (not just *at*) the end of the course. As well, ungraded assignments may be a useful part of the course, to allow learners to develop skills or participate in activities just for the sake of learning, and not only to receive a grade.

Learners should have an easy way of returning assignments to you. Some assignments might be interactive through the course Web site, so that at the click of a mouse, the assignment is sent to you automatically. Other assignments, such as word-processed documents, may need to be sent as e-mail attachments. You may need to specify which word processing software, or which versions of the software, are recommended or supported by the institution. Some assignments, such as bulletin board posts, whiteboard drawings, and chat sessions, can be created and stored at the course Web site. Yet other assignments can be uploaded to learners' personal Web sites and linked to the class site. Whatever ways of returning assignments are appropriate for your class, you need to make sure that learners understand what they are supposed to do for the assignment and how they are supposed to submit their work.

Pedagogically, the assignments should involve learners at several levels: from a basic restatement of what they have read to more thoughtful, personal responses that show how skills and knowledge have been integrated into a learner's life. All assignments should be closely related to the core content, but they should offer practical, interesting, and innovative ways to engage learners in sharing and exploring what they have read.

Evaluations or Feedback

Evaluations of the online course, teacher's effectiveness, the feasibility of the infrastructure supporting courses, and the course's marketability and cost effectiveness should all take place. Feedback about the teacher's effectiveness and the course, however, are most often a teacher's/ designer's focus during the development phase for a new course. Feedback about the teacher's effectiveness and the usability and structure of the design should be solicited during and after the course, each time it is taught.

In addition, feedback about learners' participation and competence should be provided to learners, certainly, but teachers and administrators may also be interested in some measures of learner progress and participation in the course. Learners should receive formal and informal types of evaluations throughout the course.

Feedback about Learners, Given to Teachers or Administrators

One type of feedback about learners' participation that you may wish to incorporate into the course design can be an automatically recorded count of logins. Each time the learner visits the course site, a counter records the new visit, so that the teacher (as well as learners and administrators) can see how many times each person has entered the course site. This measure of participation does not account for the learner's understanding of materials presented at the site nor of the learner's involvement in course activities; however, it does at least indicate how frequently learners (or a specific person) visited the site.

Other automatic records may be added to track the length of the learner's visit and the date and time of the last login. This type of record is important for online teachers, because they cannot take attendance for asynchronous activities (although they can for synchronous activities like chats). At least some aspects of learner participation in the course can be quantified (Bauer & Anderson, 2000).

Feedback about Learners, Given to the Learners

The feedback that teachers offer learners can take many forms, such as e-mail discussions of an assignment or posting of grades in an online spreadsheet. Different types of evaluations should be provided to learners throughout the course. As you plan the course design, you may want to see if an online spreadsheet or gradebook will or can be part of the feedback mechanisms for students. You also may check to see if counting/counter programs can be used to track individuals' use of the course site and this information made available to learners, as well as to teachers or administrators.

Learners also need to receive timely, effective feedback. You may want to develop a feedback form that can be used to return comments and grades after you have evaluated assignments. You may have a comments section to an online gradebook that allows you to highlight the strengths and areas of improvements for each assignment. Reusable, electronically available forms allow you to provide feedback consistently to all learners. They also save you time in replicating information in e-mail messages, for example, when several learners should receive similar comments.

As you design the course structure, you may want to talk with technical specialists to see what types of forms and tools are already available to you. For example, all new courses may automatically be designed to have an online gradebook or learner evaluation forms for written assignments. If these forms and tools are not standard with online courses, you need to see if such feedback/evaluation formats can be designed and implemented just for your course. Whatever mechanism you use, it is important that the courses be evaluated and results kept on hand for further scrutiny and research.

In addition, you may want to establish more informal methods of providing feedback to learners. You might write general bulletin board posts and helpful tips about upcoming assignments. You can send e-mail to the class or individuals to provide comments about works in progress or final versions of an assignment, for example. You may decide to send grades and critiques of final projects by e-mail, or to use editing software to mark written assignments.

Although these methods will be less formal and will not require any special technical design considerations, you still need to anticipate the amount of time you will need to create less formal feedback. You do not want the amount of work to become overwhelming, so that you are tempted to write only cursory comments. Feedback needs to be effective, whether it is informal or formal. As you plan the course, you need to determine the best ways to provide and receive feedback/evaluations.

Feedback about Teachers and the Course, Given to Teachers or Administrators

The feedback that learners provide about the courses, or the curriculum in general, and the ways that the teacher facilitates each course should be ongoing. However, an end-of-the-course evaluation may be a requirement and may involve forms common to all courses. Course evaluation forms (as well as teacher evaluation forms) are standard issue for most universities or colleges. You may simply need to follow guidelines provided by the institution about the number and types of questions listed on a form, which is then linked to the course Web site.

However, you may also want to encourage additional feedback throughout the course. You may ask learners to send you e-mail with their comments and suggestions for improvements for each module, major assignments, or readings, for example. Saving these e-mail messages and using them to update the course or report learners' problems with the course (from technology glitches to academic concerns) can keep you and administrators informed about what learners really think about the course.

Although end-of-the-term evaluations are useful, many learners report only their latest impression of the course, often based on their final exam, project, or course grade. More accurate comments might come from learners as they work through course materials and experience the problems and benefits of completing certain assignments. Ongoing forms of feedback, such as periodic evaluations, may provide a more accurate assessment.

Different Learners' Needs and Expectations

All course materials should be designed to meet the needs of learners with differing levels of expertise and experience with the subject matter, language skills, technical know-how, learning preferences, and physical abilities. Your course information should be accessible by everyone who will take your course. The curriculum and each course within it must meet the needs of learners with different abilities and expectations for their education or training.

Online learners certainly have clear expectations for their education. Perhaps more than students in on-site programs, online learners seem to know what they want to learn and how they want to learn it. Because online learners today are often adults returning to classes for career-specific training or a degree that will help them move into a better job, they are focused on the number and types of courses they need to take. Because these students may have at least one job, and sometimes two or three, they are often vocal about what they want or need in an online course. If they spend time, money, and effort to take a course, they want to make sure the class is worth it. Therefore, learners sometimes have a "customer" mentality that may be disconcerting to teachers.

Student customers expect a high-quality education on demand, but they also may want to determine what they do and do not need to learn and how they want to get credit for their educational experiences. Instead of passively accepting what educators give them, online learners take an active role in determining what type of education they believe is necessary for their career success.

Administrators and teachers need to provide the services and experiences that learners expect, but also retain high academic standards required for accreditation and the amount and type of coursework necessary to master subject areas. While being responsive to the needs of different learners, teachers and administrators still need to develop curricula that are competitive with that of other institutions and that cover information required in a course or toward a degree.

Adult learners like to direct their training and education, which is one reason why online education is so popular with these students. Adults engaged in the business world all week often prefer that same kind of hands-on approach when they return to classes. They want to advance through educational materials rapidly and get immediate gratification for their work. They often have little patience for drawn-out learning experiences; they prefer their educational advancement to proceed at the same pace as the rest of their busy life.

Not all online learners are adults, but even younger students face multiple pressures today. The pace of Westernized society is increasingly fast, and learners of all ages want their education to be as fast-paced as other forms of business and entertainment. Without turning your courses into the equivalent of fast food, you need to provide learners with ready access to a variety of learning materials that they can use at their own pace.

Younger students may feel more comfortable reading information on screen. They are used to spending hours in front of a computer monitor or television screen; they grew up using digital displays. As you develop course materials, you should remember that many people will complete all their work online—from reading to writing to completing activities. The computer is their medium of information gathering, creation, and dissemination.

However, not all learners want to feel stuck in front of a computer. They prefer to download information, often converting text or graphics files into printouts that they can take with them and refer to just as they would any textbook. Your course plans should take into consideration these learners, who want to download information quickly and easily and convert it into a form with which they are comfortable.

Although online courses need a linear progression of ideas, building upon skills and information gained through earlier lessons or modules, the materials in each unit should be accessible at any time, and in any order, and still make sense. Learners need to be able to return to materials they liked, but perhaps skimmed over, as they worked through a module. They may need to refer to information they used early in the course, but now need to review again to refresh their memory. They may skip around through modules, doing the activities that seem easiest, or conversely, that will take the most time, first, and then going back to complete other activities as time allows.

Learners familiar with the Web often approach educational modules the same way they approach other Web sites. They use a hypertext approach— clicking links randomly and following no predetermined order in reading or viewing information. Each linked piece of information on your site, then, must make sense as a separate chunk of information as well as have meaning as one chunk in a series of chunks randomly linked by individual learners.

Because the Internet is an international medium, and your courses may include learners from anywhere in the world, you need to think of your course site as a multinational site. Although you probably will have only one dominant language for your site, you may need a multilingual site or language alternatives. At the very least, your site should include information that reflects a multinational sensitivity.

Your site should be a model of good international communication, and the examples and links should reflect a global attitude. If you are looking for suggestions to help make your site more international, at least technically, you might want to read the guidelines and view the World Wide Web Consortium's tutorial. (Check the W3C's Web site at www.w3.org.) With this information in mind, you can work closely with the technical designers to make your site accessible and usable by international students.

Learners with Different Physical Abilities

Learners may have different physical abilities that make some forms of education easier to use, and advances in technology are making it easier for learners with different physical needs to access online information in a form that is readable and usable. For example, learners who cannot see information on a screen can have trouble if your course site features frames or uses lots of graphics. You may provide a no-frames version in addition to one with frames.

A plain text alternative can be scanned by electronic readers and turned into a form that learners can use. Information that can be heard, on an audio file for instance, may be another way to present information in a different format that is usable by everyone—those who can and those who cannot see information on screen. Audio files or plain text transcripts are good alternatives for video files. Plain text alternatives and simple graphics are good alternatives for learners who cannot hear audio files or the soundtrack to video. As you plan information for your Web site, you need to think of ways that your course site can be useful to learners with different abilities.

One place to get good ideas about information design for your site is the World Wide Web Consortium's (W3C's) Web site. They provide information about the Web Accessibility Initiative (WAI), an international program to make the Web accessible to the widest possible audience. Resources, descriptions of the initiative, FAQs, and checklists are linked. For example, the WAI is described at www.w3.org/WAI/about.html. Another valuable link is a checklist to ensure that your site's content either is accessible to persons with different abilities or that alternative formats make the content accessible; the checklist is shown at www.w3.org/TR/WCAG10/full-checklist.html.

You should view the checklist and learn about the initiative as you gather materials for your site. Then you and technical experts can create alternative formats for the information that is not readily accessible to everyone.

Learners with Different Learning Styles

Learners also differ in the way they best take in and understand information. Depending upon the learning theory you prefer, the labels and numbers of styles differ. You may, for example, prefer to use Gardner's multiple intelligences, listing seven levels of learning, or Kolb's four learning styles. You may want students to take the Myers-Briggs Type Indicator or the Keirsey Personality Inventory. Whatever learning theory or description of styles you prefer, you should make the materials found at your course site appropriate for learners with different styles.

One useful model is the Learning Orientation Model, which categorizes learners as transforming learners, performing learners, conforming learners, and resistant learners (Martinez & Bunderson, 2000). Martinez and Bunderson's classifications can help you identify and develop activities for the three types of learners (transforming, performing, and conforming) that you are most likely to have in your online courses.

Transforming learners are highly self-motivated and goal oriented. They like the autonomy that online courses provide and may feel stifled by too many synchronous activities.

Performing learners may work better in groups, especially if they are not particularly interested in the subject matter. Although performing learners may be highly self-motivated when they are interested in a subject or an activity, they prefer to let others take charge in situations that fail to interest them.

Conforming learners tend to go along with a group. They do not want to take control of a group or the learning situation, but they like to be directed or guided in their coursework. Conforming learners need reinforcement and approval; they are not highly self-motivated and may need more supervision, group activities, and direct contact with the teacher.

Finally, resistant learners may actively or passively avoid learning anything in a course. These learners may be required by an employer to take a class they consider to be a waste of time, but they usually are not motivated to take online courses on their own. They may do little in an online course or simply drop out.

Descriptions of four learning modalities can help you plan different materials for learners. These modalities are auditory, kinesthetic, tactile or tactual, and visual learners (Soles & Moller, 2001). As you build your course materials, you want to include something for learners of all types. Learners who primarily prefer one of these learning modalities should be able to find materials designed just for them; however, most learners can synthesize information by more than one learning modality. The preferred style is dominant and the easiest way for learners to take in and make use of course content.

Auditory learners like to hear information. They learn well by listening to a teacher and to other learners. They also like to discuss what they have read and get feedback from others. Information in audiovisual formats should be included in your course site for these learners. You might include a streaming audio link to an event, or an ongoing link to a radio station, for example. You might include audio and video files that can be downloaded and played again. Interviews, speeches, segments of lectures, songs—these primarily aural forms of core information can enhance the way auditory students learn. As well, audio links so that learners can hear each other can be valuable for group activities and discussions.

Kinesthetic learners like to move. In fact, some descriptions of this modality label it "mobile." Kinesthetic learners may have a hard time sitting in front of a computer to read or discuss topics in a chat room. They like to take notes during traditional lectures, and they need to keep their hands busy. As you develop assignments, you can give these students something practical to do, such as interview, build, visit—activities that allow learners to practice skills or complete a task, to try out what they have read about or seen.

Online simulations and tours, as well as offline activities and field work, are a few ways to involve kinesthetic learners. Even if your course is primarily text based, you can involve students more actively by creating role plays, design exercises, and problem-solving activities. They may prefer discussions in a chat room that allow them to type their responses. Interactive tests and questionnaires also may help them use what they are reading for class.

Tactile (or tactual, in some descriptions) learners like to use their sense of touch. Until touch screens at home or in the office become more prominent, developing touch-sensitive materials may be more difficult. However, as for kinesthetic learners, you should create activities that allow tactile learners to explore and do. They like hands-on projects and labs, so providing field or lab activities outside the online classroom are helpful. Online group activities such as chat sessions, role-plays, and simulations are also important.

Visual students seem to have the easiest time in online courses, because the majority of information online is still in print, whether you create your own information as a text or link the course site to an outside Web site. Newspapers, journal articles, government documents, research reports, and abstracts are readily available on the Internet. Checklists, guidelines, and other listed items are easy for visual learners to use and remember.

However, visual students need to do more than read, whether they download information for later reading or prefer to read off the screen. Other visuals should include graphics, either static (such as photographs, drawings, schematics, equations, and blueprints) or moving (such as film clips, news broadcasts, tours, and simulations). Videoconferencing so that learners can see the teacher and each other offers another benefit to visual learners, in addition to the immediacy of connecting with others for a discussion or a demonstration.

All learners need expediency and efficiency in their education; therefore, you need to provide information that 1) can be accessed in any order and still make sense as a stand-alone unit, as well as part of a group of materials; 2) meets the learning styles and preferences of different learners; and 3) can be used by students across a wide variety of platforms and levels of technology. An effective online curriculum includes course materials that meet all these criteria.

Summary

An effective online curriculum must be well structured, innovative, filled with usable and appropriate course content, and interesting to a variety of people who take each course and work through a series of classes. Curriculum development requires a strong, consistent infrastructure that is supported at every level of the institution. The curriculum must offer learners appropriate experiences and information that are well suited for use in a web environment.

The curricular design needs to conform to standard elements used among the institution's other programs, so that all course offerings from the same institution have a similar appearance and use similar tools. This planning takes a great deal of time and collaboration among administrators, subject matter experts (teachers), and technical specialists to ensure that the course content is sound and the course site is easy to use. Each course within the curriculum must be a well-designed link that supports other courses within that curriculum.

Although the level of technology should be appropriate for each course and the institution in general, the tools needed to access information and manipulate it should be secondary in planning the sound educational design of the course content, assignments, and activities. The tools should fit the assignment and make it workable for learners; assignments should not be created just to fit the technology. If online education is going to remain high quality, as much time should go into the pedagogy and planning as the technology and implementation.

Learners with different abilities and learning preferences should feel comfortable with the variety of assignments and activities in each course. A multicultural, international ambiance should be created so that the curriculum may be offered globally. Every module must be carefully designed to be pedagogically sound, but it also should be enjoyable and enlightening. The curriculum must reflect the current state of the discipline and offer a progression of course offerings that help learners build knowledge and skills appropriate to the mastery of that discipline.

References

Bauer, J. F., & Anderson, R. S. (2000). Evaluating students' written performance in the online classroom. In R. E. Weiss, D. S. Knowlton, & B. W. Speck (Eds.), *Principles of effective teaching in the online classroom, number 84, new directions for teaching and learning series* (pp. 65-72). San Francisco: Jossey-Bass.

Belanger, F., & Jordan, D. H. (2000). *Evaluation and implementation of distance learning: Technologies, tools and techniques.* Hershey, PA: Idea Group Publishing.

De Bra, P. (2002). Adaptive educational hypermedia on the web. *Communications of the ACM, 45*(5), 60-61.

Downey, S. (2001, January). Strategic planning of online instructional programs: A practitioner's perspective. *International Journal of Educational Technology.* Retrieved September 29, 2002, from http://www.outreach.uiuc.edu/ijet/v2n2/downey/index.html

Fuller, F., McBride, R., & Gillam, R. (2002). Degrees and programs by distance learning: Defining need and finding support through collaboration. In P. Comeaux (Ed.), *Communication and collaboration in the online classroom* (pp. 39-54). Bolton, MA: Anker Publishing.

Harvard University. (2001). Harvard DCE: Distance education: System requirements. Retrieved September 29, 2002, from http://lab.dce.harvard.edu/de/system.html

Kennedy, G. (2002). Intellectual property issues in e-learning. *E-Learning, 18*(2), 91-98.

Martinez, M., & Bunderson, C. V. (2000). Foundations for personalized web learning environments. *ALN Magazine, 4*(2). Retrieved September 29, 2002, from http://www.aln.org/alnweb/magazine/Vol4_issue2/burdenson.htm

Muirhead, W. D. (2000). Online education in schools. *The International Journal of Educational Management, 14*(7), 315+. Retrieved August 18, 2002, from the ProQuest database.

Napier, M. (2000, October 16). Making your DIGICULT web site visually appealing: An introduction to using graphics on the web. *Cultivate Interactive,* Issue 2. Retrieved September 29, 2002, from http://www.cultivate-int.org/issue2/graphics/

Parlangeli, O., Marchigiani, E., & Bagnara, S. (1999). Multimedia systems in distance education: Effects of usability on learning. *Interacting with Computers, 12,* 37-49.

Savenye, W. C., Olina, Z., & Niemczyk, M. (2001). So you are going to be an online writing instructor: Issues in designing, developing, and delivering an online course. *Computers and Composition, 18,* 371-385.

Serdiukov, P. (2001). Models of distance higher education: Fully automated or partially human? *Educational Technology Review, 9*(1). Retrieved September 29, 2002, from http://www.aace.org/pubs/etr/issue1/serdiukov.cfm

Shank, P. (2001). Out with the old. *Online Learning, 5*(8), 64, 66, 68, 70.

Soles, C., & Moller, L. (2001). Myers Briggs Type Preferences in distance learning education. *International Journal of Educational Technology, 2*(2). Retrieved September 29, 2002, from http://www.outreach.uiuc.edu/ ijet/v2n2/soles/index.html

Strom, J. (2001, May). Streaming video: A look behind the scenes. *Cultivate Interactive*. Retrieved March 12, 2003, from http://www.cultivate-int.org/issue4/scenes/

Williams, M. L., Paprock, K., & Covington, B. (1999). *Distance learning: The essential guide.* Thousand Oaks, CA: Sage Publications.

World Wide Web Consortium. (2002). Web Accessibility Initiative. Retrieved September 30, 2002, from http://www.w3.org/WAI/about.html

Updating and Developing Course Materials

As you develop the entire curriculum for a degree program, you want both uniqueness and similarity among courses. Each course should be unique, with its own purpose, objectives, requirements, content, and activities. It must have its own special place in a program.

Each course should be easily identified by learners, administrators, and teachers as unique unto itself, but the design elements and tools used among courses in the curriculum should allow everyone to be able to transfer skills from one course to another.

As well, the content and overall structure for each section within a course must be similar. If four teachers facilitate the same course (for example, Introduction to Physics), then the same content, requirements, and objectives should be found within each section being taught by each teacher. Consistency across all sections of Introduction to Physics is important for a high-quality curricular design.

Each teacher who facilitates a class invariably will create a unique learning experience for the people taking that class, because each facilitator's personality and experiences differ from others'. Learners taking a particular online course, however, should find no significant content or requirement differences among sections. For example, all the information that should be presented in Introduction to Physics will be covered, and the course interface, tools, and schedule will be similar, if not exactly the same, among all sections of that course.

Even sections of Introduction to Physics that are taught on site should be similar in content to the online sections of that course. Of course, the individual assignments, activities, and methods of interacting with the teacher and other learners will vary in each venue, but the amount of content, degree of difficulty, and numbers of assignments should be the same, no matter if the course is taught online or on site.

Online courses may be taught in a time frame different from the on-site sections' schedule. On-site courses may need to conform to a 12- or 15-week term following a seasonal academic calendar, with fall, winter, spring, and summer designations. Online sections of the same course may be offered as intensive six-week sessions throughout the fiscal year. In some institutions, courses may be started at any time, because individuals may take automated online courses, instead of instructor-facilitated classes.

Students taking an online section are expected to take responsibility for the majority of their learning, and many activities and assignments can be completed individually on an accelerated schedule. Even so, collaborative activities and assignments also require online learners to devote more time to class activities each day or week than they normally might in an on-site section.

Unfortunately, some learners (as well as administrators and faculty who teach only on site) have the mistaken notion that online classes are an easier version of an on-site course. The time frame does not indicate the rigor of the coursework or the time that learners and teachers must spend on class-based activities. Online courses are often more difficult because the same content is covered in a shorter time period, and learners must find time not only to master skills and knowledge on their own within this time frame, but also to collaborate with the teacher and other students as part of this learning process. Effective time-management skills and the maturity to meet course objectives within a short time period are required for success in an online section. Administrators, course designers, and teachers need to make sure that the quality and rigor of an online curriculum is equal to those of an on-site curriculum, but also that this fact is communicated clearly to learners and all teachers.

If learners are permitted to take both online and on-site courses toward a degree, the online and on-site courses should be the same weight and difficulty. As you develop an online curriculum, you need to ensure consistency among online courses and between online and on-site versions of the same course.

As parts of the curriculum are modified, existing courses need to be updated far more often than they are eliminated. You will seldom find a course so lacking in value that it cannot be updated. Only if the course truly has been superseded by another type of course (such as Punchcards 101 no longer is needed because the technology has surpassed the need for hundreds of operators to learn the skill of punching computer cards) should it be deleted from the curriculum. Adding new courses or updating existing courses are the more common curriculum-development changes.

Updating course materials so that course in the curriculum is relevant and accurate, as well as innovative, should be ongoing. Whole new courses should be added to the curriculum as a discipline changes and learners need new skill sets or knowledge. Information and activities that do not really fit into existing courses may become the foundation for a whole new course. That course must then meet the standards for and expectations of all other courses in the curriculum. Determining whether the course should be a new degree requirement or an elective is an important factor, too. Online students often plan their degree programs and schedules far in advance so they can fit academic pursuits into their many other activities so learners must be able to know how new course offerings might fit into their schedules.

Planning course materials, as you read in Chapter 2, is critical to the successful development and implementation of any online course. Without a sound plan and a unified idea of what the course should be and how it fits with other online courses, you have a tough time developing the proper materials. Without a sound plan, not everyone involved in the online education team may be able to coordinate activities as efficiently or understand why certain materials are important to a particular course or to the structure of the curriculum. Effective, coordinated planning provides the vision that is fulfilled with the development of useful, usable course materials.

Developing new course materials is seldom the responsibility of only one person, but teachers should have a say in adding, deleting, or changing course materials. Even if you were not the one to create the initial materials, you may be asked or allowed to add new materials after you have taught the course a few times. Most educational institutions encourage feedback from teachers who work with a specific course, so that course designers and technical specialists can assist in improving the course when it is next modified.

If you have created the course and will be responsible for updating it, you should modify the course periodically so that it remains current and technically compatible with other online courses, as well as representative of the content appropriate for a discipline. As disciplines change, so must course content and delivery methods. The job titles of people involved in maintaining and updating courses may vary across institutions, but the need for updating courses and developing new materials is a constant.

Knowing When to Update Course Materials

As you teach a course, you should keep track of learners' problems with certain assignments or tools. If you spend a lot of time each term explaining instructions or interpreting a source, those materials should be updated. When you have taught a course several times, it becomes apparent quickly if some materials are difficult to understand or tools frequently work improperly. A few learners may not understand an assignment or may have trouble getting something to work at the course site. When several students have similar problems, or if you receive feedback from site users about problems with certain areas, especially across course sections, the materials or tools need to be changed.

In a similar way, course designers or administrators should keep track of teachers' and learners' problems in using a course site. Administrators or designers can use formal and informal ways to solicit feedback about the amount of work required during a course, site access problems, lack of available software, difficulty in working with tools, or relevance of course content.

For example, user surveys sent to a sample of learners and teachers across the curriculum may provide non-course-specific feedback about the quality, relevance, and usability of materials and technology. Informally (voluntarily), learners and teachers may be requested to submit ideas for improving technology. They may help select courseware, for example, that allows them to create their online course materials. All these collaborative decisions need to be made before hardware, software, or site upgrades take place.

Course evaluations are another way to gauge the effectiveness of course materials. If a few learners complain about an assignment, you can check to see if the assignment, the student, the time frame, or competing distractions from other classes, work, family, and so on caused the problem. Again, if lots of learners submit the same complaint, it may be time to change the assignment. It may be dropped, revised, or moved to a different learning unit where it fits more logically.

You, or your institution, should periodically update courses or individual modules, even if everything seems to be running smoothly. Changing course content or tools every term is probably too often. If students have to learn a completely new way to access course information, or if a design is radically changed each term, they probably will become frustrated.

As well, if changes require learners frequently to upgrade their hardware or software, they may not be able to afford the cost, or they may not have the time to learn to use new programs or equipment. Course changes that involve a dramatic overhaul of the learner's computer system should be announced well in advance of the change. Minor changes and smaller improvements in technology should be explained, too, but they probably will not require you to warn learners about new technology requirements for their home or office computers.

Technical and design changes should be made incrementally, so that learners and teachers can easily transfer what they know about the old site design to the new. No one should have to spend a great deal of time figuring out how to find new information or perform common tasks.

As well, the technology used in online courses must be updated as new software, courseware, and multimedia applications become common in the home and office. Technical specialists, working with administrators, course designers, and teachers, must figure out how often software, for example, must be updated and which versions that the institution will support. Not all learners, or their employers, have the latest hardware and software, and some students may have low-level Internet connections. Online courses have to be kept current technically, but they also have to appeal to their target market and remain accessible to the majority of learners.

As you upgrade the technology, remember that international students may not have the same level of technology or Internet accessibility. Not only European students, but those in other parts of the globe, can find that Internet charges limit their ability to work online for long periods of time. Some students may have to share computers with many other learners, or the infrastructure may not be in place for widespread Internet use.

For example, in countries where the telecommunication infrastructure is not as highly developed as that in the United States, Europe, or Australia, working online requires special funding and personnel. The access is not as simple to gain, because the technical structure and support for the Internet are not yet well developed (Lynch, 2002). These factors mean that international students may not be able to access the level of technology you want to include in your course upgrades, or, if they have to pay for Internet access by the minute, course materials that have long load times will be prohibitive to use. Learners may not have the assistance they need if they have problems getting access to a site. You must balance the need for the latest innovations with a market analysis of your current and potential students' ability to get and use technical innovations.

Only if the course content must be updated every term to remain effective should materials be changed every time the course is taught. Current events courses, for example, need this type of modification every time they are offered. Most courses' content changes more slowly, but every course should be evaluated every year, and ideas for updating courses should be solicited or documented each time that the course is taught.

Some institutions implement a rolling schedule of changes, so that some courses are updated or taught for the first time each term. Completely outdated courses, or those not generating learner interest, may be dropped because they no longer meet learners' needs or are no longer cost effective to offer.

Changes to the curriculum also involve changes to individual courses so that they continue to fit well. Curricular design must be ongoing, so that educational programs remain pedagogically sound *and* respond to professional expectations of graduates.

Within a two-year cycle, for example, every online course may be reviewed and revamped. During this cycle, new courses are implemented, and other courses dropped. The regular scheduling of updates and implementation ensures that all courses advance, using newer tools, software, and site designs, as well as fresh course materials. Teachers, learners, course designers, technical specialists, and administrators know the schedule and regularly can prepare new courses or update existing ones.

Even if the materials' shelf life would be good for another year or two, learners expect online courses to be updated often. If any Web site—business, personal, educational—is going to be effective, it must be updated frequently, either to change the content or the design. Otherwise, people will not keep coming back to the site. The information has to seem fresh, and the design must be usable and interesting in order to attract attention.

Online courses are the same way. Even if a learner ideally takes a particular class only one time, the information and site design must look fresh and up to date. You fool yourself if you think that online learners do not compare notes about courses and assignments. Learners make friends with their online colleagues and share information about teachers, courses, and assignments, just like they do on a traditional on-site campus. Learners also compare your course site and content with the design and usability of other institutions' course offerings. To be competitive and to keep up with trends in design and usability, course sites should be updated often.

Developing new course materials can involve at least three processes:

1. Beefing up existing courses with new assignments

   If you add assignments, you need to make sure that the total amount of work is still manageable for the number of course hours and level of the subject matter.

2. Achieving a balance between new and old materials so that the overall course provides materials that meet learners' needs, learning styles, and expectations for an online course

   As technology allows more types of interaction, more hands-on activities, like simulations, may be appropriate. If more in-depth research is needed, particularly so learners can demonstrate that they have done more than reading the assigned materials, a research paper—particularly using Internet sources—may be needed. New links to materials created by others may be available; you may find additional sites that you want learners to visit. Keeping the course content fresh and providing new experiences for learners are good ways to balance new content with older materials.

3. Helping learners develop additional skills or meet specific requirements

   Curriculum changes often are the result of new learning objectives or a market demand for new knowledge and skills to supplement current learning objectives. For example, requirements for a professional certification may have become more stringent, and learners need to gain new information or practice additional skills before they can be certified. As a profession or a subject area progresses, the expectations for experts in that field also increase. Learners taking courses to gain expert status therefore need to know the latest information or work with the newest concepts. They may need a new set of skills. Your course must help prepare learners for (re)entry into the workforce, as well as for living effectively as global citizens.

When you have determined that your course fits these or other scenarios for change, you should ask these questions: What kinds of assignments should be added? Should new materials be asynchronous or synchronous? How does each assignment relate to other assignments and help learners meet the course objectives? How is each assignment unique, not more of "the same old stuff"? Your answers provide a starting point for gathering new materials.

Gathering New Materials

As you develop new materials, you first need to evaluate what you have and what else you need. Some materials are probably still useful: 1) They are not outdated; the information is still accurate and the tone still timely. 2) They have been tested and still provide learners with activities for skill development or thought-provoking ideas for discussion. 3) They allow learners to interact with them independently as well as within a group, and they permit myriad responses. 4) They are cost effective and available for use with your online classes.

For example, if you are trying to determine whether a role-playing scenario is still useful to your class, you might apply these guidelines in the following ways:

1. The scenario is generic enough to fit current situations. The language is modern, but not so trendy that it sounds outdated. The scenario also involves issues that are timeless (e.g., academic honesty, development of good interpersonal relationships, group dynamics) and are still of current interest.

2. Little skill development might be apparent in the role-playing exercise, but the way individual learners enact their roles is different each time the scenario is run. Discussion usually is lively with this activity, and it is a good mechanism for getting learners to work together in a group.

3. Each person involved in the role-playing exercise has to act out a character. The ways that character is played and he or she communicates with other characters differ because new learners bring their unique personalities to the role play. The actor determines which key discussion points will be introduced through the character's words and actions. Each learner works independently, but, because this is a group role-playing exercise, with further reports on the exercise to the class as a whole, group interaction also is important. The exercise works well at both the individual and group levels.

4. This activity is cost effective, because learners use e-mail, the bulletin board, the chat room, the whiteboard, and/or other

tools available in the classroom to complete the assignment. No extra costs are incurred, and although the technology may change, the group interactions can always take place. (For example, learners may use voicemail, voice e-mail, phone conversations, or videoconferences in more techno-logically advanced courses, but use print e-mail, the bulletin board, and text conversations in the chat room for less technologically sophisticated classrooms.)

The role-playing assignment seems like a keeper. It is effective and efficient, and it still meets the pedagogical requirements established for that assignment. The following example is one that may need to be modified.

In another assignment, learners answer questions in an online question-naire to help them determine their Internet IQ. The questionnaire has been used for four years in all introductory classes before learners have to use the Internet as a source of information for their assignments. This term, however, the free Web site with the questionnaire is not an active link, but a longer version of the questionnaire has taken its place.

Unfortunately, to use the longer version, learners (or the institution) must pay a fee for processing the responses and interpreting the results. The resulting feedback is of a higher quality than the data from the self-scored, short version of the questionnaire. The information on the questionnaire has been updated to reflect current Internet usage and concerns about information security.

As you evaluate the assignment and whether it should remain a part of the course requirements, you might consider the following:

1.   Is the information still timely?

     You might need to determine if learners need this self-assessment, or if another questionnaire would be more helpful. If the purpose of the assignment is to determine a learner's probable success in using the Internet, then the longer questionnaire or another similar assessment may still be valuable to people taking an online course for the first time. If, however, your class consists of learners who have taken online classes other places or who routinely work with the Internet as part of their business, this type of assessment may not be as valuable as it has been with groups of novice online learners.

2. What is the questionnaire's purpose? What does the questionnaire do?

It definitely requires learners to complete an online survey, which is a skill that may be useful. A self-assessment tool can be helpful to individual learners as they find out more about themselves and understand what is required of them for success in online educational programs.

Individuals could follow up by writing an essay explaining how they reacted to the results and how they might integrate the findings into their academic planning or study habits. The results of the individual or group responses could be discussed during a chat session or through a series of bulletin board posts.

You need to determine if the "bang" is worth the "buck" that learners or the institution will have to pay for using this assessment. If the activities associated with using the questionnaire are still valuable, then the newer version of the questionnaire should be used in class.

3. How are individual or group activities used to follow up using the questionnaire's data?

Results of the questionnaire are based on each learner's responses, which is an individual activity. Writing an essay, for example, is another individual follow-up activity. If the results are discussed within the group or used to develop group activities, the assignment can be useful at both the individual and group levels.

4. How cost effective is the use of the questionnaire for the skills and knowledge that learners gain from using it?

Because a monetary cost is now associated with a longer version of the questionnaire, you need to determine if the cost is worth the benefit to individual learners and to the class as a group. If learners are asked to pay an additional fee, will they do it? Will the cost be prohibitive? If the institution is asked to pay the fee, will costs for the course go up? Is the additional cost important to the educational quality of the class? Are similar fees charged in other courses within the curriculum?

You should also research whether you have only two alternatives: to use the longer, paid version of the question-naire or not to use the questionnaire. Are similar question-naires offered free at other sites? Is another short form available through another vendor or Web site? Are other questionnaires, measuring other variables, useful to the class in place of this questionnaire? Can you develop a reliable, valid questionnaire? Doing a cost-benefit analysis of this item can help you decide how to modify the current assignment, or to delete it from the syllabus.

These kinds of evaluations should take place for each assignment listed in the syllabus. You need to decide which materials are still relevant, which need to be revised, and which need to be replaced. Then you know how many activities you have to keep and how many new activities need to be developed. The overriding concern should be the continuing high quality of the course and the way the materials and activities support and develop learners' skills and knowledge base.

Creating New Course Materials

Whether you are updating an existing course or developing materials for a brand new course, you will probably work with a range of information. Much of that information may be already available on other Web sites. You may opt for non-Web-based educational materials, from printed textbooks to CDs.

Even if much of the information learners will use has already been created by someone else, you need to locate the appropriate resources and make them available to learners. In addition, you have to create at least some materials that are purely your own—most likely, assignments and activities that learners must complete to show their mastery of skills and grasp of information. Without the proverbial reinvention of the wheel, you need to assess what is valuable and available for use in your course, and what you need to create yourself, based on your vision for the course and knowledge of the learners who will take it.

Course materials that you should create include activities and assignments, plus the instructions for completing them. In addition, you need to create items like a syllabus, course schedule, reading lists, and sample documents to be used with the assignments and activities you create.

Course materials that you may find from other sources include documents that can be linked to the course site (using external or internal links, depending upon who created a document); video or audio files of important events, tours, interviews, or demonstrations; and interactive files, such as questionnaires and simulations. You also locate some samples appropriate to the course subject matter. Some corporate reports, government documents, movie clips, an essay written by a learner in an earlier section of the class, an audio clip of a famous speech, raw data from an experiment, a prize-winning photo, and a demonstration of proper lab procedures involve documents and multimedia files. Not only must these materials be appropriate for the course, but you must make sure you have copyright or other permissions to use the material within your class.

Activities and Assignments

As you read in the previous chapter, you need to plan the number and type of assignments appropriate to each learning unit or module. By the time the course is established on a Web site and linked to internal and external resources, the activities and assignments should be well defined. The activities should reinforce what learners gain from course content; a blend of asynchronous and synchronous activities, and individual and group exercises, are necessary for a sound practice of what is being presented in concept or theory. Activities may not be graded, but they should have a clearly defined purpose and follow logically from the course content for a particular module.

As well, assignments within a course should be appropriate for the level and placement of the course within the curriculum. Activities in a 300- or 400-level undergraduate course should involve critical thinking and higher skill levels than those developed by assignments or activities in a 100- or 200-

level course. The placement of a course within the curriculum also is important, for prerequisite knowledge or skills developed during previous courses must be acknowledged. Activities should be well structured within that particular course, but the entire course's structure of knowledge- and skill-building must be appropriate for its placement within the curriculum.

Assignments should be evaluated for some type of credit, even if a letter or point grade is not given. Assignments might follow from activities or course content, but again, a variety of assignment types should help learners with different styles and preferences to show their new knowledge or skills.

The work for this type of course content is completed primarily at the planning stage of the course, as the course is initially developed or updated. Of course, evaluating assignments and activities becomes part of your daily or weekly routine as you teach the course. Between these stages, you may have to provide learners with additional guidance, through bulletin board explanations, e-mail messages, or chat room discussions, about what is expected for each assignment.

All assignments and activities should be clearly spelled out in the grading policies for the course, the syllabus, and a schedule of deadlines. All learners should be aware of what is expected of them and how their work will be evaluated. These types of materials should be developed and posted to the course Web site.

Some activities, such as questionnaires, tests, simulations, videoconferences, and chat sessions, are more interactive and may require you to develop special materials, in addition to the descriptions of assignments posted several places on the course site. Olsen and Schihl (2002) noted that online course designers/teachers have to provide specific assignment descriptions, even more elaborate than those for on-site classes. Discussion questions must clearly indicate the teacher's intent, and details about written assignments must be more precise. Even if you think your instructions, discussion questions, and assignment/activity descriptions are so clear that they can only be interpreted one way, test them with real students. You probably will be surprised at the number of different interpretations you will receive. You should revise these descriptive materials after you test them and before updated materials are uploaded for the redesigned course.

Writing Activities and Assignments

As noted in the previous chapter, you should have determined the number of writing activities and other types of assignments to be manageable enough for learners yet rigorous enough for the subject matter and course level. What you need to prepare now are the assignment sheets that describe what exactly is required by learners and how and in what form the assignment must be submitted.

The descriptions should be part of the permanent course site, so that learners can easily find and work with the assignments from the first time they log into the course. You may also want to provide links with models, sample documents, scenarios, or other information that can help learners visualize what they are supposed to do. The more that learners can interact with the assignments, the better learners grasp concepts and practice skills.

Multimedia Materials

Multimedia are best used to show instead of tell how processes operate, clarify abstract concepts, and enliven new information. Your use of multimedia also can become the basis of an assignment (Ko & Rossen, 2001). For example, you may include a video clip of a speech and then have learners write a critique.

With technical assistance, you may be able to produce high-quality audio or video files so that learners can see and hear you lecture, demonstrate an activity, or give a tour. A particularly interesting lecture topic can illustrate who you are and how you sound. Learners who have never had the opportunity to meet you outside the electronic classroom may benefit from seeing and hearing you present course content as a lecture.

Although learners may not retain as much information at one sitting by just listening to or viewing a lecture, they can replay video or audio files stored at the course site, which aids information retention. Lectures are best when they are less formal, but still well organized and clearly presented. They should complement other presentational methods (Brewer, DeJonge, & Stout, 2001). A lecture as part of a module's content, and supported with other materials and assignments, may be one way to update your course materials.

Adding a video or audio file of yourself is not the only way to add multimedia materials to your redesigned course. You may get permission to record a conference session or a speech by a speaker you would like learners to see and hear. You may have traveled off site and recorded what you saw—and what you want learners to see. You can create a variety of asynchronous multimedia activities that learners can reference from the class site.

As well, you might link text versions, transcripts, or documents you have created in conjunction with or separate from multimedia materials. If you are an expert in your subject area, the materials you create, in whatever form, may be the best resources learners could find. When you develop your own multimedia materials, learners have a better sense of you as a real teacher in a traditional setting. Adding a personal dimension, especially through the use of multimedia, to the course materials you create can be a bonus for learners.

Simulations, Role Playing, and Problem Solving

Older types of online education allowed learners to be more passive in their interaction with materials. Reading, answering questions, or writing a paper or two might have been all that were required to show that learners had gone through the material. As online technology becomes more sophisticated, and as learners want to do more online instead of in an on-campus classroom, more active assignments are required. Although by the time you create course materials you should have already determined how many and what type of assignments are appropriate for the course, you need to work with course designers and information technology (IT) specialists to create more interactive assignments.

Simulations allow learners to practice skills, visit locations online instead of in the field, and see the results of their activities. These activities may be especially well suited to kinesthetic and visual learners. Because simulations may take more time to prepare, you may want to develop a storyboard, or at least an outline, of what is required in the simulation and the types and amounts of interaction required by users.

One type of simulation is the problem-solution scenario. Another is a role play. In both situations, learners must practice real work-related or "real world" tasks (Schank & Neaman, 2001). As you design a simulation, you must create problems that are interesting as well as difficult enough that students are unlikely to solve them by pure luck.

Role plays or games should be created so that learners practice skills, consider ethical options, and make decisions. Failure to complete a simulation perfectly the first time is OK. The purpose of an effective simulation is to give learners the chance to practice tasks and test their responses and decisions in a safe environment. Simulations are a learning experience; learners should not be expected to know all the answers or be able to complete tasks flawlessly the first time they go through the simulated situation.

Role-playing and problem-solving activities may be easier to create, because these can be done synchronously within chat rooms, where groups can enact and respond to scenarios, or asynchronously, by individuals or groups thinking through a problem and possible solutions. Chat rooms, whiteboards, and e-mail, as well as videoconferencing, may be useful to learners completing these types of assignments.

Although, technically, role plays and problem-solution assignments may not be difficult to set up, they still require a great deal of planning to be effective. You may want to create characters that learners can take on during the role play; you then have to create a set of realistic characters representing different viewpoints, backgrounds, and experience levels. You might want to throw in some personality quirks, too. You also can make simulations highly automated and technical, depending on the needs of the course and learners and the technical assistance available to you. If you purchase simulations from a vendor, you must ensure that the level of interaction and the subject matter are appropriate for your specific group.

Throughout the creation of characters, you must avoid stereotyping and create characters to whom learners can relate and understand. You also have to think of real problems that require thought and discussion, not just a pat response. Developing and posting scenarios, role-play situations and characters, and descriptions of problems take quite a lot of preparation. You may decide that these activities will not be a permanent part of the course site, but that you will create groups or post assignments for individuals once you get to know the class members. You may want to fine-tune these assignments to make them particularly applicable to the learners in a particular class.

Nevertheless, creating assignment sheets and descriptors is still important, because learners need to know what types of assignments they will face throughout the course and when they will receive information not currently posted or linked to the course site. You have to provide background information, instructions, and guidelines for learners, even if they will later receive additional information with specific details about an assignment.

Lab Activities

You may be able to recreate lab conditions in a virtual setting in some simulations, but you also may want streaming audio/video links so that learners can observe experiments or interviews as they happen. If learners need to complete lab activities on site, you need to make sure that learners know where they can complete the activities and how they will be supervised. These set-ups take a great deal of planning to make the arrangements with on-site administrators and proctors, as well as in scheduling learners and making them aware of the on-site requirements.

Lab activities may also require learners to go out into their communities. For example, learners may be required to interview people to gather information about the history of their city. They might talk with family members, but more likely, they interview colleagues, neighbors, and people from their hometown. They might visit a chat room or converse electronically with people outside their area. The Internet might be part of their lab setting for these interviews, but their field work can take place in face-to-face interactions with people in their area. Another interview situation may require learners to talk with professionals in the field they want to enter, or to collaborate with other professionals on a project. The lab is a Web site or physical location selected by the learner, but the activity—interviewing someone—is predetermined.

However lab activities are established for your course, you again need to make sure that the descriptions for these types of assignments are posted permanently at the course site, and that any arrangements on site are made well in advance of an incoming class.

Interactive Questionnaires

As mentioned earlier in this chapter, interactive personality or learning style inventories may be useful for you and those enrolled in the class to understand how they best relate to others and take in information. If you teach an introduction-to-online-learning type of course, one or more interactive questionnaires may be useful to help learners understand their learning preferences and personality type, so they can better understand how to use online materials effectively. As well, if you know the number of learners with a particular preference, for example, you can make sure that you have a suitable number of activities in formats useful for that type of learner.

Interactive questionnaires are also useful for quizzes, tests, and course evaluations. They are easy for learners to complete, and they can be either sent to you automatically or scored and the results sent to you. If your course content is well suited to multiple choice, dichotomous (two-part, such as True or False, questions), rating, or ranking questions, you might consider using interactive questionnaires/tests more frequently. However, you probably will not want to use one testing method exclusively.

The interactive part of these questionnaires makes them attractive for learners, who can take the tests at a convenient time and submit them automatically. Responses are easy to make and submit, and the entire testing or response time is generally short.

These questionnaires or tests are also beneficial to teachers. The responses can be evaluated and categorized electronically, so that you spend little time grading or compiling statistics. Because learners must choose from a list of possible responses, there is little room for ambiguity in answers. You know how learners responded to an item, and you do not have to worry about their problems with self-expression. Instead of figuring out what learners meant by a subjective (essay) response, you clearly know which response each learner chose.

The time-intensive factor with questionnaires is development. You need to create an effective test or survey instrument, with an easily manageable number of responses representing a range of possible answers. You cannot lead learners to a particular response, and you have to limit the number of possibilities to a scannable, easily remembered list. You also have to create effective instructions, so learners quickly understand how they are supposed to complete the questionnaire or test and submit their responses.

After you have designed the content and organization of questions, you need to test the questionnaire or exam with different groups who represent the numbers and types of learners who will be completing the form online. All questions about content and organization of the items, and the instructions for completing and submitting the form, must be resolved before the content is put online.

You will probably need to work with technical support staff to make sure the questionnaire works consistently. You may be limited in the number of questions or responses allowed with the institution's system. There may be a standard structure for each questionnaire in an institution's online courses. You may be required to use the same survey-generation software everyone at your institution uses to create your own quizzes or question-naires, which are then linked to the course site. If other teachers use similar questionnaires or tests in their courses, the overall design of all online forms should be consistent, so that learners enrolled in several classes can transfer their knowledge of how to complete and submit one questionnaire to another questionnaire used in a different course.

Another technical area is the way results will be gathered and tallied. If it is important for you to have a statistical breakdown of the number of responses to each item, you will need to discuss how statistical information can be compiled automatically. You may just need a summary of each learner's responses, or an overall grade. How the information will be evaluated, electronically or by hand, and in what form you will receive these data should be determined by you and the technical specialist.

An easier way to go might be to use survey instruments that have already been developed and tested for their reliability and validity. You need to determine if these instruments are appropriate for your course, and how you can get permission to use them. Fees or copyright permissions may be needed if you use questionnaires that others designed. Once you have permission, however, you can link the online questionnaire from another's Web site to your course site. You still need to devise a way for the responses to be returned to you, as well as a way for you to evaluate the responses.

Videoconferences, Chat Sessions, and Other Synchronous Discussions

Videoconferences, chat sessions, and other required synchronous activities must be noted in the course syllabus and described elsewhere on the course Web site. If learners need to have a certain type of hardware or software, they need to know the technical requirements. If plug-ins are available through the course site, learners need to know when and how they should use them, well in advance of a real-time activity. This type of background information must be spelled out and highlighted appropriately, so that learners know what they are required to do and if they need additional software or hardware to complete the assignment.

You also must post assignment sheets listing the background readings that learners should have completed before a discussion or meeting. Lists of sample discussion questions, instructions for behavior or course protocols for the session, and technical instructions for joining the discussion should be provided at the course site.

If you are providing numerous sets of instructions at the course site, be sure to test them before the course begins, to make sure the instructions are correct and are easy to understand. Simple alpha and beta tests with learners, staff, and other teachers should help you troubleshoot the instructions. Once the course begins, you, along with class members, should also make sure everything works as expected.

Evaluations

Whether you are using interactive questionnaires or written evaluations, learners and teachers should evaluate each class as soon as it is over. The evaluations can be done anonymously, if the institution prefers, or they may be a course requirement like any other assignment. If you are using interactive questionnaires, these should be planned and tested before learners are ever asked to complete them. Most institutions have already established forms for evaluations, which have been tested and approved. You may just need to make sure that your course site contains links to these previously established forms.

As with all other assignments, learners must understand how and when they complete evaluations. Any instructions or descriptions should be part of the course site.

These types of activities and assignments require you to create the appropriate descriptions, reminders, instructions, and guidelines in order for learners to understand their assignments and to complete them successfully. You might be actively involved in developing more technically sophisticated materials, such as simulations or audio or video files, or you might enhance the course materials with more multimedia examples and applications as the sophistication of the technology available to you increases. In addition to these types of materials, you also need to conduct research for outside information and materials to supplement what you provide learners.

Descriptive Information to Help Learners Complete the Course

Several universities or colleges provide excellent documentation of course content and ways to use course Web sites. They highlight the types of information that you may need to write or design so that prospective learners know which courses are offered, if the course is taught purely online or involves other distance learning methods (such as televised class sessions or on-site proctored exams), and which hardware and software are required for course participation. The syllabus, assignment sheets, grading criteria, course and institutional policies, and contact lists of e-mail addresses and phone numbers, for example, are permanently and prominently displayed at the course Web site.

In addition, the institution's Web pages guide teachers and learners through all kinds of academic procedures, such as registering for classes, paying tuition, accessing course information, and logging into the online education system. Additional information, about accreditation, course designs, and the institution's mission, for example, also might be provided at the university's or college's Web site. By looking at the ways other universities or colleges display information, you and administrators at your institution can develop ideas for a usable design for your own programs or institution.

Washington State University (www.eus.wsu.edu/DDP/courses/outlines.asp) uses icons next to course titles to indicate which type of distance learning activities are used in each course and if the course can be taken completely online. Links to additional course information allow prospective learners to find the syllabus, course outline, description of class sessions, or other helpful items.

The Connecticut Distance Learning Consortium (www.ctdlc.org/Help/index.html) allows students, instructors, or guests to log into the site to find more details about specific programs offered by members of the consortium. Several Help links offer assistance to visitors who are looking for a specific type of information. Not only are the technical requirements listed (a System Requirements link), but contact information for technical support is also provided. Tutorials and instructions (Course Help and Conference Help links) show learners what they can expect from online courses. A link to downloads lets learners install the browser or plug-ins they will need for a course. Links to other course-related information and FAQs make up the rest of the page.

One page on the site of the Canadian Virtual University/Universite Virtuelle Canadienne (CVU/UVC) offers links to online demonstrations hosted by several Canadian universities (www.cvu-uvc.ca/sample.html). This type of page is useful for learners who want to see which course designs and technical tools best suit their interests and level of expertise. These examples also prepare prospective learners for taking courses offered by one of the universities affiliated with the CVU/UVC program.

Through these effective yet simple ways, academic institutions document the courses they offer and provide technical assistance. The information gives prospective learners (as well as teachers and administrators develop-ing online curricula) great ideas about the quality of online courses and the level of technology required. Although the way the information is presented varies among institutions, you or someone else within the online programs at your institution should develop and regularly update similar pages. Documenting your institution's policies, programs, and technologies not only is a service to teachers and learners, but it helps market your programs and courses. The information answers questions about the curriculum and individual courses. It illustrates how this curriculum fits within the institution's mission and with other programs of study.

Institutional information also helps potential students compare your college's or university's curriculum with curricula offered by competing institutions.

Locating Materials Created by Others

As you develop a curriculum, you should be on the lookout for suitable materials to use in individual courses. If you teach online, you are probably very familiar with the Web, and browsing for samples and examples is second nature. You might find additional readings archived at outside sites, or used by another teacher at your institution. You might locate questionnaires or demonstrations that are appropriate for the course content. You may try out several chat rooms to see if any are appropriate—and safe—for learners to use during an assignment.

Finding information on the Internet, and connecting the site with that information to your course site, is an important task for online educators. Of course, you want to ensure that the person or group providing the information is reputable and that the owners of other Web sites know and approve of your linking a whole classful of learners to their site.

In addition to Internet resources, you may require one or more textbooks or popular books as background readings for assignments and activities. You may require learners to purchase other peripherals, or the institution may provide them, so that learners have multimedia learning experiences away from the course site. CDs, for example, can include samples, tutorials, and instructions that supplement the information found on the course site or available through printed texts. You, or more likely, someone else, created these peripherals, but you select them and make them available to learners.

Each course within the curriculum should have similar requirements for the types of materials available to learners and the number of peripherals needed per course. Naturally, the subject matter plays a big role in determining the suitable materials for studying a particular discipline. However, there should be similarities among the number and types of materials used in each online course within the curriculum.

Teachers expect the freedom to select the books and other materials that learners will need for their class. Those decisions are part of the academic freedom that teachers expect. However, all sections of an online course are generally taught the same way—with the same required texts, CDs, or Web-site supplements. Individual teachers most likely will not be allowed to switch textbooks between terms or select materials different from those supported by the online program.

To ensure that the teachers who will facilitate a particular online course will be satisfied with the materials until the course is next revised, as many teachers of that course as possible should be involved in selecting or approving materials. As a course is modified, the people who teach that course should be consulted about changing the materials.

As well, the standards for the curriculum must be upheld. Any substantial changes in expectations for one course must be evaluated in light of the effect on the entire curriculum. Because online programs require planning and Web-site preparation before a class can be offered—and the modification process is more demanding and often technical—teachers and administrators need to consider the whole curriculum as they modify the individual courses within it.

Approved Web Sites

Some institutions want administrative approval for all sites linked to a course Web site. Others rely on teachers to review site information and determine if it is appropriate for dissemination to all class members. As well, there may be policies about what can or cannot be posted to a course site or a learner's Web site that is shared with other class members.

Approval may need to be granted by determining the following:

1. What is academically sound to link to the course site

    Each URL/URI should link learners with information about appropriate course content or an activity (such as completing a questionnaire) that meets a course objective. The information should also be checked for accuracy and timeliness.

2. What is unique to that course

Each URL/URI should be used only in a particular course. If learners find the same links in multiple courses, the effectiveness of the information will be lost. Each subject matter, and each specific course within the curriculum, should have its own series of links that provide learners with interesting, appropriate information to be used only in that course.

3. What is technically sound to link to the course site

Each URL/URI should be available for use throughout the course; there should be no broken links. The material at the linked site should be easily used or downloaded and not require any special software or hardware to use; if the site does require additional plug-ins, for example, they should be the same plug-ins required by the institution or for the course in order to access general course information.

4. What is economically sound to link to the course site

Free information from a reputable source is generally all right to link to an academic site. Information from for-profit sites or sites that include advertisements that may not be appropriate for an academic course site may not be advisable to link to the class site. Institutions generally frown on a site that promotes a particular product or service, at least without some type of disclaimer that one company is being advocated over another. Another aspect of economical information is that which does not cost the institution or learners fees for accessing.

As you browse the Web, you should bookmark or make lists of sites with source information useful in your courses. You need to evaluate the quality of the source, as well as its bias.

For example, you might find information that is ideal for a topic covered in your course. A corporate Web site provides background and readings that learners should find useful to their understanding of the topic. However, because this is a corporate site, you expect a positive bias toward that business and the corporation's policies. The information probably is designed to advance the corporation's image or ideals. That does not mean that you should not link this information to your course site, only that you will need to balance this point of view with links to information from a site providing a different perspective on the topic.

The Internet is a useful source of information *if* that information is critically evaluated. Before you link any site to your course site, you want to make sure you know where the information is coming from and the accuracy of what is published online. The information linked to your site should provide balanced content within a similar style. For example, you want the reading levels of all textual information to match learners' comprehension and literacy levels. You want the visual content, such as graphics or streaming video, to match the technical requirements for the course. Information from outside Web sites should be as accessible to all learners as any information designed specifically for each course's learners.

You also need to know that the information will be available throughout the course. Before you link a site to your course information, you should see if it will "always" be available at that link. By checking course links frequently, you can avoid problems with missing information or broken links. Information that changes rapidly, such as press releases or news reports, probably will not be available at the initial URL/URI for very long. However, these types of information may be archived indefinitely at a more stable URL/URI. If you want to use newsworthy information several times, across more than one term, you may want to use the archival links.

Your institution may want to approve the links to your course site, especially those that are used from one course session to the next. You may also be limited to the number and type of links provided to learners. It is useful to maintain a list of links you want to add to your site and to share this list with others who develop and maintain other courses in the curriculum. If you are not able to use all links at once, you can substitute links as the course materials are updated. If your institution does not want to include some links, you have a list of alternatives readily available.

You should also check your institution's policy for posting links to mailing lists, e-mail messages, and bulletin boards, for example. As the teacher, you may be able to post useful URLs/URIs that may be available only temporarily (such as news) or to a new Web site not available when the course was originally designed. Posting information as it becomes available or as you locate it can be helpful in keeping the course relevant to learners' interests and quickly updating course materials. However, you may need to have the Web site approved before you post it, even temporarily, for the class.

A similar situation may occur with learners' posting of their personal Web sites' URLs/URIs. You may have the final say on whether the information at a site shared with the class is appropriate. Information posted by learners about a personal Web site or other external sites shared with other class members may be harder to control. You have to use discretion in reviewing all locations posted to class members and supporting any recommendations for sites you did not suggest for learners to use. You may need to establish policies about what is appropriate to share with class members or to post on a personal Web site that is then made available for class members' viewing. Similar policies may then need to be followed in other courses in the curriculum, to ensure consistency across the program.

Keep in mind, too, that when learners click an external link at the course site, they may not quickly return to the course information. As you plan to link information to your site, you should determine how much time you want learners to spend away from the site. Is it more important that they visit many external sites, or that they primarily work at the course site alone? Can you add more internal links to documents or graphics, or do you need to direct learners outward to the Internet at large?

In addition to content links, you may need to include links to other departments or services within the institution. For example, you may want to link learners with a technical help service located at a site within the institution's network. You should see which links to the institution will be useful for learners, and secure permission to list those URLs/URIs as direct links to your course site.

Preparing to Teach a Course You Did Not Design

Many online teachers begin their career in distance education by teaching one Web-based course. If that goes well, and the teacher, administrators, and learners work well together using this format, the new online teacher takes on additional courses and may begin to develop new courses. Some teachers, however, prefer to teach already established courses and never develop their own course.

Even if you never develop an online course, you can make someone else's course design your own. By modifying materials, within the institution's guidelines, of course, you can add information that you think learners need to know. More importantly, through your personality and course-management skills, you put a distinctive stamp on each class you teach. First, though, you must become familiar with the course content, educational design of the course and Web site, and the computer tools used in the course.

Familiarity with the Materials

Before you ever teach an online course, the university or college should train you in using the course design. You also should be given an overview of the curriculum, so you can see where your course fits into the master plan. You need to receive the textbook or other materials that accompany the online coursework, so that you can become familiar with the course content.

You also may be required to take an online course designed for potential instructors. This type of class allows you to practice using the tools in the online programs, but it also gives you the opportunity to go through the materials and tools that you will be using in the course that you will teach. As a learner, you then experience what your students will go through in an online course.

Before you teach subsequent courses, you should receive the textbook and information to access other teachers' course sites so that you can study the materials. You also can get a feel for the scheduling and content of each learning module well in advance of the time you teach that course, as well as a greater awareness of the entire curriculum. This level of preparation should help you understand not only the content that you will be teaching, but also the online format, schedule, course objectives, and assignments.

Many administrators of online programs provide this kind of training and overview to teaching an online course, whether that instruction is provided via the Web or on site. Unfortunately, not all online programs operate this way. Teachers who are not provided specific training or information about the way an online course has been designed have to create their own training program.

If you can, take an online class similar to the one you will be teaching before your course begins. Each institution sets up its courses differently, even if they use a standard brand of courseware, like WebCT or Blackboard. Although you may be familiar with these programs, the tools may be used slightly differently, or the arrangement of icons may not be the same as you have used before. Become familiar with the way your specific program is set up.

Then locate all the linked information to which learners will have access. Although the IT support team, as well as the faculty and administrators who designed the course, should make sure all links work, take a few minutes to check each link. Note any problems, and check the site later. Sometimes between courses new information is added to the course site and broken links are fixed or removed. If after a few tries you cannot get a link to work, you should check with the person supervising the course you will teach to report the problem.

Find out which books (if any) are required for students, and get a copy. Read the book at least once, and match the reading selections against the required assignments listed on the course Web site. You might usually download the assignment list, too, as well as a schedule or syllabus, to make sure that you are familiar with deadlines and course objectives.

Familiarity with the Technology

If you can access another teacher's course site, you may be able to see the course content and basic tools with which you will work. However, you may not be able to play with the technology. If possible, see if you can access a lab or get passwords so that you can work with the technology as you will use it in class.

What can you expect to work with? Most institutions encourage, if not require you, to post grades to an online gradebook. You will need to know how to enter, modify, and save grades. You will need to know how to post messages to the bulletin board, both as a new thread and within folders or existing threads; you will also have to learn to create folders or start a new thread of conversation. Working with a whiteboard may take a little bit of practice so that you can hand write comments or draw pictures or diagrams.

You may be familiar with using chat rooms and sending e-mail, so your only concern will be to do those tasks within the context of the course Web site.

Some institutions want you to set up a personal home page with information about your schedule, contact information, and relevant personal information, including a photo. If you have not uploaded and downloaded files, used FTP, or worked with XML, HTML, or XHTML, you may need to be familiar with basic tasks so that you can create and upload the information required by the institution.

Check with the technical support staff to see how personal pages are set up and what kind of information you need to provide. For example, sometimes you need something as simple as a plain text resume that can be uploaded through a form developed by the university or college; all you have to do is prepare the initial text file and follow the instructions on the form. Other times you may have to upload HTML files to a group site.

If you need to create your personal Web site and have little technical support, find out first what is required. How much space will be allocated to your home page? What types of interfaces are required (e.g., Are students using a specific browser or a required version of a browser?)? How much space should be allocated to text and how much to graphics? What kinds of graphics files are appropriate (e.g., .JPG, .GIF, or other formats)? Answers to questions like these are important as you prepare your home page. Then look at other teachers' personal pages to see how they set up the information and what they included. You can use these models to prepare the files needed for your personal site.

Although online teachers usually do not have to solve technical problems students have during a class, you probably want to know some basic troubleshooting. For example, if a student cannot log into the class bulletin board, what are some possible reasons? If a student gets bumped out of the class chat room, what should he or she do? Some problems are undoubtedly human error, like typing in a password incorrectly or clicking the wrong link. However, some problems are real technical glitches.

As a teacher, you should be able to provide basic troubleshooting suggestions to students, who may panic or at least become frustrated when they cannot use a tool or access information. You should be able to tell the difference between a problem you and the student can solve and one that requires the assistance of technical support personnel. If some serious technical assistance is needed, you should have a handy list of e-mail addresses or phone numbers of persons designated to provide this kind of help.

Checking the program's, institution's, or course's FAQ list is a good idea. These are the kinds of questions that new students (and teachers) typically ask. Read through as many of these help guides as possible to answer your questions first. Then you can check with others to get answers to questions not covered by the FAQ list.

Rapid Changes in Design

Even seasoned teachers have to keep up with changes in technology and course design. Just like you update materials for on-site classes, you—or someone else—updates the course files and links to make sure they work, are within copyright permission, and still relevant. Newer materials need to be uploaded or linked, too.

In addition to content-related changes, teachers also face changes in Web site design. As new tools are added to the site, the arrangement of tools probably will change. Procedures for getting into a chat room or bulletin board, sending bulk e-mail to a whole class, or posting grades on the site's gradebook may change as frequently as each term the course is taught. Although the pedagogical design of the course may not change dramatically from term to term, technical design changes may occur rapidly.

A new version of software is installed. A completely different interface or software is selected. Completely new tools are added to the site. Old tools are deleted. These are just a few possible changes to a course Web site. How do you keep up with rapid changes?

Most institutions provide faculty bulletin boards, mailing lists, or online newsletters that describe upcoming changes. Make sure you read all the updates pertaining to your course. Also, read any supplementary mailings, such as print newsletters or brochures, that describe programs and courses to make sure you are up-to-date with all news items. You may be invited to participate in group discussions online, via a conference call, or in an on-site meeting. These are places where you can discuss upcoming or recent changes and problems and learn how to use a new system. Just because you teach online, you should not feel isolated from other colleagues. Get into the loop; make sure you are on the electronic and surface mailing lists for all new information.

Effective online teachers embrace new technology and expect to learn new skills rapidly. You must be flexible and allow yourself plenty of prep time before you teach an online course, even if you have taught the course before. Chances are that something has been changed, even slightly. To avoid any confusion or frustration, make sure you know the latest information about your course before you log into the classroom.

Philosophical Differences Between You and the Designer

If you did not design the course or the curriculum, you will probably wish some things had been done differently. You might have chosen other links or files, in addition to or in place of the standardized ones, but you are not allowed to change them. You might want a different organizational structure for assignments, because the order of concepts just does not seem quite right to you. You may find some procedures too restrictive for the way you like to run a class—or not restrictive enough. Any time you are hired to teach a course someone else designed, you will probably have differences with the originating designer or curriculum developer. You may have a different vision for the program and ideas to change the direction or emphasis of the curriculum.

In online education, you are probably going to have some philosophical differences concerning the technology, too. You may have worked with another interface you prefer, but now you are stuck with a different system. The institution may have contracts that prohibit you from using different software. You may have some great ideas that you want to implement in the course, but you cannot add information because the course is already "set."

Working online often means that you accept the design as it is—at least for this go around—but you offer suggestions for changes the next time the course is updated. You find out what you can do in addition to what is already offered at the course Web site. For example, if only two bulletin board posts are required for a course, you might provide additional non-credit discussion questions or reviews to encourage students to use the bulletin board more frequently. If you are required to use required class readings placed in files at the class site, you can ask for approval to mention some additional files that students can access, even if they are available at your personal Web site, which is not part of the institution's domain.

Keep up-to-date about curriculum changes, and determine if your proposed changes fit with the vision of the entire degree program. Also keep an open mind about existing course designs and materials, as well as the technology used to present them. Your initial resistance to materials or tools may come from lack of experience with them; give the design a chance. Then, after you have worked with the course at least once and probably more often, you can see if your suggested changes can be implemented. Also, you can talk with administrators and other faculty to find out how much you can add to a current course, to enhance the materials and activities already created for the class. If you are a permanent part of the faculty, use your influence to suggest a newer vision for the curriculum and the way it mirrors changes within a discipline. Online courses and curricula must move forward if they are to survive.

Effectively Making a Course Your Own

If you are hired as adjunct faculty for a course or two, or if you are asked to teach online courses you did not design, you may wonder if the course will ever feel like your own. Although you may be able to provide additional activities and materials for learners online, most institutions do not want individual instructors tampering too much with their established courses and designs. Nevertheless, you can make your course stand out from the rest, simply because there is no other teacher just like you.

You alone are responsible for creating a learning community within your classroom. You must guide students to learning materials and activities and facilitate these educational experiences. You determine the tone and pace of the course through your e-mail messages, bulletin board posts, chat room persona, and whiteboard markings. You reveal your personality through your messages and the number and type of communications. You can establish an environment in which learners feel free to discuss and question, but yet are respectful of other learners and the teacher. The way you phrase messages and the speed of your responses to questions and comments, for example, illustrate your willingness to work with students and develop a true learning community.

Anecdotal information from my teaching colleagues at Franklin University and Embry-Riddle Aeronautical University who did not design the online course they teach indicated a wide range in the amount of time that they spent in course preparation. They reported up to eight hours per week preparing to facilitate the course. Some preparation included posting bulletin board threads or folders, reading through the materials to check for any changes in content or design, and sending e-mail to learners to alert them to upcoming assignments. Although these teachers did not have to prepare new materials or update course information for a module before they could teach it, they did have to spend time familiarizing themselves with the materials and communicating with learners about the next module.

Spending less time in materials preparation allows you more time to prepare learners for working with assignments and discussing course content. Although you may not have designed the course, you can put your unique stamp on the course through your discussions with learners about the material. Your perspective and experience differ from any other teacher's or designer's. With more time for communication with students, you can more actively participate in discussions and perhaps share additional resources with learners. You will need some preparation time as you teach, but your focus can be directed primarily to meeting learners' needs and guiding the class to new materials as well as through the current course content.

Working with a Faculty Mentor

New online teachers, including adjunct faculty who live far away from the physical campus, may feel left out if they work on their own, almost in a vacuum. In a completely online university or college, all administrators and faculty may work at home or in widely dispersed locations, depending upon where their computers are based.

In these types of situations, the well-designed online program includes one faculty member or administrator who leads a program and oversees the courses taught by online faculty within a particular discipline. Having a mentor and contact person especially is important for new faculty, although that lifeline is important to each teacher. You should feel free to ask this contact person your questions about the course design and the mechanics of running the course. You might also provide feedback about courses and curriculum development as you learn more about the overall structure of online education at the institution.

A mentor also should alert you to opportunities to work with other faculty. Mentors who are already familiar with programs and special events, such as an annual series of training workshops, can let you know what types of activities take place or how often they are offered. Mentors can introduce you to other faculty or suggest ways for you to get up to speed about the institution and its inner workings. The quality of your teaching experience is left up to you. By working with a mentor and developing a network of colleagues and friends online, you feel more like the faculty who teach full time or on site.

Summary

As you read the next chapter, you will learn more about the daily workings of a class, whether you have designed the course or you are teaching a course someone else designed. Having a positive, adaptive attitude and being willing to learn quickly are key attributes for all successful online teachers.

Online courses should encourage learners to interact with materials, ideas, and each other throughout the term. Your job is to design materials and activities appropriate to the subject matter, the level of the course, and the best ways for learners to understand information and develop skills. Materials should be unique to that course but appropriate for the skills and knowledge levels learners need at that point in the curriculum. Your course's subject matter should not overlap that presented in other courses, but should be a logical extension of previous courses and a bridge to more advanced content.

You need to direct learners to the linked information and activities. You may need to write instructions, assignment sheets, guidelines, sample documents, and other informative pieces to help learners understand how to use the course site and find what they are looking for. Many of these descriptions and instructions should become part of the text permanently stored on the course site.

Throughout a course, you will need to provide individual assistance and facilitate learning through your presence as an instructor. Your e-mail messages, bulletin board posts, chats, and videoconferences, for example, are necessary to provide a human link to the technology and to elaborate, explain, discuss, share, and otherwise interact with learners and the course materials.

Developing course materials is an ongoing job. Just because a course is approved should not mean that it becomes static term after term. As technology, subjects, and teacher and learner expectations change, so should the course. Keeping an eye on what you want to add or modify in a course is an important, continuing part of course and curriculum development.

Often, updating one course requires further curriculum modification. The changes made to one course may have a ripple effect to other courses. Keeping an eye on the entire curriculum and assessing the changes needed within individual courses are important activities in the curriculum-development process.

References

Brewer, E. W., DeJonge, J. O., & Stout, V. J. (2001). *Moving to online: Making the transition from traditional instruction and communication strategies*. Thousand Oaks, CA: Corwin Press.

Canadian Virtual University/Universite Virtuelle Canadienne. (2002). Online demonstrations. Retrieved September 30, 2002, from http://www.cvu-uvc.ca/sample.html

Connecticut Distance Learning Consortium. (2002). CTDLC technical support. Retrieved September 30, 2002, from http://www.ctdlc.org/Help/index.html

Ko, S., & Rossen, S. (2001). *Teaching online: A practical guide.* Boston: Houghton Mifflin.

Lynch, M. M. (2002). *The online educator: A guide to creating the virtual classroom.* London: RoutledgeFalmer.

Olsen, R., & Schihl, R. (2002). Beyond demographics, content, and technology: The impact of culture on the design and implementation of a distance education program. In P. Comeaux (Ed.), *Communication and collaboration in the online classroom* (pp. 55-71). Bolton, MA: Anker Publishing.

Schank, R., & Neaman, A. (2001). Motivation and failure in educational simulation design. In K. D. Forbus & P. J. Fettovich (Eds.), *Smart machines in education: The coming revolution in educational technology* (pp. 37-69). Menlo Park, CA: American Association for Artificial Intelligence.

Washington State University. (2002). Course information online. Retrieved September 30, 2002, from http://www.eus.wsu.edu/DPP/courses/outlines.asp

Part 2.

Implementing the Curriculum

Implementing the modified curriculum involves the day-to-day tasks of teaching. In Part 2, you will read about the tools you will use in your class and the day-to-day tasks involved in keeping a class running smoothly. Although curriculum and Web-site design are critical areas to plan, the implementation of the course is equally important. A sound plan may be useless without an effective means of putting it into operation.

As a teacher, you may have been involved in the course design and curriculum planning. If that is the case, you are already well ahead in understanding how an online course operates and why your course has been designed in a certain way. You are also probably familiar, at least theoretically, with the tools and techniques required to make the course run smoothly.

If you have been hired to teach an existing online course, you will need a little bit more preparation before you begin teaching the class. Before the class starts, learning the specifics of the course Web site and the tools you and learners will be using is time well spent. If you have not been involved with course design, you may pay special attention to the way this class was set up. You may want to compare it to other online courses you have taught or online course sites you have visited. Providing insight into what makes an online course effective can help you not only when you teach a class, but also in recommending ways to enhance the course or materials the next time the curriculum or Web site is updated.

In Chapter 4. The Tools of the Trade, you find information about the tools you will use in teaching, especially at the low-tech level. E-mail, bulletin boards, chat rooms, whiteboards, and online gradebooks are discussed. In Chapter 5. The Daily Work of Teaching, suggestions for teaching online and descriptions of ways to use these tools effectively are provided. Chapter 6. The Aesthetics of Teaching, lists ways to help you build online learning communities. Communicating effectively with your students throughout the course is crucial, and in this chapter you will read about some strategies for group and individual messages, discussions, and chats. Ethics and academic honesty are also discussed in Chapter 6. These three chapters guide you through the practical and ideal workings of online courses.

Implementing the carefully designed curriculum is important, because the Web site, course materials, and "published" communication (e.g., through bulletin boards, whiteboards, gradebooks) are the elements that learners first see when they log into an online course. Once the course has begun, learners take their cue from the tone and pace that you set.

Although learners have the primary responsibility for directing their participation and ensuring that assignments and activities are completed, you have an important role as facilitator. The way you communicate with learners and create an inviting educational setting directly affects learners' perceptions of the course and its importance to you. If you show that you truly care about online education and students' progress in a course, and if you become involved in helping learners meet their objectives (and have a positive learning experience along the way), students are more likely to take the course seriously and to care about their work.

Throughout Part 2 you should get ideas for making your daily and weekly teaching activities more enjoyable and creative.

The Tools
of the Trade

4

Once a curriculum has been established and new or existing courses modified to reflect any curricular changes, the courses making up the curriculum must be successfully implemented. The effectiveness of the technical tools in presenting materials is important to the success of a course. Each segment of the curriculum should work as well as planned. The pedagogical design and its implementation are of primary interest to teachers and administrators.

However, learners approach courses differently. They determine a course's and a curriculum's effectiveness by the ease with which they use a course and institutional Web site. Students often determine the value of a course by how much they enjoy using the tools and how well the teacher helps them interact easily with other learners and the materials. Learners do not care why a specific brand or type of tool was chosen; they want to make sure that it works, is easy to use, and meets their expectations.

The day-to-day use of technology has a big impact on the way learners perceive a course. Technology and accessibility also frame learners' perceptions of the rest of the curriculum and the institution. As a teacher who facilitates a course, you want to make sure that you use tools well and can help learners successfully use the technology for a positive educational experience.

Not all online classes use the same tools, and currently, many online education programs rely heavily on writing-based tools such as bulletin boards, chat sessions, and e-mail. Some teachers, working with full-time course designers or on their own, are implementing more interactive designs, such as streaming audio or video, two-way voice communication, and two-way online video. All these tools provide real-time communication that appeals to learners with different learning preferences and styles.

Many learners who take courses through colleges or universities lack access to higher-tech forms of instruction and communication. To ensure that the course design can reach the broadest market possible, the educational design generally favors low-tech communication. As online courses presented by an institution progress, and as market analysis shows that the program's potential online students have more access to advanced technology, more interactive media are introduced. This plan allows learners gradually to upgrade their home or office computer systems. It also helps accommodate learners who do not have their own computers and still rely on public access to computer technology, through on-site university or college computer labs or public libraries.

Online training may involve much higher levels of technology, especially if the business requiring the training is actively involved with e-commerce or specializes in some aspect of computer technology. Higher-tech communication and instructional options may be offered by commercial vendors of training programs or in-house departments created to customize training for employees. Educational institutions may rely on program vendors, but they are more likely to use courseware or other "do it yourself" options.

Because, for the time being, at least, many colleges and universities emphasize the use of e-mail, whiteboards, bulletin boards, written chat sessions, and word-processed assignments, the print-based forms of communication are highlighted in this chapter. Tools used to facilitate chat sessions, create bulletin board messages, draw on whiteboards, send effective e-mail, and keep track of evaluated work with online gradebooks are discussed.

Keep in mind, too, that not only are you expected to be familiar with course tools and to use them accurately in teaching/facilitating the course, but you also may need to instruct learners in ways to use these tools. Although many learners are increasingly sophisticated in their use of technology, and some may have computer knowledge and skills that far surpass yours, at least some learners may be novices in using the Internet or course Web sites. For example, adult learners who may be taking their first online class and who may not work with computers at home or very often use them at work may need some assistance in learning to use all tools.

Learners in purely online classes typically span more than one generation (although learners taking classes in a curriculum requiring both on site and online coursework usually are younger adults). In some classes, students' ages might range from late teens to 60s. (This information may be disclosed informally when individuals participate in an informal chat session or through an e-mail comment. Otherwise, you probably will not know someone's age, although from assignments and comments in online discussions you may receive hints by learners' choice of topics or personal frame of reference about an event.)

The experience levels among learners range from barely computer literate to highly literate, such as those who are studying Web site design or computer programming. Typically, at least a few people will need assistance and a friendly online presence to help them troubleshoot technical problems.

Therefore, you may need to provide some basic instructions for at least some class members. As well, not everyone may know all the fine points of working with course-site tools, so you may want to provide helpful tips to the class as a whole. Part of your role as teacher is to make sure learners know how to use all the tools available at the course Web site. If you cannot provide the appropriate level of technical assistance, you need to have a list of phone numbers and e-mail addresses for the technical support staff who can help learners solve the problem.

The Teacher's Roles as Communicator and Facilitator

When you are teaching an online class, you must communicate frequently with learners. Of course, you can call them, send them a fax, or otherwise set up non-computerized forms of communication, but the point of an online course is to deliver materials and interact with participants through the Internet. The most common tool, therefore, is e-mail. Popular second choices are chat rooms and bulletin boards. It is important not only to be able to use the tools required to communicate with learners, but also to communicate effectively. Technical and communication skills are both necessary for you to work well with all learners.

Online learners tend to take responsibility for much of their education. They have to read and study online materials, complete the assignments, and integrate feedback mostly on their own. Because they work any time and from any place, these learners may feel isolated from you and other students. Your job as an online teacher may require you to be an educational facilitator. You need to make sure learners have access to materials they need for the course and to guide learners to key points and major skill areas.

However, an effective facilitator also must be a wonderful communicator. Without a way to bring learners together for discussion and camaraderie, the online class will not be as interesting or engaging as an on-site class. Although using the tools of the trade is important to your effectiveness as an online teacher, the tools are powerless unless you use them to build a community of learners.

The following sections explain some typical tools and the skills required to use them efficiently in class. Communicating by using these tools is an important, ongoing skill. Although you can master the basics and the communication theory of working with these tools, remember that you need to keep up with changes to the specific hardware and software required for your classes, as well as with trends on the Internet. Adding to your technical skills as the technology changes is important, too.

Asynchronous and Synchronous Communication and Activities

If the course has been designed to be user (student) centered, rather than teacher centered, your role primarily will be to guide learners in creating meaning from course materials. They may do this by working alone on some assignments, but more often by sharing ideas and discovering connections among ideas through collaborative learning. Group activities, such as discussions and simulations, allow learners to collaborate within the course structure. However, individual and group activities should take place within an online course.

Both asynchronous and synchronous communication and activities are important in an online class. You will use both types of communication to build a learning community. As well, a group of learners with different preferences and styles should find a variety of individual and team activities and assignments. In this way, each learner should have at least one type of activity that matches his or her preferred learning style or method of communication.

Asynchronous communication and activities take place outside of real time. For example, a learner sends you an e-mail message. You later read and respond to the message. There is a time lag between the time the learner sent the message and you replied, even if the lag time is short. Bulletin board messages can be added at any time and read at your and the learners' leisure; you do not read someone else's message as it is being created, and you can take as much time as you need to respond to the post. Asynchronous activities take place whenever learners have the time to complete them. For example, viewing videos linked to the course site, reading a textbook, and writing a paper are all asynchronous activities.

In contrast, synchronous, or real-time, communication takes place like a conversation. If your class uses only writing-based tools to communicate, the only synchronous communication possible is a chat session. Everyone gets online in the same chat room and types questions, comments, and responses in real time. Synchronous activities may include chat sessions, whiteboard drawings, and other group interactive work.

If your class involves multimedia tools, synchronous communication might involve audio or video feeds to the computer. Some "online" courses require learners and teachers to get together at least once (or sometimes several times) in person, by conference call, or through closed-circuit television links.

Although these examples of synchronous communication take place offline, they may still be important communication tools for distance learners who spend the rest of their time working online. Occasionally, group synchronous activities take place on site, too. For example, lab sessions or proctored testing sessions may require learners to complete activities with other class members in real time.

Learning communities may use chat rooms for discussion, interviews, Q & A sessions, and team work sessions. Community members often prefer real-time communication instead of asynchronous communication for work sessions, although both synchronous and asynchronous communication are used frequently. Location, personal/work schedules, and time zones determine which forum is best for a particular situation or community. Group members also keep in touch through notices and responses tracked on bulletin boards or posted to a community's Web site, mailing lists, and bulk and individual e-mail.

Chat Rooms

Unless your class uses a multimedia chat room, in which you can hear or see each other during the discussion, your chat sessions involve typing lots of information. You type questions or comments and post them immediately, where the class reads them. Class members respond individually with their own comments or questions. The entire conversation can be seen scrolling down the screen for immediate reference. Many chat rooms are designed so that a transcript of the session is made available to the teacher and learners after the end of the session or within a short time (such as within 24 hours).

Some course sites have more than one chat room. If several rooms are available to learners, you have to make sure you explain which room will be used for a class discussion. Making empty rooms available to learners for smaller group projects or learning communities' discussions may become a regular part of your job; posting schedules of smaller groups' meetings as well as the entire class' discussions can help keep learners in the correct room. As well, you can encourage learners to use chat rooms more frequently if more than one is regularly available.

Chat rooms are ideal for class discussions, learner study sessions, group work, your office hours, and review sessions before a test. All or only some members of a class may meet in the chat room. Although it is probably a good idea to require some sessions, visiting the chat room should be an ongoing, easily available way for learners and teachers to get together informally to discuss the course.

Two types of chats should be encouraged in a course: structured discussions and social get-togethers. The purpose of each should be made clear to learners before a chat session takes place. Structured discussions may be study sessions and reviews, required assignments, analyses of course readings, or formal presentations by class members. As facilitator of a structured discussion, you keep the conversation on target for a meaning-ful session about course content. The tone and format for this type of chat are more formal and serious. However, the social get-together chat is far from being a waste of teachers' or learners' time. Course topics may be discussed informally, but this chat's purpose is socialization. The session helps learners get to know each other and take a break within a safe chat environment (Collison, Elbaum, Haavind, & Tinker, 2000). Learners may meet on their own for either structured discussions or social get-togethers; you do not have to facilitate every chat activity.

The institution may provide other safe havens for chat sessions outside a course chat room. Online coffee houses or lounges may be established exclusively for students or faculty and staff, or everyone working within the university or college may be invited to participate. Password protection should limit participation only to those belonging to the institution, so that people who chat feel safer in knowing who is likely to be online in the chat room. If out-of-class chat spaces are available for learners, you might encourage class members to take advantage of them so that they feel a part of the wider university or college community.

Office Hours

One of the best ways to bond with online learners is through a chat session. Weekly office hours (at least one or two per course section per week is a good idea) should be posted on the course Web site so that learners know when you are online and ready for synchronous communication. You should arrive in the chat room a few minutes before any learners log in, and then stay until the last person has logged out of the chat room after a session has officially ended. If no one shows up during the first quarter of an office hour, you may want to post a notice that you will return in a few minutes. Then check the class bulletin board or e-mail to make sure that no one has been trying to get into the chat room but could not log in and then posted a request for help. If there are not any messages requiring your immediate attention, return to the chat room for the remainder of the class time.

Like office hours on site, when you sit in your office and await learners who may need some extra help or just want to chat, what goes on during online office hours may be unpredictable. Sometimes almost everyone in a class may show up to chat. Other times no one visits during the entire session. Some online office hour sessions are very chatty, with no class content, just friendly conversation among people getting to know each other. Other sessions are content heavy, with learners asking precise questions about assignments or materials.

Especially during an office hour, you should let your personality shine through. For example, do not be afraid to appear more human to learners: The group might commiserate over favorite sports teams, discuss plans for the weekend, talk about the weather, critique the latest movies—just as you would do if you talked with learners on site in the student center or hallways. The office hours provide a way for learners to get a little extra attention, and for teachers and learners to learn more about each other.

However, you also need to come across as "the teacher"—someone who understands the assignments and the objectives for them, who is prepared with additional resources for further exploration of a topic, and who has had experience with the course materials and their relevance to professional career pursuits. You can be approachable and get to know students without losing your authority as the teacher/facilitator.

To encourage attendance during office hours you should permanently post the days and times (with time zone notations) in an easily seen spot on the course Web site. On the day of the office hour(s), send e-mail to the class to invite them to attend. You might suggest some possible topics for discussion. Reminding learners of these sessions and inviting class members to participate are effective ways to increase the number of visitors to your online office.

Also send e-mail to learners who asked questions during a session or disclosed some personal information (such as "I'm leaving on a business trip this week" or "my son is having surgery on Tuesday") to follow up on their progress or to learn how they are doing during a difficult time. Learners who understand that you look forward to talking with them and are interested in them generally come back to chat during office hours.

Although when you hold an office hour at home, you could have the TV blaring in the background and a bowl of snacks on the printer, you should treat an online office hour just as professionally as you treat an office hour on campus. Your demeanor may be friendly and casual, but your focus is on the learners and their questions and concerns. Even if the group goes far off topic in a chat, you can stay focused on the discussion if your attention is not split among several distractions. Of course, one benefit of teaching and learning online is that you can do so at home in a comfortable atmosphere. You may not wear a suit when you work online, but try to act as professionally with those learners who cannot see you as with those who can.

Class Discussions

Some online classes are huge. If you are holding a required discussion session, you may want to split the class into at least two or three different groups, each with their own chat session. Having a chat with 25 people at the same time can be at best difficult, and learners who have trouble typing or spelling may get lost in the avalanche of messages. Chatting with eight to 10 learners is manageable, even if you cover the same material with several smaller groups. Smaller groups are the ideal, because learners tend to participate more often, and you can more easily manage the flow of the discussion.

The group's makeup, the way they communicate, and the personalities of the different people in each chat create variety in the discussion, even if you ask similar questions or make similar comments as you hold chats about similar topics or for the same assignment but for a new group of learners. If you hold several similarly themed chat sessions, it is a good idea to have learners read the transcripts of each discussion session, not just their own. Key points, insights, and shared experiences differ from group to group; to get a feel for a "full class" discussion, all transcripts should be read.

If you plan to set up several required chats throughout a course, you may want to assign learners to different groups, just to make sure everyone has a chance to meet other class members. Project or discussion groups should be varied to allow a different mix of learners to interact. Although some combinations will be more successful than others, it is a good idea to facilitate the interaction of as many learners as possible within the course.

During chats early in a course, if you know that some learners have a great deal of difficulty in communicating clearly or quickly, you may want to group learners with similar difficulties in the same session. Once learners become more familiar with the chat environment and improve their skills, they should chat with learners who have greater skill levels. You also do not want to advertise that a chat is set up for the slow typists, for example. You need to build a learning community and self-esteem. Providing learners with a safe environment in which they can respond effectively is an important step in building a community. Sometimes you have to give smaller groups a chance to succeed before they join larger discussions.

Even if you have carefully grouped learners for projects and discussions, setting up a convenient time for everyone to participate in a chat can be tricky. Scheduling online discussion times can be challenging, especially if learners live in different time zones or have widely divergent work schedules. At the beginning of the course, you should find out where your learners live and work. You can also ask if there is a preferred time block for chats.

For example, you might schedule an early evening time block for discussions with learners living primarily in the Eastern and Central U.S. time zones, if you also live in one of those time zones. Learners living in another continent will have another block of time better suited to early evening in their time zone, which means that you may need to set your alarm for a time that is inconvenient for you. Of course, you cannot please everyone. You can set up office hours at a few different times, if not in the same week, at least across the duration of the course, to help more learners be able to talk with you online. You can vary required discussion times to include some weekends, late nights, or daytime hours to accommodate everyone at least once and preferably most people several times.

You can also find out if learners have permission to access the course chat room from their workplace. Some employers, especially those who are paying for their employees' continuing education, may not mind if learners use the office computer for an hour-long chat. Other employers may just request that the chat take place during a scheduled lunch or dinner break, or before or after regular work hours. However, firewalls and other security safeguards may prevent learners from accessing a chat room from the office. Any technical glitches should be worked out between the learner and his or her employer, as well as with the university offering the course.

If many international students are participating in required chat sessions, learn about the customs and protocols for chat sessions within that culture. See if there are different expectations for the use of language or the appropriate structure for a discussion or conversation. Not all learners come from cultures in which discussions or especially dissenting views are encouraged. These students may be reluctant to offer ideas that differ from the teacher's or each other's. As well, not all learners worldwide will have easy access to an hour-long chat. Those learners who share Internet access with others or pay by the minute may find chat sessions prohibitive. All these factors should be considered not only as chats are initially planned in the course design, but also as the chat sessions are facilitated. You may need to be flexible with requirements for chat sessions.

Facilitating a Chat Session

Most universities and colleges require you to post a syllabus (or one is automatically posted for a particular online course). The due dates and assignment descriptions should include a list of upcoming chat sessions, so learners at least have in mind a general time frame for required chats from the start of the course.

At least a week before a required chat session, you should make sure learners know about the chat. In addition to sending a group e-mail detailing the date, time, and topic of each chat session (if more than one will be offered), you should post a bulletin board message and other Web-site bulletins (such as on the home page for the course site). A required chat should not be a surprise to anyone. Remember, too, that some learners may be traveling out of state or country and may not have their laptop along. The more advance notice you can give of an upcoming chat session, the better.

A few days before a structured chat session, you should ask learners to practice logging into the chat room, just to make sure they know how to get into the room and to maneuver once they are inside. You also should list guidelines so that everyone knows the protocol for the chat. One important guideline should be that learners use their complete (and real) names as they log into the chat room. That way you do not have to wonder which Heather is speaking, or if this is the female Chris in a class with both male and female learners with the same first name. It also solves the problem of learners entering the chat room under a cute, or even an inappropriate, nickname.

Although learners have to prepare for a chat by reading required materials or completing specific assignments, you too have homework. You should prepare a list of more questions than you could possibly ask during a chat session. You want to stay on target with the discussion and make sure all core concepts are discussed, but your list can also help you give learners a different approach or another perspective to the topic.

To lead an hour-long chat, for example, you might prepare a list of 30-40 open-ended questions. You do not need to ask them all for the chat to be successful; prioritize questions by categories of information or a sequence that you want to follow. However, if you get "dead air" with some questions, be ready with restatements or new questions that may prod further discussion. With a long list of possible questions, you can also vary the questions asked of different groups studying the same subject. That way the questions remain fresh, and learners do not know exactly what you are going to ask them, even if they have read the transcripts of other chat sessions about the same subject.

Collison et al. (2000) suggested asking a full range of questions to help learners delve more deeply into a topic and make connections among ideas.

They recommended five categories of questions, from the "so what?" variety to questions that clarify, explore assumptions and values, show the relationships between and among cause(s) and effect(s), and help learners plan what to do or how to act. Chats must not only show that learners have read course materials, but also that class members are connecting what they have studied with other concepts and life experiences. Chats should emphasize critical thinking instead of students' rote recitation of what they have read.

A few minutes before the chat, enter the chat room. Being the first in the room allows you to test chat room features, post a quick welcome message, and take roll as learners enter the room. You might also have a few extra minutes to take off-topic questions from learners new to the chat environment.

When you are ready to start the chat session (and you should start on time, even if some learners have not arrived), take a minute or two to review the guidelines for the chat session. For example, make sure that learners know the topic for the chat. Tell learners, both before and at the beginning of the session, that you will pose a question and then wait for their answers.

If you want to call on one person only, write that person's name (or use the chat room feature of selecting a name from the chat list) before posing a question or asking for clarification or explanation of a previous comment. The group then should wait for that person to respond before commenting further or asking a different question.

Visual cues are also important during a chat. Explain that you will use boldface, color coding, or all capitals (boldface or color coding is easier to read, if your system provides these types of options) so that learners can see your questions or comments within the longer, scrollable text. You need to make sure that whatever format you use to highlight your information can be seen by all learners. Some systems or browsers may not display all types of highlighting, so you need to check to make sure that everyone can see the highlighted information. If you use all capital letters for your comments, explain that you are not shouting—just making sure that your questions and comments can be seen.

Remind learners to stay on topic and to offer constructive comments. If a learner needs to ask a question, ask her or him to write QUESTION so that you can slow the discussion and request the learner by name to ask the question.

You may require learners to use other visual cues to help facilitate the discussion. For example, especially with a larger group, you may receive dozens of responses right away to a question. It may take a few moments for you, and the class members, to read all the information. If new comments are posted rapidly, you may not be able to keep up with all the comments and ideas being presented.

To slow the conversation to a manageable pace, and to help you keep track of who wrote what, you might ask learners to "raise their hand" if they want to respond to a question. You might ask them to type a ? to indicate that they want you to recognize them. Then you can type the learner's name so that the person can answer the question.

If you use a series of terms, such as QUESTION, or symbols, such as ?, to have specific meanings for your classes' chat sessions, make sure everyone knows how to use these conventions ahead of the session. You may post a list of procedures to the bulletin board, or you may remind learners at the start of a chat which symbols or phrases should be used during that session.

Some novice chat participants may need a little reassurance. Explain that everyone will probably make a few typing mistakes, but learners should try to proof a comment quickly before sending it, just to make sure it is readable. Remind learners that you are not evaluating their typing ability, only their knowledge of the subject and level of participation.

Because chat rooms require learners to type their responses, poor or slower typists may not provide complete ideas or sentences. Their cryptic comments may be difficult to understand unless you prod learners to type a little more and give them the time to respond more fully to your question. As the chat progresses, you may want to call on or give more time to those learners who need to clarify their ideas or take a little longer to express themselves adequately.

If anyone has trouble keeping up and needs a break, suggest typing HELP! to alert you to stop or slow the conversation for a minute. Also note that sometimes, no matter what you do or the learner does, a computer glitch, power surge, or power outage occurs. If someone is thrown out of the chat room and it is possible to re-enter in a few minutes, that person should log on again. By going over these ground rules at the beginning of a chat session, you can remind learners how to type their responses responsibly and readably, and while you are doing that, you are also allowing late arrivals to enter the chat room before the discussion starts.

During the chat session, you must truly be a facilitator for the group. At times, you may want to summarize the past few minutes of conversation. Definitely, at the end of the session, you should ask learners to summarize the key points of the discussion, or you submit a summary for consensus. Sometimes you may have to slow down the discussion so that everyone can read recent comments and finish the comments they are typing.

As with all classroom discussions, you have to determine how much to let the group digress or follow a tangent. Sometimes you have to pull the group back into focus about the subject matter you are supposed to be discussing. If the discussion moves into an inappropriate topic, or if some learners are not as sensitive and politically correct as they should be, you may need to steer the discussion in another direction or even stop the conversation and ask that language or topic selection be changed. Everyone in the class should feel comfortable about participating in the discussion, and decorum and consideration for others are essential elements of a useful chat session.

Chat sessions can move quickly, and lots of good ideas can be lost in the barrage of messages posted at about the same time. You may want to post a PAUSE message to allow learners to catch up with their reading and to finish the message they are in the process of typing. Then you can ask clarification questions about what has been written, highlight important ideas that may have been overlooked, or pull together what may seem like diverse threads of conversation into a common theme.

Some learners may post information that is incorrect, not just a different interpretation of the material. You have to correct wrong information without stifling the learner's participation. One way to do this is to focus on the information, not the learner who provided it. You might add to the information or explain the concept in greater depth in order to provide a clear, full discussion of the topic. Chat sessions should allow everyone to participate, but there has to be some semblance of organization and purpose for the information gained through the chat. A session should do more than generate lots of different ideas; it should be used to help learners make sense of these diverse ideas and how they fit together in the bigger picture.

Throughout the session, you should be aware of who is in the chat room and who is participating. Generally, that is fairly easy, because the names of participants appear somewhere in the chat window, as well as within the participants' comments (usually before the comment). If one learner hogs the conversation, you need to direct the conversation toward other learners without abruptly dismissing the talkative participant. If some learners are lurking, but not typing, you can specifically ask them a question or ask for their opinion.

You may want to comment on a response or tie new information with what has been previously discussed. You may need to request clarification or elaboration of a point. Positive, esteem-building comments are helpful, too. A "good point" or "excellent suggestion" not only builds up the learners who wrote the original messages, but they provide a model for additional positive comments. You need to keep everyone involved in the conversation, and although a chat tends to take on a life of its own, you can guide the participants into a fair, friendly discussion.

Before participants log off after the summary, you might thank everyone for joining in the discussion. A helpful reminder when the transcript will be available is also appropriate. Because you are the facilitator, you should be the last person to log out of the chat room.

Figure 4-1 summarizes some tips for facilitating chat sessions.

Figure 4-1. Tips for Effective Chat Sessions

Pre-chat Activities

- Set up several convenient sessions, and allow learners to sign up for the session they prefer.

- Limit the number of participants in each session to eight or fewer, if possible.

- Promote each session through bulletin board posts and e-mail messages.

- Provide instructions for using the chat room and procedures for participating in the chat.

In-chat Activities

- Make sure your questions and comments can be seen (e.g., use highlighting).

- At the beginning of the session, review the rules for the chat session.

- Follow the protocol you have established.

- Ask open-ended questions.

- Allow time for learners to respond to these questions and to make comments regarding previous messages.

- Provide positive feedback about the responses, even if you need to correct a misconception or steer the conversation in another direction (i.e., emphasize activities to do, rather than "don't" actions; restate information so that it is correct; summarize a topic and lead into another area).

- Keep track of who is and is not participating.

- Ask for summaries (or provide a summary of the content) at the end of the chat.

- Pull a session to a close by describing the outcomes (e.g., the way learners will be evaluated for the session) or follow-up activities (e.g., a written assignment about chat topics, encouragement to read chat transcripts).

- Thank everyone for participating.

- Be the last person out of the chat room.

Post-chat Activities

- Review the transcript of each chat session.

- Send feedback to the chat group and/or individual class members.

- Use the information and experience gained from the previous chat session to help you prepare (or modify your protocols or procedures) for the next session.

Class Projects

The chat room is useful for learners who need to collaborate on a group project. Typical class projects include role plays, discussion of reading materials, preparation of a document or design, or development of a Web site. Everyone in the group should have individual tasks to perform, but the group needs to coordinate these activities and eventually turn in a gradable project.

Although other communication methods may be used (e.g., in-person meetings for groups in the same locale, fax messages, videoconferences, closed-circuit TV meetings, e-mail, bulletin board posts), most learners in online classes like to use the chat room when they have to work together. A great deal of work can be done in synchronous time, when the group members can find a convenient time to get together.

You can help groups find suitable times to work by publishing a schedule at the class Web site when different groups plan to meet in the chat room. If only one chat room is available for learners in your class, posting a schedule of times when learners plan to get together helps all groups know when the chat room will be occupied.

You can also help by limiting the number of people in a group. A group of four can get a great deal of work done on a project, if they share the workload. They also are less likely to have scheduling conflicts than a larger group would face.

You might remind learners that you can view the group's transcripts (or you may want to ask permission if you cannot automatically view each transcript) so that you can keep tabs on the group's progress and help troubleshoot any problems. However, work groups who meet in the chat room should determine their own facilitator and create their own little learning community. If you are invited to participate, you may, but you should respect the group's protocols.

Transcripts

Transcripts might be made of individual discussions or those that took place within a certain time period, such as 24 hours. The transcript may be linked to the course Web site, so that learners can read, download to disk, print, or cut and paste individual transcripts, or they may be requested from an archive or a site administrator. The transcript provides a permanent record (at least throughout the course) of the ideas discussed in a session and the names of the people who participated. If the transcript automatically lists increments of time, such as an hour and minute listing in 10-minute increments, you can see how much conversation was generated during the session and how much time individuals needed to express their ideas. You can determine the pace of the conversation, too, by looking at a timed transcript.

This transcript helps you record who participated and how often each learner added to the discussion. You have a record of the total time of each session, if multiple sessions took place on the same day, but at different times. You can review the topics, questions, and comments to make sure that learners grasped the key concepts for a unit, and that you answered all questions.

For learners who type or read more slowly than the pace of the conversation, transcripts provide a way to review and catch up to everything that occurred in a session. Even the fastest typists or readers in a class often have a hard time keeping up during a fast and furious conversation. Transcripts help everyone remember the conversation accurately and completely.

Here is an example of sections of a transcript from a small group discussion with the teacher. Sometimes the pieces of different parts of the conversation overlap. Although the example includes few typos, misspelled or missing words are common as the pace of the chat increases or with the number of participants who have difficulty typing.

In some chats, smilies and abbreviations provide additional cues to indicate the speaker's expression. For example, <bg> refers to a big grin, and :) shows a group member's expression. Other typical abbreviations in a chat might be LOL for "laugh out loud," OT for an "off topic" comment, and BTW as shorthand for "by the way." In addition, some participants may shorten "for" to 4, "are" to r, and "you" to u.

The flavor of a typical chat can be depicted in this short, simple segment, which represents only a few minutes of a session. A complete hour-long discussion creates transcripts of dozens of pages, depending upon the topic and the participants' writing speed.

Figure 4-2. A Transcript Example

(This is an example of a short section of a typical chat session requiring learners to discuss a topic about which they have studied and completed other assignments. This is not an actual transcript, but an example based on typical discussions held in online classes. The names do not refer to real learners.)

Lynnette Porter:	**Hi. How is everyone tonight?**
Amie Lynde:	Fine.
Sam Archer:	OK. How are you?
Lynnette Porter:	**I'm fine. Is everyone ready to get started?**
Amie Lynde:	Yes.
Jay Sandburg:	Yes.
Zhue Li:	Yes.
Sam Archer:	Sure thing.
Cameron Martinez:	I have a question.
Lynnette Porter:	**Yes, Cameron?**
Cameron Martinez:	Were we supposed to write our paper about the Olympics before tonight? Or after this discussion?
Amie Lynde:	Oh. I sent mine already. Is that OK?
Lynnette Porter:	**Cameron, Amie. If you wanted to write the paper before class tonight, it was OK. But if you thought the discussion would help you write the paper, you could do that instead. It was up to you.**
Cameron Martinez:	☺
Amie Lynde:	OK. Thankx!
Sam Archer:	Due Saturday?
Lynnette Porter:	**That's right. I have to receive the paper by Saturday night's deadline.**
Sam Archer:	Sounds like a big weekend 4 u!
Lynnette Porter:	**Hey, I like reading your papers! <bg> Let's get started on our "official" topic: the Olympics in the 20th and 21st centuries. Here's my first question: For a nation, what are some political benefits of sending athletes to an Olympics?**
Zhue Li:	To show everyone that your country's the best.
Jay Sandburg:	Athletes as ambassadors
Cameron Martinez:	Get on TV.
Cameron Martinez:	And show off the country.
Lynnette Porter:	**Jay, how do athletes act as ambassadors?**

Figure 4-2. A Transcript Example (continued)

Sam Archer:	The athletes get together throughout the Olympics and have a chance to talk to each other. They learn that the have some things in common.
Amie Lynde:	I'm not sure there are political benefits from an Olympics. It's just a bunch of people trying to convince everyone else that they're great.
Sam Archer:	I meant they, not the.
Lynnette Porter:	**Amie, why do you think that countries host an Olympics if there isn't some political benefit? Are there other benefits that outweigh politics?**
Jay Sandburg:	Athletes who are heroic are looked up to by other people. They're the best of the country. They represent the country. That's why they're ambassadors.
Lynnette Porter:	**I see, Jay. That's a good point.**
Cameron Martinez:	QUESTION
Lynnette Porter:	**Yes, Cameron?**
Amie Lynde:	I thought that the Olympics weren't supposed to be about politics. But about fair play and good sportsman ship. Good PR. Plus they
Amie Lynde:	make lots of money by selling stuff. Maybe better economics than politics.
Cameron Martinez:	Isn't an Olympics always political, even if its nt supposed to be? Like the one before WW2.
Jay Sandburg:	Good point, Amie. I agree. Shouldn't be about politics.
Lynnette Porter:	**So, in general, an Olympics may not be overtly created to be political, but it might have some political implications or reflections anyway. And there might be other benefits, such as economic or public relations benefits, that are more obvious. Cameron brought up a good example of one Olympics. Let's talk about it in more detail. What was most interesting to you from the video clips you saw about the Berlin Olympics?**

(This type of discussion could go on for a long time, as the topics are covered.
Here is the final segment of the example, once the discussion has begun to wind down.)

Lynnette Porter:	**Let's summarize some key points you've talked about tonight. What is important to remember about the Olympics?**
Cameron Martinez:	That it reflects our culture, what we think is important.
Sam Archer:	It's symbolic. We remember certain athletes and what they represented.
Zhue Li:	The Olympics in general should be a genuine display of worldwide sharing and good sportsmanship. That's the olympic ideal.
Jay Sandburg:	You can't get away from world events, even when you take time out for something like an Olympics. Other events overshadow.
Sam Archer:	Worldwide viewership in modern times
Cameron Martinez:	Instant celebrities. Who's getting the Wheaties box?

Figure 4-2. A Transcript Example (continued)

Jay Sandburg:	I agree with Sam and Cameron. Lots of sponsorships now. And endorsements.
Zhue Li:	But that's not the way it always was. The Olympics has evolved during the past century.

(After a lull in the posts)

Lynnette Porter:	**These are all important points that we've discussed. Do you want to add anything to this list?**
Cameron Martinez:	Nope.
Sam Archer:	Not me.
Zhue Li:	No.
Jay Sandburg:	No.
Amie Lynde:	No. I think I'm done for the evening.
Lynnette Porter:	**You've done a good job with the discussion. Before you leave tonight, let me make just a few comments...**
Lynnette Porter:	**First, you'll receive full points for this assignment. You were all well prepared for the discussion....**
Lynnette Porter:	**Also, you need to read the chat transcript. Just to make sure you caught all the discussion points. You might want to use some of this information in your paper, which is due when?**
Sam Archer:	Saturday. ;>
Lynnette Porter:	**Do you have any other questions about the class in general, or tonight's discussion?**
Jay Sandburg:	When is the transcript up?
Lynnette Porter:	**By tomorrow. I'd check in the afternoon, just to be sure.**
Jay Sandburg:	OK. Thanks.

(Another lull in the discussion)

Lynnette Porter:	**OK then. You did great tonight. Thank you! If you have questions this week about the assignments, be sure to send me e-mail. I'll be the last one out of our chat room. You can log off at any time. Thanks again. Good night!**

(All participants write goodbye messages and exit the chat room.
When everyone else has logged off, the teacher logs out of the chat room.)

Bulletin Boards

Another popular tool for online classes is bulletin boards. You should post information important for all class members to see and reference throughout the course. You can also encourage learners to discuss key topics and share experiences and information. Bulletin board postings can be part of your required writing assignments, optional opportunities for sharing ideas, or both.

If you require learners to post information, you owe it to them to read the posts at least every few days. You might read the bulletin board a little less frequently than you read e-mail, but visit the bulletin board at least three times a week—more if required postings are due. Each time that you read the bulletin board, post comments or replies to the entries within each thread or folder (depending upon the way the bulletin board is set up). Not only do learners know that you are reading the bulletin board posts frequently, but you also join in the discussion and comment as a participant in the course, not just as "the teacher." Joining the discussion and providing your insights about a topic not only may help guide learners to new perspectives or materials for further study, but can also help you develop a learning community among class members.

If you require bulletin board postings, you may need to establish cutoff dates for posting information, so that learners can keep track of a discussion and meet the requirements for the assignment. Requiring a certain number of posts about a topic, or a number of responses to what others have written, by a deadline not only forces learners to get in the habit of reading the bulletin board frequently, but it helps the group move from one discussion topic to another.

You definitely need to organize the posts into folders or threads so that all postings about the same subject can be easily tracked and read. You may set up a series of bulletin board posts that mirrors the materials learners are using in a module and sequence the topics so that the discussion stays fresh and up to date with other activities in the course.

Although bulletin boards offer only asynchronous communication among you and your learners, the posts can create a lively discussion forum and a well-written history of class activities. They allow learners to express themselves freely and frequently, but within an edited print format. The date and time stamps on posts also alert you to the time frame within which learners published their comments. You can tell, for example, if the majority of the group completed a required bulletin board assignment on the day it was due, or if the discussion took place over several days.

Although most learners post interesting, informative messages in response to your lead in discussion threads or to meet a required assignment, you occasionally may find a few students who post flames or carry on an argument through a series of posts. Bulletin board messages are a permanent record of a comment and the responses to it. The words can be analyzed, and new or multiple meanings might be interpreted when readers study the comments over several viewings. Unlike a spoken comment made during a heated classroom discussion on site, which is said once and is not as easily or thoroughly analyzed by class members, written bulletin board messages can be decoded, shredded, reconstructed, and otherwise scrutinized by a whole group for several days or weeks. The message can take on a life of its own.

Robertshaw (2001) reminded teachers that the ability for learners to read messages several times or out of context can intensify readers' responses to messages. A spoken message is given in context one time and is more difficult to analyze as thoroughly. Bulletin board posts only show written comments and a name; it is almost an anonymous medium, and it certainly is a faceless one. Arguments in print may become prolonged and angry on a bulletin board moreso than in a face-to-face classroom.

If inappropriate posts or flaming arguments start to take place, you need to cool down the situation immediately. You may need to post guidelines for using the bulletin board and remind all learners to be sensitive to the ideas of others. You can call or send e-mail to individuals to defuse the situation and advise against hurtful posts. If you cannot seem to control the situation by yourself, enlist the help of your supervisor, chair, or another administrator to help stop an escalating argument and, if students refuse to stop posting inflammatory messages, remove students from the class.

If you do not have the ability to remove incendiary posts from the bulletin board, you should know who has this capability and under which circumstances posts can be removed from a course bulletin board. It's not your job to act as censor, but you must be able to keep the bulletin board as a place for lively, but not harmful, discussions and friendly sharing of ideas.

Course Announcements

An important use for the class bulletin board is the posting of announcements. For example, a welcome message provides introductory information and a friendly greeting when learners first log into the course site and visit the bulletin board. In later posts, also highlight the important points of upcoming assignments and remind learners of due dates on the bulletin board. It is a good idea to post at least one such introductory folder each week as learners start a new unit. During some modules, you may post several folders, one for each assignment or discussion topic.

In those classes in which learners work at their own pace in a more open-ended structure, before the course starts, you might post a folder for each unit. Learners then can read your comments or suggestions pertaining to the learning module as they begin that segment.

Even though assignment or activity information appears elsewhere at the course Web site, such as in a syllabus or schedule, the bulletin board highlights notices and allows you to draw learners' attention to a folder or highlighted subject line that leads a thread of postings. Within an assignment folder or new thread, learners may post general questions about the assignment. Because your answer may be important to many learners' understanding of the assignment, you can answer the question in a single place. That saves time from answering the same e-mailed question posed individually by several learners and gives all class members the security of knowing that your answer to the question is uniform to anyone who asks.

If a change to the schedule must be made, the bulletin board is a good way to document that change and the date it was made. For example, if you have to change a due date on an assignment or be offline for a few days, you can post the announcement, as well as contact learners in other ways.

Other announcements are more interactive. At the beginning of each class, you should post an introduction to yourself and the course and invite learners to provide their own self-introduction. This activity should take place the first week of class; then the folder can be locked or closed to further posts once everyone has had a week to read everyone else's posts and to submit his or her own message. Keeping all introductions in the same folder or within the same thread allows learners to read all introductions quickly and get a sense of who is in the class and what common interests they share. It also gives learners practice with posting messages.

You might also list proposed dates and times for required chat sessions and other synchronous activities. You can then ask for feedback about these times, or get an idea of how many learners can attend each chat session if you offer more than one discussion session about the same topic. If there are scheduling problems or concerns, learners can suggest alternative dates or times. You might even use the bulletin board as a way for learners to sign up for synchronous activities, if multiple times are available. All types of announcements and course-management information can be high-lighted through bulletin board postings.

Each announcement should be placed in a separate folder or located at the start of a new thread for posts. You must choose a unique, brief, but descriptive title for your message. For example, use descriptors like Module 1 Assignment Notes, Chat Session Signups, and Introduce Yourself as headings for folders. You should request that learners who want to post a response to a topic do so within the same folder where you started the topic. That way all similar posts are kept in the same location.

Most bulletin board posts automatically receive a date, time, and name stamp. If any of this information is not added to your post automatically, you must make sure that you add it as part of your message.

Like effective e-mail messages, bulletin board posts should be well written but brief. You may need to edit (and definitely at least review) the information before you submit it. As a teacher, the number, type, style, tone, and accuracy of your messages serve as models for learners to emulate in their posts.

Finally, you should limit the number of announcement folders you post at one time. You may need more posts at the beginning of a class, so that learners know what is expected of them and have their basic questions answered. Even at the start of a new class, however, try to limit the number of folders or threads on the bulletin board. Overwhelming learners with messages defeats the purpose of the bulletin board and makes this important tool something to avoid rather than use. By using the bulletin board to highlight important notices, and by crafting these notices carefully, you can encourage learners to read and respond to posts.

Discussions

A good way to hold an asynchronous discussion is to keep a running thread of posts about the same topic. These discussions may be required, with learners having to post a certain number of messages within a specified time frame. You can also start discussion folders with optional posting requirements. These folders may provide learners with additional practice in submitting messages, a forum for a less serious discussion, or a place to post their questions and suggestions. Both these types of discussions can be started by you, acting as the facilitator and catalyst for discussion.

However, more spontaneous discussions can be started by learners themselves. You may need to circulate some guidelines for starting a discussion topic, just to make sure the discussion is pertinent to the course. For example, learners working together on a project may create a separate folder or thread of their small learning community's discussion of the project.

Because some topics may be timely, you may want to establish a limit on the time when learners can respond to a topic. Depending on the type of bulletin board used in your course, the folders or threads may disappear from the bulletin board, or they may be locked or closed from further postings but left in the bulletin board window so that learners can read what others wrote.

If you require learners to post messages as part of an assignment, you should clearly state in the assignment (and within the first message in the folder) your expectations for posting. How long should messages be? When are they due? What kind of information do you want to have posted (e.g., suggestions for accomplishing a task, possible solutions to problems, an analysis of reading material, a description of a project the learner has done)? How many posts are required? Are learners required to respond to others' messages? If so, how many responses do you require? These are the kinds of questions learners will have about a bulletin board assignment. If you can answer those questions in your assignment sheet and within the folder where messages are posted, you encourage learners to create more thoughtful posts that further discussion.

Faculty Bulletin Boards

In addition to the class bulletin board (one for each class you teach), you may be required to participate in discussions on faculty bulletin boards. Just as this tool can be an effective way for learners to share information, so too can you learn from other teachers and share your ideas for improving classes.

Even if you are not required to post a certain number of messages or log into the bulletin board so many times during the course you teach, you should get in the habit of reading other teachers' posts at least once a week. These messages are valuable for getting answers to course-management questions, suggesting curriculum changes, and sharing ideas for assignments. As well, through your posts, you help nurture a learning community of teachers that can help bridge the geographical distance among online faculty.

Whiteboards

Whiteboards allow you to draw, write cursively, figure, doodle, take notes, or whatever you need to write longhand. At the end of your writing session, you can save the information or delete it. You can show it to learners during a chat or use it on your own as you document what you are reading or recording online. Similar to a whiteboard, marker board, or chalkboard in an on-site classroom, the online whiteboard can be a creative tool to communicate visually, but not necessarily verbally.

Whiteboard information can be shared during a chat or a videoconference, so a group can brainstorm ideas and save the session. Individually or with a group, a whiteboard is a good tool to capture thoughts, ideas, sketches—information that is more visual than textual.

Learners who like to brainstorm ideas visually and draw or storyboard rather than write ideas in words often enjoy whiteboard sessions. This can be an entertaining way for small groups to brainstorm ideas for a project. They also can supplement chats held at the whiteboard, allowing visual learners print and graphics options for presenting and viewing ideas created by the group.

On many whiteboards, you can use different colors to represent different people (or ideas). At the end of the session, or when the board is full and you want to start again, the information on the board can be saved, printed, or simply erased.

Whiteboards are especially useful when you want to represent ideas that are difficult to describe in words. You might want to illustrate an idea for learners, or yourself, to supplement printed discussion. You can create flowcharts, small schematics, equations, symbols, drawings, charts, and other graphics. As long as you can draw it by hand, you can create it on a whiteboard.

Whiteboards can also be helpful for you or your learners when you need to jot down notes. Keeping a whiteboard window open can be easier than setting up a separate word processing window and typing notes. Short notes and visuals can help you note the highlights of what you are reading. You can save a worthwhile note session, or delete the notes after they have served their purpose.

E-mail

E-mail is probably the most useful tool for most online teachers (especially those who do not have multimedia tools with which they converse with learners). How you handle e-mail may be left entirely up to you, or you may have to meet requirements set by course designers or administrators. Because online teachers are not available in person and perhaps are not typically available by phone, e-mail becomes the lifeline between learners and teachers.

Some institutions require you to respond to learners' e-mail messages within 24 to 48 hours, or at least to notify learners if you will not be able to respond to e-mail within that time. Even if you are not required to respond quickly, it is still a good idea to check e-mail at least once a day. You might typically check e-mail in the morning and evening each weekday when you have an online class, or more often when assignments are due or learners seem to be having more difficulty mastering a concept or skill. On the weekend, for example, you might check e-mail only once.

E-mail novices (and there still are some) initially may have some unreasonable expectations for your response time to their messages. After all, in a society with pagers, instant messaging, and phone-accessed e-mail, why should there be much of a lag in response time? That is why you should try to socialize learners to the online classroom environment during the first week of class. Explain when you generally check e-mail, what types of messages you send, how often you send individual and group messages, and what type of attachments you need to receive. This information should go out in e-mail messages and is placed in a bulletin board folder available on the first day of class.

Socialization may also involve teaching learners how to write messages. Although most learners know the mechanics of sending and receiving e-mail, they may need help in writing effective messages. For example, you may need to explain the protocol of sending messages: Each message should have a clear point; messages should be phrased clearly, grammatically correctly, and politely; and spamming is a big no-no. You also must discourage flaming other learners (or the teacher!), sending multiple messages about the same subject, and adding class members to personal mailing lists. Because many people have multiple e-mail addresses, you need to require learners to provide an active e-mail address for an account they check regularly. (Some institutions create an e-mail account that learners use during the course.)

In addition to helping learners communicate more effectively, try to act as mentor and role model through your messages. Rapid response is important, even if you do not stay up to answer e-mail from distant time zones. If you do not know the answer to a question, at least send a message that you are checking on the answer and will send a message with the answer as soon as possible.

The important idea is to make sure learners know someone (preferably the teacher) is out there and willing to assist with feedback on assignments, answers to course questions, and solutions to problems. Messages must be written precisely, concisely, and accurately, and you have to ensure that your online persona is concerned, friendly, and open to ideas.

At the beginning of an online class, as you post information about the course, you should also create a "how to contact the teacher" folder or send a group e-mail message. You need to provide an alternate way of communicating with learners and receiving their written assignments, in case your e-mail account fails or the server has problems.

For example, give learners a backup e-mail address that you can access from any computer. Web-based e-mail accounts are easy to set up, and some accounts are still free. As insurance against e-mail problems, you should set up at least one backup account and let learners know to use this address only if the primary address bounces back their messages. That way you can eliminate duplicate messages and assignments going to both accounts. If you also want to provide learners with a phone or fax number for use in emergencies when computer systems are not available or working properly, you can add this information to the folder or e-mail, and encourage learners to print a copy of the emergency contacts.

You may also want to provide learners with important e-mail addresses for the institution. Learners may need to keep on file technical assistance or help desk e-mail addresses and phone numbers, in case there are technical glitches in accessing course information. You might also provide e-mail or Web addresses for the institution's online library, bookstore, registrar, or other important administrative services. Before you widely publish someone's e-mail address or phone number, however, you need to make sure it is OK for this information to be given freely to learners.

In-Class Mailing Lists

Many universities or colleges automatically create a group e-mail list of addresses that learners provide or addresses assigned by the institution for learners enrolled in a class. This in-class mailing list allows learners to contact one or several learners and the teacher at one time. As well, it is a useful tool for you to send bulk e-mail announcements to all students.

If such a list is not created for you, create your own mailing list with the preferred address for each learner. You may also want to keep track of a backup address for each person, in case the original address is not working when you want to send an important message.

You may need to remind learners that if they change e-mail addresses, the address has been entered on the list incorrectly, or they do not check that e-mail address often, they will miss important course notices. Of course, you can post a backup message on the bulletin board, but e-mail is generally a faster method of communication and one that learners check more often.

Typically, you should send group e-mail when a new assignment is introduced or needs further explanation. Then send a reminder e-mail when the assignment is coming due. If you need to change a due date or will be unexpectedly unavailable to answer e-mail for a couple of days, send an announcement to the group. At the beginning of the course, send a welcome message, with important introductory announcements; at the end of the course, mail a farewell/thank you message.

Anything that needs to be explained to the class at the same time is a good subject for an e-mail message. However, to make sure learners read the message and to underscore the importance of group messages, send only one group message a week. Sometimes you may need to send additional messages, but never overwhelm learners with several important group messages. The "cry wolf" theory of announcements does not work well in online classes.

If you need to call attention to a particularly timely or important message, add a higher priority setting to the e-mail message. Many e-mail programs allow you to set a priority rating from low to medium to high to urgent. The message is then highlighted appropriately when the recipient receives it. Of course, tagging a message as urgent is no guarantee that all class members will view the information immediately, but your message is more likely to be noticed when learners scan their e-mail.

Individual E-mail to Learners

Although group messages can save you a lot of time in copying and pasting the same information to each learner, sometimes you need to send individualized messages. Even if you use an online gradebook to post grades for each assignment, feedback on writing assignments requires more than just a grade. For example, learners may use a recent version of Word to create their written documents. These Word documents then can be sent as an attachment to an e-mail message to you.

When you read an attached assignment, either immediately when you read the e-mail or later, after you have downloaded the file, mark changes and add suggestions to the written assignment. Word's reviewing toolbar provides the features for marking, highlighting, tracking changes, and adding comments. These marks are saved within the learner's assignment.

When you return a document, summarize comments in an e-mail message and tell the learner the grade for the assignment. (This practice helps learners keep track of their letter grades or points, which they can compare with the online gradebook as a safeguard that the information was entered and displayed correctly.)

In case the learner's computer cannot read your comments on the document, the e-mail message provides an overview of feedback about the assignment. Then attach the marked file to the e-mail, so learners have a fuller record of your comments and, you hope, will use the marked document as a learning tool to improve future assignments.

Individual e-mail coming from a teacher needs to be supportive and positive, even if the learner needs a lot of help. The old compliment sandwich may be a useful format for e-mail in which you provide feedback about a learner's performance. You can start with a positive overview comment, followed by specific suggestions for improvement, and conclude with encouragement to do better on the next activity or assignment. Focusing on specific ways to improve performance and good points in the current assignment is crucial to building learners' self-esteem and having them actually follow your suggestions.

Learners often save e-mail and refer to it as they complete a course. You may want to save your e-mail correspondence with learners, too, especially if there is an ongoing problem or concern. You can document a learner's effort and progress, and your and the learner's efforts to solve a problem, by saving the series of e-mail messages through the end of the course.

You may become a learner's confidante about a personal matter, because some students like the anonymity of e-mail and feel better asking for personal advice or explaining a personal problem if they can send e-mail instead of talking with an authority figure face-to-face. You should be professional, but as helpful as you can legally and ethically be, in your e-mail messages. E-mail tends to be a self-revealing type of communication, and although you want to maintain a friendly persona with your learners, you also need to be careful about being too much of a buddy and too little of a teacher. In some cases, just like with on-site classes, you may choose to develop a friendship with adult learners once they have left your class.

Messages Among Learners

E-mail among learners is useful for group projects. Although learners may choose other forms of asynchronous or synchronous communication to facilitate group work, e-mail is often a popular choice. If learners have access to the class mailing list, it should be easy for them to send messages to group members. Otherwise, you may have to make sure that everyone in a work group has the others' e-mail addresses.

You may need to establish some ground rules about sending e-mail to other learners. For example, collaboration is OK for group projects and general discussions, but doing one's own work is critical for individual assignments. (Plagiarism policies should be discussed in class.) Learners can create their own learning communities and set up their own guidelines for sending e-mail back and forth. Spamming and flaming are unacceptable. (Some teachers impose sanctions against learners who send these types of messages; if you plan to do that, you need to let learners know what will happen if they abuse e-mail.) You may need to remind learners not to give out others' e-mail addresses without their permission or to link others' addresses to mailing lists outside of the class.

Any rules or guidelines for course-related e-mail messages should be explained to (or set by) the whole class. You may want to post the guidelines on the bulletin board, send group e-mail with a list of the rules, or make the guidelines a permanent part of the course syllabus or other standard introductory information about the course.

If you are on learners' mailing lists, you should indicate if you are willing to send and receive e-mail with former students once the course is over. Learners who meet in an online class and hit it off, especially if they will take other online classes together, may want to establish an e-mail network of friends and colleagues. You should let learners know if you are interested in being a part of their ongoing network.

Volume and Quality of Messages

As you read earlier in this chapter, you should use e-mail when you need to send group or individual messages, but you should keep the number of messages manageable. The quality of your written work should be excellent so that your messages are models of good e-mail.

As well, you should let learners know how often they should respond to e-mail and what types of response are expected. You might require learners to check in with you once a week, or to send at least two messages to group members as they work on a project. Even if you do not require a certain number of messages per week or course, you should encourage learners to ask questions if they need to clarify an assignment or have a course-related problem. Learners should feel comfortable sending you messages when they need help or have some news to share. You need to develop a learning community in which everyone feels safe to send appropriate e-mail and can send well-crafted messages.

Off-topic messages that have nothing to do with the course might be discouraged, but messages with information that might help students learn more about a relevant course topic should be encouraged. For example, in history or cultural studies classes, you can encourage learners to share their reviews and recommendations of special historic or anthropological exhibits, museums, re-enactments, and events. Adults in professional communication classes might post bulletin board items or send e-mail announcements about job fairs for writers and editors, upcoming national conferences, or recently published articles about Web design. The message might not be directly related to their current readings or required e-mail or bulletin board posts for that week, but it pertains, even indirectly, to the course content.

Although your institution may require you to keep certain types of e-mail for more than the duration of a course, you probably have limited storage space for old messages. Once a class is over, delete any messages that you no longer need as samples or models for another class or a series of e-mail needed for legal or professional purposes. E-mail can become the worst kind of electronic clutter. If you are not going to need the message after the class has ended, you should delete the message. If you are really attached to your messages, you can download them to disk, but save space online (and time searching through old messages, even if you have archived carefully).

Archived messages, as well as new messages you need to keep at least temporarily, should be moved to clearly marked folders. For example, create one folder for each class' (or section's) assignments. You also may want to use an e-mail filtering system to route messages to the appropriate folder. Microsoft Outlook Express, for example, allows you to determine rules to sort/filter your e-mail. Setting up a filter may save you time from personally sorting messages every time you sit down to read your e-mail (Turner, 2002).

Suggested titles for folders in online classes might be Module 1 Assignments, Questions about the Whiteboard, General Course Info, or Departmental Info. Whatever titles you create should indicate only one type of message. You might have a series of highly specific folders, as well as some that are more generic, depending on the number of messages you receive and the frequency with which you get messages falling into one category.

Stock messages, like welcome messages, can be stored in a Group Messages folder. Different types of messages are grouped together, either by the person/group sending them or the content of the message. If you organize your e-mail as you read and respond to it, you save lots of time in trying to find old messages and sorting through a list to find new messages. Neatness truly counts with e-mail.

Preventing E-mail Flames

As mentioned with bulletin board flames or inappropriate messages, some learners vent their frustration by sending several complaints or angry messages to you, other class members, administrators, or even people outside the institution. You cannot stop every learner from sending an incendiary message, but you can try to head off learners' frustrations, which often lead to flaming e-mail. Encourage learners to ask you questions about assignments or tools, and answer as promptly as you can when you get such requests. Post a list of e-mail or phone numbers for official Help services, such as technology support or library assistance, so that students are more likely to find a friendly, competent professional available to assist them. Automated help is a good backup, but nothing is better than a person when a frustrated student is looking for answers.

Hailey, Grant-Davie, and Hult (2001) suggested that teachers keep in touch with learners and visit the course site often. Knowing what is going on can help you spot potential problems and resolve them before they get out of hand. You should post messages often and respond quickly to learners' questions. Finally, calling learners and listening to them can support frustrated adults and help them solve a problem quickly. Although these suggestions may not keep a flame from appearing, they should help you deal with a matchstick instead of a forest fire.

E-mail Security

You may want to limit learners' use of your multiple e-mail addresses. (For example, you may have four or five different addresses but only want learners to use one primary institutional address and one free or low-cost Web-based account.)

Make sure that any e-mail address learners will use automatically scans messages and attachments for viruses. Also, use your computer's virus-protection scans often on your whole system, to prevent any problems from opening or downloading information. Update your virus-protection soft-ware at home; institutions usually update their programs frequently and make patches or new software available to online teachers. You should not open any attachments that have strange extensions that do not match the programs that you or class members regularly use, such as .doc for a Word attachment, .wpd for a WordPerfect document, or .ppt for a PowerPoint presentation. These extensions sometimes are a tip-off about viruses masquerading as or in attachments.

In addition to these simple security procedures, keep track of administrative e-mail notices regarding security issues, including viruses. Most institu-tions send messages as soon as a problem has been reported within the system. By frequently reading your e-mail from the university or college, you can be aware of any potential problems you may face with your home computer and can protect it accordingly.

Scan your e-mail for messages from people you do not know, and delete messages from unknown senders. Tell learners to use one e-mail address consistently from which they send messages, or to use their institutional account instead of a personal account. Let class members know that you need to be able to identify the sender of the message, and you probably will not recognize strange names or nicknames.

Also, to help you identify senders, remind learners to write a standard subject line, such as *Question about Module 2* or *Assignment 4 for Week 3— Bart Allen*. Even if you do not recognize the address, chances are that spammers or people promulgating a virus will not use these kinds of subject lines because they are specific to online learning. Learners may need to include their name, course ID, and the topic of their message in a subject line.

You may not want to give your institutional e-mail address for personal messages or online subscriptions. Your institution also may have established policies that limit the ways you can distribute your e-mail address. It helps to limit the number of people who will send messages to your institutional account. If you keep the account as private as possible, not only do you limit the possibility of security problems with your e-mail, but you also reduce the number of unwanted messages in an account that you review regularly. You save yourself time and trouble if you keep your institutional address for business only.

If you have any problems with e-mail, or you see a suspicious message in your mailbox, you should report the problem to the technical support staff, who can better check out the potential problem. They then can report to administrators and the educational community at large when a bona fide problem has been spotted and how to deal with it.

Viruses are an important security problem, and you need to protect your e-mail and your computer as much as possible. However, this is not the only security issue you need to be concerned with academically. Keeping information confidential is another hot topic.

Your institution may have policies regarding the type of information that can be sent by e-mail. For example, you may not be allowed to send a grade through e-mail, although you can send comments about an assignment. Grades may only need to be posted to an online gradebook. If it is OK to send grades through e-mail, you should send individual e-mail to a learner's institutional address. That way you are more likely to reach the learner directly, without others viewing the grade or other private information.

Try not to send private information to a business account or a general e-mail account; use the individual's academic account. Also, send only one message at a time—do not send specific comments about an individual's performance to the class or a group. Keep evaluation-related information as private and secure as possible.

These security measures are not designed to make you paranoid, but to help keep your online information, hardware, and software safe. They also save you time in troubleshooting technical and course-related problems.

Outside Mailing Lists

If you teach a class in which professionals outside the institution may be helpful to learners, you may want them to join a mailing list outside the class-based learning community. For example, students in technical writing and editing classes may be encouraged to join professional mailing lists to supplement the information provided by textbooks, the teacher's shared experiences and anecdotes, and learners' experiences. Adult learners can participate in the discussions on a technical writing mailing list, for example, so they may network with professional managers, writers, editors, information designers, and others involved in technical communication. Even if learners just lurk on the running conversations through posts to the mailing list, they gain a better insight into what goes on in their career field and what is being discussed as hot topics.

Before learners participate in discussions with professional colleagues, you want to make sure that they are comfortable with the protocol of writing effective e-mail messages and bulletin board posts. They should also focus their communication on specific questions, comments on previous posts, and requests for information; it helps if learners identify themselves as students interested in a particular topic or the career field in general. You want learners to make a good first impression with their messages, so that they are more likely to get appropriate, timely responses and to make contacts that build their professional network.

Most careers or subject areas have several mailing lists from which to choose. You may need to scout which lists are best suited to learners' needs before you provide the class with the subscription addresses. Getting learners to join several lists at once creates the problem of having too many posts to read each day. If you want learners to join more than one mailing list, you might suggest that they subscribe only to a journal or an archive so that they receive a summary of messages in one long post, usually each week. You can also suggest that learners choose to join only one list that seems most closely related to their career interests.

Collaborating with Other Professionals

Some classes are well suited to mentoring by professionals in the learners' career fields. If you have the capability for streaming audio or video, you may want learners to watch or listen to a special event, such as a speech or a news conference. If you have the capability for two-way audio/visual communication, you might set up interviews or discussions between professionals in the workplace or at a conference and learners logging into the discussion from home or their workplace.

Without this real-time multimedia feed, you still can tape segments that can be stored at the class site and downloaded as video or audio files. Of course, you have to secure copyright permission to use interviews, discussions, speeches, and coverage of special events before you can link your class to the files. Panoramic views of work sites, such as an archeological dig or an operating room, and taped descriptions of work in progress can be useful supplementary materials. You can be creative in finding the best ways to link in the online classroom the information from professionals doing the jobs learners will one day have.

Online Gradebook

An important tool that you might not think of as a communication device is the online gradebook. No matter how interested learners are in the subject matter for its own sake, they need to be evaluated for their work and given academic credit. Even if you are teaching a non-credit continuing education course, the participants need or want some way to show that they have completed the course successfully. Employers who want their employees to take credit or non-credit classes to gain skills and information they will use on the job need to document employees' progress. Letting learners know grades for individual assignments and cumulative point or grade values is useful to teachers, learners, and administrators.

Online gradebooks should have confidentiality and security safeguards so that only the teacher can enter grades and each learner can view only his or her grades. Some systems allow you to submit final grades from the course site. Others only keep a running tally of accumulated points so learners know their current cumulative grade. At the end of the course, you then have to transfer grade notations to a paper or electronic form that is sent to the appropriate administrative office.

You may decide to post grades in the online gradebook after the entire class' set of assignments has been evaluated, or simply record grades as assignments come in. Instead of posting grades one at a time as learners complete an assignment, you might individually grade each paper and return feedback by e-mail within 24 hours of receiving the paper. Most learners in online classes submit papers sporadically as a deadline approaches. In a class of 30 or fewer learners, for example, you may receive four or five papers on the first day of the week when an assignment is due. About half the class turns in assignments by the end of the week; you may find one or two new papers each time that you access your e-mail. On the day the papers are due, there is a flurry of activity. Unless you are overwhelmed with a number of assignments at the same time, you probably can evaluate papers as they come in and post grades soon after an assignment's due date.

Whatever is your common practice, you should publicize your grade-posting policy, so that learners know how frequently you record new grades and when they should check the online gradebook. They also have a better idea how long it may take you to evaluate assignments.

For example, send e-mail with feedback about the assignment and a note about the learner's points for that assignment, in addition to posting the grade to the gradebook. Being able to match what you have written in e-mail with what appears on the grade screen is a good double check that the grades are posted accurately and that class members and you agree on assignment grades, as well as final course grades. However, only send this private information to the learner's institutional account, in order to keep the information as confidential as possible.

Keep a hardcopy backup record of the grade or points for each learner, in case the online system fails. After grades have been listed in the online gradebook, notify the class that all grades have been posted. If there are questions or discrepancies between the point value listed in feedback e-mail messages and the posted grades, learners quickly let you know. They also alert you if they sent an assignment, but you have not posted a grade for that assignment. E-mail problems or security problems may have prevented the assignment from arriving in your mailbox. By checking the gradebook, learners know if there is a problem with an assignment and contact you right away.

Online gradebooks that automatically total points and assign grades based on the total points accumulated by a learner throughout the course should be printed or saved to disk. You may want to print a final hard copy to save as a backup record for each class.

If you do not have a secure gradebook that limits each learner to viewing only her or his grades, you might create a variation of your own and link it to the class site (if this is permissible by your institution). For example, you might create a spreadsheet, but instead of listing learners by name, give each learner a code or number that only that person knows. Of course, your numbering system should be something other than alphabetical order or an equally easy system to decode. You might use learners' class or school ID numbers, for example, and post grades under learners' numbers, instead of names. However, an automated version is superior to such a simple system. Nevertheless, it is important for you to post grades so that learners have an ongoing, easy-to-find record of their performance in the class.

Summary

When you teach online, you rapidly become familiar with the tools you need daily to communicate with learners and maintain your classes. Before a new section begins, you should test the tools and links at the class site, just to make sure you are up-to-date with the technology and information provided at the site. As technology advances, and learners have more expectations for multimedia tools in the online classroom, you will undoubtedly have to learn to use additional hardware and software.

Keeping up with technology is a given in online education, and learning the mechanics of using a new tool takes some time and practice. However, your more important job is knowing how to work with learners effectively. If you have mastered the basics of effective electronic communication and have a plan in mind about the ways you and your learners will work together, learning which menu to click or how to input data should be easy. Good communication skills are a key to effective online teaching.

References

Collison, G., Elbaum, B., Haavind, S., & Tinker, R. (2000). *Facilitating online learning: Effective strategies for moderators.* Madison, WI: Atwood Publishing.

Hailey, D. E., Jr., Grant-Davie, K., & Hult, C. A. (2001). Online education stories worthy of Halloween: A short list of problems and solutions in online instruction. *Computers and Composition, 18,* 387-397.

Robertshaw, M. (2001). Flame war. In D. Murphy, R. Walker, & G. Webb (Eds.), *Online learning and teaching with technology: Case studies, experience, and practice* (pp. 13-20). London: Kogan Page Ltd.

Turner, E. S. (2002). Organizing e-mail. *Learning Online, 3*(2). Retrieved September 30, 2002, from http://www.learnersonline.com/sample/0202LOL.pdf

The Daily Work of Teaching

5

So far, you have read about the tools you will use on the job, a little bit of theory about how online teaching is supposed to operate, and the role of the facilitator/teacher. Another part of implementing an online curriculum is critically evaluating work tasks using these tools and planning how you want to approach online education. You evaluate how well your experience with online courses matches the expected outcomes for learners who take that course. At the completion of your course, are learners ready for the next part of the curriculum? Do you think that students were prepared to take your course—both in their knowledge of the discipline *and* their ability to complete course objectives online? Your daily work is a good measure of the curriculum's strengths and weaknesses.

If an online curriculum is effective, most learners coming into your online course are prepared both to work online with this level of technology and to learn new concepts that bridge effectively from what has been learned in previous courses. If you find that most of your daily work revolves around remedial work for the majority of class members, the structure of the curriculum is weak. Somewhere in the linear arrangement of courses, either more skills development is needed earlier, or perhaps course content needs to be modified in one or more courses. Perhaps a prerequisite course needs to be identified.

Of course, many factors may lead to learners being unprepared to take your course. Poor teaching methods, ineffective materials, a flaw in the curricular design, learners' difficulty in mastering basic concepts and skills—these are just a few possible reasons indicating a need for remedial work as students enter your course. Also, some learners know how to work the educational system so that they pass course after course without truly mastering anything. However, by monitoring your workload and the types of tasks each time you teach the same course, you have a good idea of the entry-level skills and knowledge needed for success in your course and if students usually arrive prepared to take the course.

You may receive feedback from former students about the effectiveness of your course's materials and activities in preparing learners for subsequent classes they took. Getting feedback after students have gone to the next sequence of classes gives you a better idea of the effectiveness of your course within the curriculum.

Understanding the daily tasks of online teaching helps you not only plan your weekly schedule, but it also can help you monitor the health of the curriculum and be able to suggest improvements in curriculum redesign.

Daily Teaching Tasks

Online teaching is just as detail oriented as teaching on site. You still have to maintain files, solve problems, communicate frequently with learners, and oversee their progress. These tasks take up the majority of your typical teaching week. Although you may have an entire course prepared on a Web site and not have as much day-to-day content preparation as on-site teachers, you still have to discuss the current learning module and guide learners through it.

You usually post folders or start new bulletin board threads to explain and discuss the content area. If you lead a videoconference session, you still may prepare a presentation before all or part of a class. However, the majority of your work will involve facilitating learners' work, troubleshooting any technical problems or learner difficulties in understanding the material or assignments, and evaluating learners' work and progress.

You usually are required to spend fewer hours "in the classroom" than your on-site counterparts to complete synchronous activities, such as lectures and discussion sessions. Your off-the-course-site online work, however, takes up the majority of time. Unlike on-site teachers, who may talk individually with learners around class time or discuss assignments and provide feedback during office hours, you have to do these kinds of activities through e-mail, bulletin board posts, or other written communication. These messages take time to craft carefully.

Even if synchronous activities, such as chat sessions or videoconferences, are used to provide one-on-one guidance for learners, you need lots of time to respond to questions, explain course content, or comment on drafts of assignments. Seldom will an entire class be online at the same time for synchronous activities. The logistics for managing online teaching duties are thus different and require you to schedule teaching tasks differently than you might for on-site classes. You have much to do to keep the class functioning smoothly day by day and to make sure that learners are progressing at a rate by which they not only understand the materials but also can complete course requirements within the allotted time.

Daily and Weekly Communication

Although community building is an important, if loftier task than the day-to-day job of responding to learners' messages (as you will read in Chapter 6), daily communication is a big part of building a successful learning community. Learners need to know that someone out there cares and can help them through the course. They need a way to get together with you and other learners. As Palloff and Pratt (2002) expressed this important concept, the best online teachers are those who create a learning community and build an empowering educational environment that encourages learners to work together. Ongoing communication—whether to prod, discuss, acknowledge, praise, announce, or clarify—gives the necessary personal touch to a computerized course.

The need for reassurance is especially strong with first-time online learners during the early days of a course. Although they may be competent businesspeople and experienced on-site learners, even the most computer-savvy new learner wants some reassurance that her or his perceptions of what is expected match your perceptions. If there is a problem with a computer novice getting into the course or successfully attaching e-mail, for example, your work as a friendly guide is critical. You not only make sure that everyone can access course materials and complete assignments, but you also help ensure a positive online learning experience.

New learners may have preconceptions about online education. Although they look forward to the freedom of working independently at home to get a degree or to take a single course, they also worry that they will not be able to keep up with highly sophisticated computer users. Making sure all learners feel comfortable with the tools used in the course and your expectations for learner performance is an important sidebar to the first week's communication.

Motivating learners is a big part of online teaching, and some students require more encouragement than others. Miller and Corley's (2001) study of online learners at Augusta State University (Georgia) showed that receiving e-mail from the teacher increased the learner's motivation; learners who were not doing well in a class benefited from faculty e-mail and thus were usually motivated to do better. These researchers found that some online learners benefit from more structure, and e-mail from faculty can help provide that structure.

Feedback about assignments may help students who are more familiar with an on-site class in which teachers remind students of upcoming assignments, discuss learners' progress, and often can observe how quickly or well students are working toward the completion of a particular assignment. Online teachers may not be able to supervise individuals' coursework as closely, and learners are largely responsible for completing work independently from the teacher's guidance. However, online teachers can help those learners who need more supervision by sending more e-mail and generally keeping tabs on students who procrastinate or have difficulty understanding assignments.

Your workload may increase dramatically when you need to motivate learners by sending e-mail frequently. Savenye, Olina, and Niemczyk (2001) added that the time spent teaching online, as opposed to on site, is often twice as long, in part because of this need to send plenty of e-mail to learners. Because e-mail is usually a one-on-one form of communication, sending e-mail frequently to many learners is highly time consuming.

E-mail is not the only way to motivate learners, but it is highly popular. The National Education Association (NEA, 2000) published a survey of higher education faculty that showed 83% of faculty who facilitated a Web-based course sent e-mail at least once a week to each student. As expected, e-mail rated highly among the surveyed faculty who taught Web-based classes. Sixty-one percent used e-mail to communicate with a student more than once a week.

For an informal survey, 25 teachers working with online courses at Franklin University (Ohio) volunteered their responses to the open-ended question, How many hours per week, on the average, do you spend sending e-mail to students? Teachers were not given guidance about the way to respond; they reported the following amounts of time spent per course per week sending and responding to e-mail.

The minimal time reported was one to two hours, although higher numbers—all the way to 18 hours a week—were listed. The teachers who reported the minimal time had the fewest essays to grade; they taught courses that required fewer written assignments, although they did have to answer questions about assignments and activities. The higher numbers were reported by teachers who taught classes in which more written assignments were required. Even such an informal anecdotal survey indicates that e-mail takes up a big chunk of a teacher's weekly work time. Teachers who work with learners on written assignments, or who respond to writing and documentation questions, seem to need the most e-mail correspondence time.

Posting and reading bulletin board notices takes less time for most teachers, according to the 25 surveyed teachers from Franklin University. Responses were solicited to a similar question, How much time, on the average, do you spend each week posting and reading bulletin board messages? The majority of teachers (20) spent four or fewer hours on this activity, although one teacher reported spending eight hours each week working with the bulletin board.

Toward the end of this chapter you will see a chart with some typical time schedules for facilitating online activities. You may want to track the amount of time you take with these activities, especially communication tasks, so that you can better plan your time.

Early in the week, for each week of the course, you should send a group message to outline the week's assignments or activities. If you need to create a signup sheet for an upcoming chat or another synchronous activity, such as a group project, you can establish a bulletin board folder or discussion thread with instructions. If everyone in the class seems to need the same explanation of an assignment or is having difficulty with the same material, create a Help folder or thread to provide links to sites with similar information and descriptions or explanations that elaborate on the instructions or materials.

In online classes in which learners work at their own pace and seldom work within a group, you can still send e-mail early in the week, just to say hello and check on the learner's progress. By initiating the communication, you not only remind learners that you are monitoring their progress, but you also show interest in that progress. If you make a habit of writing first, and you come across as sincerely interested in each student's concerns, progress, and achievements, you are more likely to receive more commu-nication from class members, whether a question or just assurance that everything is going well.

When you send e-mail, whether to individuals or to the whole group at once, try to limit the total number of messages. For example, send messages on the first date of a new learning unit to preview the module and explain difficult concepts or assignments. Send a reminder when an important deadline is approaching, or if new information has been added to the bulletin board. Make each message count.

You should stick to the point in your message. Keep the message short enough to be easy to read, but cover the salient points, and create short, effective subject lines.

Most e-mail systems allow you to set the priority for messages, although you do not want to make every message high priority. Some messages are "nice to know" information that can be sent at regular priority. If a deadline is approaching—or has passed, if you need to contact a learner right away, or if your information has another reason why it must be read immediately, set a high priority for that message.

E-mail should be friendly and helpful, and they should show that you genuinely care about individuals taking the course. Through the tone and frequency of your messages, you can provide a personal touch without becoming just an e-mail buddy. You can be a facilitator and mentor without losing your professionalism; you can be a friendly authority figure whom learners can approach confidently.

Office Hours

Before the first day of class, list your office hour(s) and time zone. Although an hour time block may be effective, especially if learners drop in and out of a chat room, you may want to set up several shorter blocks of time throughout the week. Few learners will stay online just to chat for an hour—at least with their teacher! They may want to meet other learners and talk informally for a few minutes, ask questions, or request some help. Setting up a series of convenient, but varying times, may be more effective for learners.

If you set hour-long blocks of time, you should state in the syllabus or otherwise post a notice if you will stay only as long as others are in the chat room. If you plan to stay for an entire session, whether learners arrive or you are left talking to yourself, you should state that policy. Your policies, as well as office hour time slots, should be published in the syllabus or in a "meet the teacher" notice through e-mail, on the course Web site, or in a bulletin board folder or discussion thread.

You should try to schedule an office hour early during the first week, so that new learners, who may have lots of questions, can talk with you in real time. Setting up a schedule when learners can talk with you is important to begin in the first days of the course. Because online courses may be short, such as four or six weeks, you want to establish a routine for regularly scheduled synchronous activities as soon as possible.

Although consistency is important in establishing your office hours, and knowing that you will be available at the same time(s) each week is comforting to learners, you may want to set up office hours at different times or on different weeks to accommodate learners who have a class on site one night a week or who live in a time zone far from you. For example, you might have two office hours, one early in the evening early in the week and one late in the evening late in the week, or you may have hours that shift from week to week on a published schedule.

If you only hold one office hour a week, you might vary the schedule, so that on even numbered weeks in the course you have an office hour, for example, on Tuesday at 7:00 p.m. and on odd numbered weeks you are in the chat room beginning at 10:00 p.m. on Thursday. The objective is to make your office hours as convenient for many learners as possible.

If you have international students, you may have to set up alternate ways of communicating regularly, perhaps once a week, so that you can accommodate these learners' needs within a "normal" time frame. Setting up an office hour for 3:00 a.m. in the learners' time zone is not going to work—if you really want students to participate. However, you might set up a very late or very early time for you once a week or every few weeks, just so you can talk with these learners at a time convenient for them.

Most learners (and teachers) prefer nights other than Friday or Saturday for office hours, and some people rule out weekends entirely. That is up to you and your students. Other teachers and learners like these days because many people are away from the office and can participate in synchronous activities that they are too busy to complete during the work week. You may want to ask learners about their work schedules, so that you and they can plan (or vary) office hours as needed to ensure everyone can meet with you at least periodically.

You should not make any new announcements during an office hour, because not all learners will be able to attend, and not everyone may read a chat transcript for an office hour. However, you can emphasize certain important points, and by answering learners' questions, you get a sense about the type of announcement you may need to make for the whole class. For example, if you are swamped with questions about a particular reading or assignment, you can bet that learners not in the chat room also have similar questions. After you answer the questions during the office hour, you should repeat the explanatory information in an e-mail message to the whole group.

Keeping course information handy is important during a chat session of any type, but especially for an office hour chat. You may not be able to open a window with the class information you need to reference while you are in a chat, so having a printout handy may be a useful reference. Keep a course schedule and list of assignments nearby so you can give everyone the same information about point values, URLs/URIs, and due dates. Because learners who cannot attend an office hour chat may read the transcripts later, and because you do not want to confuse students, you must be accurate in your responses to questions during an office hour. Keeping notes or printouts handy can help ensure consistency in the information you provide.

Lectures and Discussions

If you have the responsibility of designing a course, you may have created audio files of your short lectures (nothing that lasts anywhere near an hour!) or demonstrations. Not all core information should be provided through downloadable lectures; that is not a good pedagogical strategy, much less a space-efficient one. However, if some lectures or demonstrations are important for learners to see and hear, you may have made them available on the Web site. Even with such material available at the course site, you still preface lectures with bulletin board posts or e-mail messages. You may need to post an outline for the presentation, or create study questions based on the lecture.

Vary the supporting materials by class. Some groups require additional supporting materials. You will not know what kinds of supplementary assignments or guides your class needs until you have gotten to know this group of learners better. Your daily tasks therefore may include new materials preparation, even though much of the core content already is linked to the course site.

If you teach a course that was designed by someone else, you still can add your "lecture" touches by posting some text through bulletin board posts. You might provide background information through initial bulletin board posts, for example, and then comment on learners' responses to your written lecture.

If the core content is too long to be feasible as a bulletin board post or series of posts, you may want to provide the URL/URI to your personal/ professional Web site, where a longer, scrollable or chunked document can be read. This information can be given to learners through a group e-mail message or a bulletin board post. Of course, you should check with administrators or your program coordinator to make sure that the content of your added lectures or notes is consistent with the course's objectives and there are no legal, logistical, or consistency problems with adding new materials to existing course content. Check with your university or college to learn the rules for linking personal Web sites to a course site. Do not assume that such a link is permissible; verify that permission before you create a link.

Some supplements can be designed to lecture without a lot of text. For example, learners who must complete research papers may be expected to cite references for their papers. They may be required to use American Psychological Association (APA) style or Modern Language Association (MLA) style. Some learners may be well versed in at least one format and have no trouble with parenthetical and Reference or Works Cited page citations. Others, however, probably have little idea about what APA or MLA style is or how to cite sources. They may understand the importance of citing sources, and they definitely want to avoid plagiarism, but they do not know exactly how to do that.

In a separate bulletin board folder, you can post some examples of full-text and parenthetical citations. You should choose models that pertain to the sources learners will use most often in their research papers. You also should provide a brief explanation of each citation, along with the example. Although this bulletin board post may be longer than most you will create for the class, it still can be a short, but detailed summary of the elements of citation style that learners need to understand first.

Learners who do not need this type of instruction can ignore the folder or thread, but learners new to the citation style may post questions to the folder, asking for clarification of some points or additional examples. This running dialog through a series of posts in the same folder (or linked to the same thread) in effect creates a "lecture" similar to those on citation style that you may have given in on-site classes.

Another way to lecture is to offer a special discussion about a narrow topic for a weekly chat or office hour. The Q&A format is generally considered more of a discussion, but the length of your responses—in effect, short paragraphs—can be read together in the transcript as a mini lecture.

Learners who prefer online classes often say they like to get away from long, boring lectures in three-hour night classes, for example. Of course, not all lecturers are boring, and not all online classes are scintillating. Online readers generally do not like to scroll through long documents. However, if you break up longer documents into manageable segments, with organizational links and appropriate navigation tools, you can incorporate longer "lecture" documents into the course materials. As well, by using multimedia and creatively designing bulletin board and chat messages, you can effectively provide lecture information in an appropriate online format.

More appropriate for learner-facilitated education, however, is discussions, and you can generate online discussions in lots of ways. Both synchronous and asynchronous forums should be used in an online class. Two-way multimedia can be used so learners can see or hear each other, in small groups, or as a large class. Chat sessions, better held to a small number of learners, can be guided, as you ask questions and let learners take the conversation from those initial questions. Of course, as with any discussion, you will probably have to get everyone back on track at some point, as discussions tend to digress over time. Bulletin board discussions can be tracked by thread or folder, and you can close the discussion after several days of comments. E-mail, chat, or bulletin board discussions are useful for learners who want to collaborate on a project.

As with all ongoing activities, your daily teaching tasks involve small parts of the lecture and discussion set up. If you plan ahead, and break activities down, you can manage your class more efficiently and enjoy the activities with your learners.

Facilitating Assignments

As you (or someone else) designed the course initially, the number of assignments was determined, based on the amount of coursework to be covered, course objectives, and the time frame for the course (e.g., six weeks, 15 weeks). An equal amount of work per week helps learners keep pace with assignments but not feel overwhelmed or forced to fall behind. Nevertheless, as you go through a course, you may need to explain assignments more than you originally thought was necessary, and you may want to add some optional assignments.

Online learners seem to either work quickly on their own and follow their own assumptions about an assignment (even if they have misread what was provided in the syllabus or assignment sheet) or need some guidance before they start to make sure they understand what you want and how you expect assignments to be formatted. Online learners are not poor learners, but they tend to want some reiteration of what the assignment entails before they begin. This may happen even if you carefully worded the original assignment sheet and had lots of editors helping you refine it.

A few days before a new course week starts, post a message to the bulletin board with an elaboration of the assignments, special tips, or guidelines for formatting papers. Add information about working as a group or submitting assignments for evaluation, for example. Learners should know to expect this extra guidance a few days before they officially begin work on an assignment. Of course, some learners want to or, for work or personal reasons, need to work ahead on assignments and may contact you privately if they need some assistance long before they are scheduled to begin an assignment. In your announcement, you might include the following:

1. Title of the assignment

2. Description of the assignment (e.g., a five-page paper; a Web site with four internal links and three scanned photos)

3. Due date

4. Format in which the assignment should be submitted (e.g., a Word document following MLA reference style, attached to an e-mail message; the URL/URI of the Web site posted to the class bulletin board; group e-mail with copies of the scanned photos)

Although the assignment may seem self-explanatory to you, and even though it may be well written, students like this reinforcement to save them time in completing the assignment and making sure they are meeting all requirements.

Online classes may include international audiences with different language skills. Learners who are not native speakers may need help understanding idiomatic phrases used in the syllabus or assignment sheets, as well as in learners' messages. You may need to explain some assignments or responses in other terms so that all students understand what is required and how others stated their ideas. If you can provide examples or models, preferably on the course Web site, learners who may have difficulty understanding the written assignment can see what is expected of them.

Some groups seem to hit it off and want to share all kinds of ideas with each other. Others may need additional practice with a certain type of assignment. Both types of groups may benefit from additional short assignments. You do not want to inundate learners with lots of extra work, or confuse them as to what is required and what is optional. If you suggest too many optional activities, learners are not likely to do them, because they have enough to do as it is. However, you might have an extra weekly discussion of a relevant topic that interests the majority of learners, or you might start a bulletin board discussion by posting a scenario and asking learners how they react to it.

These types of assignments should be as carefully thought out as the formal, permanent assignments on which the course grade is based. They should be short, to the point, and require little advance preparation before learners complete them. They might be fun, like games or role-playing activities. They should complement the course design but offer students additional ways to learn something new and share their ideas with others. Participate in these extra activities with your class; you can have fun while you learn something new, too. Above all, take each assignment, whether optional or required, seriously, and help learners understand the objectives for each assignment.

Once learners know how to log into a course and understand its overall makeup, most questions will focus on specifics. After the first week, your daily communication will probably be centered around questions or comments about course assignments.

Collecting and Evaluating Assignments

If you set a deadline for an assignment, make sure you respect that deadline. Let learners know that you have received their assignment; a short e-mail message should suffice. You should also tell learners when they can expect feedback and when grades will be posted. Then stick to those arrangements.

Teachers vary on their grading preferences, like anything else. You may prefer to evaluate assignment one at a time as they come in before a deadline, just so you are not overwhelmed with assignments at one time. Instead, you may be one of those teachers who prefers to wait until all assignments have been turned in, so you can evaluate the assignments as a group and get a better sense of the class' mastery of the subject. Whatever your preference, you must be sure you provide feedback and post grades within the time frame you have established. Students will be looking for your comments, and their grade, as soon as possible.

The way that teachers evaluate assignments varies, too. You should post your grading criteria, preferably in the syllabus or course description. If not there, at least provide the information somewhere easy to find. Learners should know the grade scale, evaluation criteria, and point values for each assignment well before they start each project.

You may download learners' papers to a hard drive and use a marking tool, like Word's reviewing toolbar, to add comments about the content and organization of the document. Marks and comments are a practical visualization of what should be improved in the next assignment. Although you also may print copies of learners' papers, this process adds a great deal of time to the grading process. If you print papers, you then have to transcribe comments into an e-mail message to send to learners. However, if you do not have computer access when you want to grade papers, or you do not feel comfortable reading and marking papers only electronically, download and mark papers the traditional way. (Recycling the paper appropriately should be a given.)

Keep a copy of the marked file on the hard drive for the duration of the course, in case there is any question about your marks or the evaluation process. At the end of a course, you can download these files to disk, just in case there is a question after the course about a learner's work. If you are keeping paper copies of assignments, you may want to establish a similar filing system of hard copies.

Assignments that do not involve papers, usually sent as attachments, can be graded online. For example, in a Web design class, learners usually post the URL of the site they have created. You can make sure that the site can be viewed as it was intended, all the links work, and the site meets your design criteria. If learners complete a role play as a group assignment, request a summary, whether through e-mail or attachment. If learners post work to their personal Web page, visit the site to read, view, or otherwise interact with the posted materials.

The temptation with grading online is to make fewer comments. When you mark an essay using editing tools, for example, correct what is wrong and mark problem sections. You should edit the work for grammatical correctness, as well as accuracy in presenting information and an expressive, interesting writing style. Because it is easier to cross out wrong information or highlight trouble spots, the overall effect for learners who view your marks is that the paper is "bad." Learners whose files have few or no editing marks may think their essay was "perfect." By focusing on negative areas that are easy to mark as right or wrong, you may give the wrong impression about the quality of the assignment or the learner's mastery of concepts.

If you use marking or editing tools to correct written assignments, be sure to add comment files or send more elaborate comments by e-mail to learners. These comments should help establish a dialogue between you and the learner about the subject area, not just about the assignment or the quality of the writing, for example. You should praise the best points in the assignment and suggest ways to improve skills or knowledge areas that were weak.

No matter what type of assignment, comment on the overall effectiveness of the learner's performance, highlight the most successful areas, and guide the learner toward improving weak areas. Even if you cannot mark an assignment online (for example, change a learner's Web page design), you should make a note of the good points and areas that need improvement, and then send feedback as soon as possible.

Although it seems like online evaluations and feedback should be faster to create than hardcopy or in-person evaluations, the opposite is often true. Byington (2002) compared experiences from online to on-site teaching and noted that many more hours were needed to assign and grade work and return feedback online. The greater time commitment was attributed to the change from providing spoken comments face-to-face with comments that need to be written. You need to find a way to provide feedback quickly without getting bogged down in the grading process, but yet help learners to understand how they can improve as well as receive assurance about what they do well. Online evaluations and feedback should be vehicles for effective learning, not just information skimmed and disregarded by learners. Your grading process should encourage learners to be interested in more than the point value or grade you awarded for each assignment and to discuss ideas with you throughout the course.

The Importance of Flexibility with Deadlines

Although you read earlier that you should list and stick to deadlines, some exceptions are necessary for online learners. Because more online learners tend to work at least one job, have family responsibilities, and take one or more online courses at a time, their time is limited.

Of course, on-site learners may have these demands, too, but online learners as a whole tend to be older adults with multiple responsibilities. In addition, their work schedules may vary because of job changes, shift changes, unexpected travel demands, and unexpected overtime. Online learners may find it difficult to have computer access all the time, especially if they travel or have to work strange hours. Not all workers travel with a laptop or have time on the road to complete assignments, much less participate in group activities.

Because skill and knowledge levels progress in most courses from easier to more difficult, learners cannot successfully complete assignments all at one time—either to work ahead or to make up for lost time. Time management is always an important skill for online learners, but job changes can throw off even the most carefully planned schedule. Learners who become frustrated with the job/classroom time conflict often choose to give up an online class, at least until their work schedule eases up or becomes more stable.

As well, sometimes computers fail at the most inopportune times. Networks crash, files die, servers are out of commission, and so on. Power outages or bad weather prevents learners from getting online when they have time to work on course materials. Because online education depends on hardware, software, and networks, at times equipment failure will cause learners and teachers to get thrown off schedule.

Keeping to the established course schedule is important, but so is flexibility in knowing when to grant an extension and when an assignment has to be forfeited. Being flexible requires insight into learners' needs, learning preferences, and work schedules. You have to keep open the lines of communication to negotiate any changes or discuss problems with deadlines.

Try to be as understanding as possible when job-related changes interfere with class assignments and activities. In that way you encourage learners to discuss their concerns or scheduling problems, so that you can negotiate a mutually agreeable solution to potential problems. However, a learner's constant procrastination or the request for a last-minute extension on the final class date may be exceptions to the flexibility rule. Whatever your guidelines for granting extensions and keeping deadlines, you must make sure that your rules are well known, fair, and consistently applied.

If you communicate with learners at least each week, you probably have a good idea how each person is progressing in the course. If someone seems to be falling behind, you need to send some gentle prods to see if there is a problem and, if there is one, how it can be solved. Many learners fall behind in one unit, but quickly make it up—or they may work ahead if they know that they will be offline for a week. Keeping track of learners' participation and gauging whether stronger messages or other measures are necessary to ensure that everyone will finish the course are part of your course-management activities.

Usually learners only fall behind if there is a serious problem, such as a change in work schedule, illness, or an increase in family responsibilities. However, sometimes students may not grasp a new concept and become stuck in one module. In these situations, be flexible with the timeline in which learners catch up with the group or make progress toward completing the course.

Learners occasionally are such gifted procrastinators that they may put off turning in assignments until the end of the course, and then attempt to complete all assignments in a few days. You may not be able to motivate dedicated procrastinators, but you should discuss with these learners the need for making steady progress in an online course. Even if it is possible for someone to complete assignments within a few days, turning in assignments is not the same as learning the subject matter and showing the required depth of understanding for mastery of a subject. You may need to explain to learners who believe that online courses are easier and can be done almost overnight that this plan is not the best way to learn information and develop skills.

A related problem is taking several online courses at one time. The online curriculum should be structured so that only a few courses can be taken at the same time. However, learners in a hurry to complete a degree program may attempt several online courses at once. This practice should be discouraged. Either prerequisites can be set to make sure that students' progression through a program is regulated, or a limit can be placed on the number of online classes that students can take at one time.

Flexibility in online classes usually involves time. However, you may also need to be flexible with the topics learners select for their assignments. Allowing learners some choice of topic and format for a few assignments is a good way to meet the needs of people with different learning styles. Again, frequent communication with learners as they select topics and work through assignments can help you gauge how much guidance that learners need with the assignment and if there are inherent problems in the choice of topic or project. You should allow learners to direct their coursework as much as possible, but you should also help them troubleshoot any potential problems with their selections.

Testing

If you have designed tests or quizzes as part of the curriculum design, learners need to know about them long before the testing date arrives. Informing learners about the number and type(s) of tests and the testing procedures is especially important if students can take the tests whenever they feel ready.

Reminder notices of tests and instructions for taking them online or on site should be sent about a week ahead, if the tests must be taken at a certain time or date. Before learners take an online exam, they have to know when they can log on, how much time they have to complete the test, what it covers, and how they submit the information to you. If learners take tests at the end of a learning unit, but on their own schedule, they need to know where to find the tests (or how to make arrangements for on-site proctoring, if that is part of the process) and how they will be evaluated. Your regular e-mail or bulletin board correspondence can take care of these messages.

As with on-site testing, online testing can cause anxiety for learners with poor test-taking skills. You may want to provide a practice test or sample questions to help learners overcome some worries about taking exams. Learners not only get an idea of how questions will be phrased and what type(s) of questions will be used, but they also practice the mechanics of taking the exam.

For example, your course exam might require learners to click on their response to multiple-choice questions. Learners unfamiliar with the process may need instructions and practice sessions to make sure they know how to record their responses and submit the form. Although a good online instructional design provides clear instructions and an intuitive interface, new online learners may feel more comfortable if they know exactly what they will have to do during the real test.

You also may schedule a review chat session when most learners have completed a module or set up a Q&A forum during part of each office hour to prepare learners for the next exam. Helping learners understand what is expected of them is a big part of your role as a facilitator, especially when it comes to testing.

If online tests are sent to you automatically for grading, you will need to keep a log of when tests were taken, when you graded them, when the grades were posted, and how each learner fared. If objective tests are graded electronically, you may have little to do but post grades and keep track of how many learners have taken each exam. If subjective tests, such as essays, are used, you will need more time to evaluate and grade the responses before you send feedback. In any of these situations, you should summarize comments about each learner's performance and provide individualized feedback as soon as possible.

Some online gradebooks allow you to create a short personal message next to the posted grade or score. Even if you use this space to provide feedback, you may still want to send individual e-mail to provide a personal touch. Learners usually read e-mail more often than they check grades posted to a course site, so e-mail provides another practical benefit for learners.

Browsing the Web

The tasks described to this point in the chapter emphasize everyday work that pertains directly to your course. Browsing the Web may not seem to have a direct impact on your daily or weekly teaching, but it is an increasingly important part of being an effective online teacher.

Browsing anything or everything that grabs your interest is a good idea at least once or twice a week. Serendipity may lead you to innovative Web sites or an example of a new design concept, even if the subject matter has nothing to do with your course. Keeping up with trends in design and technology not only helps you note improvements that should be made to your course site, but allows you to keep pace with what learners are seeing and using on the Internet.

No matter what your area of specialization, you should keep informed about what is going on in the world of online education and other forms of distance learning. Bookmark sites that provide newsletters, news briefings, and technology reviews, just to help you keep up with other areas of online education.

State-of-the-art is fleeting, and it is easy to become complacent by being familiar only with your institution's level of technology or course design. You should keep learning more about distance education in general, and online education in particular. Checking bookmarked sites for the latest news, and conducting searches to find new clearinghouses, e-zines, and e-journals, for example, are activities well worth an hour or two a week.

Many institutions offering online instruction provide at least one sample or demonstration site, so that prospective learners get a feel for the course design and required tools. You should visit other online course sites, for other institutions as well as within your own, to compare your course's design with other courses'. Also visit sites offering courses similar to yours (or ask to visit the sites of teachers who facilitate other sections of the course you teach), so you can see how other designers and educators present similar course content.

You might experiment with demonstrations of educational software. Test drive new products, so that you can recommend their inclusion in your course the next time it is updated, or compare what you are using now with what else is available. Developing a broader understanding of trends in technology and the specific differences among similar hardware and software can help you determine what would be most useful in your course.

Finally, you need to keep up with professional standards for online courses and teachers. Even if your institution has been accredited, you need to be aware of any changing standards or trends within education. You might want to keep tabs on governmental Web sites, for example, to be aware of any bills or regulations that will affect online education and Internet usage. You may want to join a mailing list or subscribe to a newsletter produced by educational associations or other groups related to specific professions (i.e., those related to the subject areas you teach). In addition to updating your knowledge of technology, online education, and your course subject areas, you also need to understand the status of your profession.

You may not always have extra hours in the week to devote to these online research activities. However, as you have a few minutes when you work online, search or surf as long as you can. If you find something that warrants further investigation, possibly when you have more time, print a copy of the information or design or bookmark the location so you can check out the site when you do have more time.

For example, each morning, after you have checked e-mail, spend a few minutes browsing the Web while you finish a coffee. You might not be able to spend a long time online, but regularly schedule these few minutes either to browse as your interests dictate or to look for a particular site or type of information.

Ongoing research should not be haphazard; it can be highly focused. However, even when you have a few minutes to play online, you can look for new sites or designs that become a starting point for more focused research at a later time. Conducting research and working with the Internet are important tasks that you should complete weekly, as time allows.

Conducting Course-related Research

When you have time for more focused research pertaining directly to your course, you want to look for additional sites that provide course-specific links for learners. You also need to see that old favorites are still operating and their information is still worthwhile for your course.

As you locate new information and new URLs/URIs of effective sites for learners, make lists of sites that may be added to your course materials the next time the course is updated. Information of immediate use, such as news reports, feature articles, and multimedia files showing what has been told in course print materials, may be discussed and the URLs/URIs posted on the class bulletin board or in e-mail. Compare the addresses of sites that you want to use in your class with those required in other classes within the curriculum. You do not want revised course content to overlap too much with the content of other courses.

Your research also may help you find models or samples that you can use in class. Positive examples should be listed, and their benefits explained or discussed. (You do not want to post the locations of bad Web sites, for example.)

You should also encourage learners to send you new information or URLs/URIs as they find them. Check the site or information for suitability for the whole class to read or use before you post a notice about it. However, learners should be encouraged to share information relating to course topics as they find it. You cannot check all sites on the Internet, but by having a network of learners who also actively conduct research about course topics, you can better canvas more sources and make that information available to everyone in the class.

Time Management

Figure 5-1 shows you two sample schedules that indicate the numbers and types of activities you will need to build into your personal schedule. Both samples show two required chat sessions (splitting the class into two groups, probably to discuss the same topic). The samples also block out only times when the teacher is online doing activities other than grading. Additional activities, like grading work and posting grades, are not shown on these schedules.

Figure 5-1. Weekly Schedules

Sample 1

Time Frame	Monday	Tuesday	Wednesday	Thursday	Friday	Saturday	Sunday
6-8 a.m.	7-8 Check e-mail	7-8 Check e-mail	7-8 Check e-mail	7-8 Check e-mail	7-8 Check e-mail		
8-10 a.m.						9-10 Check e-mail	
10 a.m.-12 p.m.						10-11 Post bb messages	
12-2 p.m.							
2-4 p.m.							
4-6 p.m.	5:30-6 Check e-mail	5:30-6 Check e-mail	5:30-6 Check e-mail	5:30-6 Check e-mail	5:30-6 Check e-mail		
6-8 p.m.	7-8 Office hour		6-6:30 Post bb messages				7:30-8 Check e-mail
8-10 p.m.			9-10 Required chat (first group)				8-9 Required chat (second group)
10 p.m.-12 a.m.							

Sample 2

Time Frame	Monday	Tuesday	Wednesday	Thursday	Friday	Saturday	Sunday
6-8 a.m.	7-8 Check e-mail		7-8 Check e-mail		7-8 Check e-mail		
8-10 a.m.							
10 a.m.-12 p.m.							
12-2 p.m.	12-1 Required chat (first group)						
2-4 p.m.							
4-6 p.m.							
6-8 p.m.		7-8 Check e-mail					
8-10 p.m.		8:00-8:30 Office half hour	9:30-10 Post bb messages	9:30-10 Check e-mail		8-10 Check e-mail	
10 p.m.-12 a.m.			10-11 Required chat (second group)	10-10:30 Office half hour			10-11 Post bb messages

If the class size is larger than 16 people (two groups of eight), you probably will need to set up a third chat session. Only one office hour is listed for the week, but you may want or be required to establish more hours. E-mail, as the most time-intensive activity, takes up the greatest number of blocks. You may need a different number of e-mail sessions, depending on the subject matter, number of learners in the course, and personal preferences of class members. Sample 1 shows nine hours of e-mail time per week, whereas Sample 2 only provides six and a half hours for working with e-mail.

Sample 1 is a very traditional schedule and operates with the assumption that learners have an eight to five business day, Monday through Friday. No allowances have been made for international time zones, although all continental U.S. time zones, for example, might work into this schedule if the teacher were working in an Eastern or a Central time zone.

Sample 2 offers more variety, with a lunch hour chat for people in the same time zone as the teacher. A few later times are offered for office hours and chats.

You may need a very different schedule, depending on your available time and the free time of class members. As well, you may teach more than one online class at a time, so your schedule may be filled every evening as you juggle multiple chat sessions and office hours for different classes. However, these samples give you a starting point for blocking out your weekly schedule.

It is a good idea to create a schedule like either of these for each week, or a few weeks in advance. That way you can more easily keep track of your daily schedule and be able to post signup folders and notices for upcoming synchronous activities.

How much online time is enough for each class? That is a question only you can answer, and the response probably will change from class to class. It may be a matter of focus, not so much the total time. For example, you may get a lot done by answering short e-mail or easy questions for 15 minutes each weekday morning. You can save the more time-intensive e-mail, such as evaluating written assignments and sending feedback, for response when you have more time. The first few minutes each morning can be spent weeding out the urgent messages from those that either do not need a response or that require a much longer time commitment.

In the same way, if you have an office hour, videoconference, or chat scheduled in real time, you know what you have to prepare for that session, just as you know what you have to do to prepare for the next on-site class. Keep track of upcoming synchronous activities in a calendar, and plan materials needed for those sessions. The total amount of time is equal to or even greater than what you spend in an on-site classroom or office, but the time commitment is broken into smaller chunks. Being online all the time is not necessary or desirable; being focused on learners when you are online is the key.

E-mail is probably the easiest way to provide a touchstone with class members. At least once a day, when you have computer access, read and respond to e-mail, both individual messages and group notices. You may need to download assignments for later viewing or spend a few minutes deleting old messages. If you plan to view assignments immediately instead of later from a disk or hard copy, allocate a few hours for evaluating work and sending feedback.

Many learners work late at night, after they complete their job and home responsibilities, or early in the morning, when they come in early to the office to work on course materials. By answering e-mail early in the morning, you can help solve problems early in the day for people sharing your time zone, as well as get a good idea of the number of assignments that you need to evaluate later. If you will be holding an office hour, check e-mail immediately before the session to make sure that there are not problems with or panic messages about the upcoming chat.

The number of e-mail messages and assignments can be overwhelming at times, but try not to enslave yourself to the computer. By taking care of the most urgent problems once or twice a day, and downloading assignments to read when you have more time to evaluate them, you can avoid becoming overwhelmed with messages.

You also can read all the bulletin board messages that have been posted since the last time you logged into the bulletin board. Spend at least an hour twice a week working on new folders and reading bulletin board information.

If you are planning to monitor a discussion, for example, you will need to allocate more time on the bulletin board that week. The bulletin board takes up far less time than e-mail, but you cannot neglect it. Setting aside a couple of sessions a week is a good way to keep up with recent postings. Learners who need to talk with you immediately tend to send e-mail or to call; they seldom post urgent messages on a bulletin board, except as a last resort or to enlist the help of other students.

To determine how much time you may need to spend on various activities, you might want to compare your workload for an online course with that required for an on-site course. When you teach an undergraduate class on a university campus, the class may meet from one to three times a week, depending on the type of course. However, the total time spent in the classroom is three hours, not counting the time it takes to get to the classroom, set up activities, and close down a computer lab after use. In addition, you probably hold at least two to three office hours per week for each class. Without counting preparation or assignment evaluation time, you spend at least six hours a week communicating with your on-site class.

The hours spent online for a three-credit class are similar. If you spend an hour each weekday on e-mail per class and hold a one-hour online office hour per class, that is six hours right there. Adding your time using the bulletin board and sending e-mail over the weekend means that you have spent more hours communicating with online learners than on-site students. Of course, you also may receive e-mail from on-site students, but your primary means of communication with on-site learners is in person through class sessions and office hours.

To avoid spending several hours a day with online activities, you may want to develop some measures to save time. One such method is to recycle some e-mail messages. Of course, you do not want to become impersonal, but some group messages can be saved, with slight modification, for use with another group at another time. For example, you generally want to open the class with a welcome e-mail message similar to the text shown in Figure 5.2.

This e-mail message is long, and you do not want to rewrite this information each time you begin a new class. The structure is effective, and the content provides the most important information you want learners to have during the first days of the course. You can make changes to the announcements, add a personal or seasonal comment, or otherwise slightly vary this message each time you send it. However, if you have saved the basic message, you can quickly make changes and send the revised message to the group.

Figure 5-2. Welcome E-mail

Welcome to the class! I'm looking forward to working with you in this course. Before we get started, here are some important announcements:

My office hours will be held on Mondays from 7:00-8:00 p.m. Central time and Thursdays from 10:00-11:00 p.m. Central time. I hope you'll join me in the chat room.

The first assignments are listed on the course syllabus, but I've added some comments in the Unit 1 Assignments folder on the bulletin board. Please read the information in this folder before you begin your first assignments.

If you need to get in touch with me outside of e-mail, you may call my office at 555-555-5555. Voice mail is activated if I'm not in the office. I'll return your calls as soon as possible.

I'm looking forward to this class. Please send me e-mail if you have questions this week.

(Add your name and signature line, indicating how you want to be addressed by class members.)

Figure 5-3. Welcome Bulletin Board Post

Welcome to the class! Please read the information on the syllabus and assignment sheets for the first unit. If you have questions, please send me e-mail at myemail@school.edu.

In this folder, please briefly introduce yourself. Here's my introduction:

My name is Lynnette Porter. I've been teaching this course for the past three terms, and I'm looking forward to working with you in this class.

I live in the South, but I've lived several places around the U.S. and traveled throughout North America, so many of your hometowns were familiar to me. In fact, I just returned from a conference in Toronto, so I'll be sharing some career links I discovered at that conference. I'm a technical communicator, and I'll also be sharing some information about this profession as we get into the career-development unit.

Once again, welcome to the class!

You can save similar reusable files from the bulletin board, for example. Figure 5-3 shows a similar welcome message posted to the bulletin board before the class begins. The message may be altered slightly each time it is used, but by saving standard bulletin board messages, you save time in remembering what needs to go into a message and when it should be posted.

You may want to save commonly used bulletin board messages, just as you archive standard group e-mail.

Your descriptions of APA or MLA style and examples of different citation formats probably took a long time to create. Save that information so that you can update it and post it for the next online class, which will need similar instruction. Models of documents or lists of additional resources or links might also be saved and updated as needed, especially if they cannot be directly linked to the course site.

Developing effective assignments, responses to typical questions, and information about new resources takes time and should be ongoing activities. They help you not only implement the current curriculum, but plan ways that the curriculum can be modified in the future. You need to save your work and use it with other groups, as appropriate. You do not want to reuse old, stale information.

However, effective, still-current information can be helpful to more than one class. You must carefully evaluate your messages and supplementary information before you teach each online class. Materials that are still interesting and relevant and that can be easily modified to fit the next class' needs should be saved. This measure not only saves you time, but it also helps ensure a high-quality, well-developed set of messages and lectures, for example, that have been reviewed and tested by learners.

Summary

Keeping up with your teaching responsibilities is easier when you break down tasks by week or day. Schedule your time so that you enjoy synchronous activities with your learners, and spend some time almost every day doing the asynchronous tasks. Make sure learners know when you will be online, and then stick to the arrangements you have made. Being methodical and consistent is a big part of making your online teaching responsibilities manageable and keeping learners motivated.

In addition to these pragmatic tasks that require you to keep up with immediate teaching responsibilities, you also need to conduct research as often as possible. Scheduling Internet-based research activities into your weekly workload is an important ongoing teaching task. As well, creating disks with saved information that can be used in future classes can also help you save time in writing effective instructional information and standard group messages.

References

Byington, E. (2002). Communication: The key to success in an online writing and reading course. In P. Comeaux (Ed.), *Communication and collaboration in the online classroom* (pp. 192-206). Bolton, MA: Anker Publishing.

Miller, M. D., & Corley, K. (2001). The effect of e-mail messages on student participation in the asynchronous on-line course: A research note. *Online Journal of Distance Learning Administration, 4*(3). Retrieved July 9, 2002, from http://www.westga.edu/~distance/ ojdla/fall43/miller43.html

National Education Association (NEA). (2002). *A survey of traditional and distance learning higher education members.* Retrieved September 30, 2002, from http://www.nea.org/he/abouthe/ dlstudy.pdf

Palloff, R. M., & Pratt, K. (2002). Beyond the looking glass: What faculty and students need to be successful online. In J. Bourne & J. C. Moore (Eds.), *Elements of quality online education* (pp. 171-184). Volume 3 in the Sloan-C series. Needham, MA: The Sloan Consortium.

Savenye, W. C., Olina, Z., & Niemczyk, M. (2001). So you are going to be an online writing instructor: Issues on designing, developing, and delivering an online course. *Computers and Composition, 18,* 371-385.

The Aesthetics

of Teaching

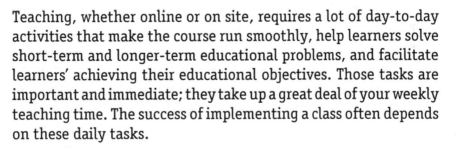

Teaching, whether online or on site, requires a lot of day-to-day activities that make the course run smoothly, help learners solve short-term and longer-term educational problems, and facilitate learners' achieving their educational objectives. Those tasks are important and immediate; they take up a great deal of your weekly teaching time. The success of implementing a class often depends on these daily tasks.

However, the "aesthetics" of teaching are equally important and can help determine how well the learners enrolled in your courses actually gain knowledge and develop skills. Ideally, you were involved with the course design process, but even if you were not, you still can create an online learning environment where learners feel safe to disclose information about themselves and their work, both to you and to other students. You also can gather information to help with future curriculum development by talking with learners about the course and their major areas of study.

A supportive, professional learning environment cannot be created through the course design alone. A nurturing environment is built when you work well with students and facilitate their educational experiences. This part of the curriculum-implementation process is more esoteric and may be forgotten by teachers who are overwhelmed with the daily tasks described in previous chapters. Nevertheless, you must find time to relate to learners and really think about how the course is coming across to others.

An online class by definition meets electronically, not in a physical classroom. Nevertheless, learners and teachers must feel there is a place that belongs to the class alone. Learning communities, of the class as a whole and of smaller groups of class members, are one way to create this educational space and time. Expecting honesty and ethical standards from learners, and upholding your and your institution's standards for fairness and equality, are other ways to build an aesthetically pleasing, sound educational environment. The people who come together to take a course, even if their number is limited, should feel secure enough that they can disclose personal information, when appropriate, with others. They should believe that they belong to the online group and have responsibilities to it.

Although throughout the course you probably will deal with issues of academic integrity or class members' interactions with each other, you should start the course by explaining your expectations for class members and showing by example how to work effectively with other members of the learning community. The aesthetics of teaching may be intangible and subtle, but they affect learners in profound ways. When learners feel secure in a classroom and share information in positive ways, they not only can learn more effectively, but they also build networks of friends and colleagues to further support their academic and professional development.

Creating a Positive Learning Environment within Different Times and Spaces

Online classes vary in the number of learners and the time frame for the course. Some programs continue year round. For example, in the design and structure for one online course, learners may work on their own and turn in assignments to a teacher who evaluates the materials. There are no required chat sessions or other forms of synchronous communication. The learners in this type of program like the freedom of completing assignments at their own pace, as long as they finish within the parameter of the course's final due date. E-mail keeps teacher and student in touch, but there is little learner-to-learner communication, and the amount of learner-to-teacher or teacher-to-learner communication varies with the student's needs and personality.

In this example, the teacher and learner have to develop a tiny learning community. They define what makes the class real, and they mostly create a sense of the classroom through their individual work spaces.

The student creates a time and place for completing course activities and basically builds his or her "classroom" individually. The teacher does the same. However, the connection between teacher and learner—the rapport, shared insights, and suggestions for studying a subject—makes the class a true educational experience. Creating a learning community, even with two people, is a big part of creating a sense of classroom and "real education."

Other institutions treat online classes similar to on-site classes, with one group of students taking a course during the same time frame and working on at least some projects together. Working entirely alone is not an option, if learners want to complete all assignments successfully. For example, enrollment in one class may be limited to 15-20; some classes may be smaller, but most courses are filled to the cutoff number.

Learners in this scenario have a clear start and end date for each course, but the courses may vary in length, anywhere from a minicourse of three or four weeks to a short six-week course to a more traditional (in terms of on-site education) 12-15 weeks. Learners are expected to facilitate their own learning, and the readings, whether linked to the course site or found in a hardcopy textbook, are a large part of the coursework. However, learners also participate in group activities that allow them to discuss ideas with each other and to complete team projects, such as papers and role playing.

Required chat sessions, videoconferences, conference calls, and voluntary group chats help learners create a sense of camaraderie. They build a classroom within the time frame of events, such as a chat session, in which all participants work together. When the event involves synchronous communication, like a chat or a videoconference, the classroom is the electronic network that joins members of a learning community. Although the place varies, with learners from different geographic locations participating in the chat or videoconference, the shared real-time framework creates a sense that everyone is in the same classroom.

When learners use asynchronous communication to work with others, they lose the connection of time as the foundation of their classroom. However, they still have other experiences that bond them to other learners: Because they are working as a group, independently doing the same assignments and sometimes meeting to talk with each other and complete a project together, they have a sense that they belong to the same class. Learners may have to create their personal classroom when they work alone at home, in the office, or another computer-accessible space, but they retain a connection to the larger group.

You have a personal classroom space, too, but your role in building a classroom is especially important during synchronous activities. Although asynchronous communication should be used to give learners a sense of belonging to a class while they complete learning activities on their own, the synchronous activities give you that much more opportunity to pull the group together.

Your persona, as evidenced through asynchronous and synchronous messages, makes the class seem professional, yet friendly. Your online personality indicates how formal or informal the class will be, how approachable or remote you are from learners, and how seriously or frivolously you take the course materials—and the job of teaching.

If you teach from home, you should develop a work space in which you are comfortable; reserve this space for your work. Keep all the information about the class close to your computer. You should act as professionally while you are working in this space as you do when you enter an on-site classroom or your office on campus. Getting into a professional state of mind helps you to build the learning community and to create a formal space and time for working online.

Whether the program model you follow encourages learners to work mostly on their own or at least sometimes as part of a larger class, you can build a learning community each day through your teaching activities. *You* create the sense of classroom, even without a common building or location. *You* ensure that learners' communication and learning activities are not completed in a vacuum, but that their work is just as valuable in an online class as it is in a class where learners physically see each other and others' assignments.

Building Learning Communities

As an educational tool, the Internet provides useful resources and opportunities for communicating with others. However, the Web is only a repository of information, and Internet technology provides only a glorified answering machine unless they are used to create a community. Online technologies can help you create a true communication forum if they are used to develop interactive learning communities. Anyone who has the technical capability for connecting with the Internet is connected automatically to the "global" part of the hyped global village, but educators and learners need to work more carefully to build effective communities.

An online learning community can be defined as a group of people who communicate with each other across the Internet (or sometimes by intranet) to share information, learn more about a topic, or work on a project of mutual interest. The community may come together for a brief time or last for years, depending upon the group's needs and interests.

Within an online classroom, the group as a whole should be a learning community, although several smaller communities can also be formed within the larger group. Learning communities within the context of the course are *internal learning communities*. Learning communities involving people outside the course, such as mentors, businesspeople who work with learners in the class, subject matter experts, even family members and friends, are part of *external learning communities*, whose influence may last well beyond the length of the course.

Jonassen, Peck, and Brent (1998) defined online learning communities as a way of learning that is based within a supportive environment. Trust and respect for others' differences help students work together well to achieve common course-related objectives. This definition seems much gentler and more nurturing than what you may perceive as online business teams or political academic groups working to promote one product or viewpoint over a rival's. Instead of emphasizing conformity to a group norm or competition for an edge over another group, *community* in Jonassen et al.'s definition describes an empowering environment.

A learning community can be more than a group of individuals who come together to share knowledge and experience. Especially in an online classroom, the learning community should serve as the medium used to build self-esteem, as well as skills and knowledge. Each student has diverse skills, resources, or information to share with the rest of the learning community. This diversity should be highly valued by the group.

Therefore, a wide range of viewpoints should be invited. This does not mean that rude behavior or flaming others by e-mail or bulletin board posts should be tolerated. It does mean that different perspectives on the subject matter, different approaches to solving problems, and shared experiences based on previous projects should be discussed to provide a broad spectrum of information about a topic.

Milson and Chu's (2002) netiquette guidelines were initially designed for younger students who should be instructed in character building and ethical use of the Internet in order to live as virtuous global netizens. However, adult learners may need these guidelines, too. They may serve as the basics of initial socialization in an online learning community. They can foster discussion and help learning communities within the class establish their own behavioral guidelines. Some of Milson and Chu's guidelines advocate responsible use of the network, respect for other members' privacy and ideas, honesty in online work, and abolition of offensive language. These general rules can be broadened for adults. For example, responsible use of the network can refer to intranets as well as the Internet and involve issues like use of corporate computers to complete personal homework during business hours with/without the boss' approval.

Jonassen et al. (1998) noted that learning communities can be strengthened through communication and the appreciation of a shared culture. Dialogue and access to resources bring group members together. When learners work on a project, for example, each member of that learning community should communicate with all group members at least twice a week for the duration of a project. They may send bulk e-mail to the whole group, set up a convenient time for a chat, or post messages to a project folder on the bulletin board. Specific or required amounts of communication may initiate discussion among group members, but the true community aspect of the group develops as they communicate with each other more often.

The need for communication initially binds the group, but as members share information and learn more about each other (especially in an intercultural environment), additional communication, not always focused on the project, creates a community. Sharing or developing common interests with other members of the community brought participants together initially (Brown, 2001). A requirement may get a group started, but community building takes place as group members get to know each other and work together. Learning communities usually send more e-mail to each other or otherwise surpass the number of required messages.

Ideally, learning communities should provide a human touch. Encouragement and feedback are two important services that class members can provide each other (The learning community and online instruction, 1999). If the purpose of education is to allow each learner the ability to grasp new concepts and develop skills in a supportive environment, online learning communities certainly support this mission statement. Unlike other team environments, which may encourage competition, online learning communities should foster cooperation and mutual support.

Building a learning community, or several communities, is critical to the success of an online class. Even if the learning community is tiny—one teacher and one learner—the benefits can be the same. Learners may modify their perspective of a topic by coming in contact with another's (or others') ideas that differ from theirs; they share experiences and information and, you hope, gain insight into how a particular topic affects their lives. Online education, when it is done well, links students with teachers and other learners who may have not otherwise had the opportunity ever to meet or exchange ideas.

However, hearing or reading about other perspectives is not all that is important. Critical evaluation of what is being heard or read is part of the educational process. Just about anyone today can dump information onto a Web site and have others read the information and, perhaps, learn something from it. Anyone who wants to learn about a subject can download lots of information from the Internet, go to the library and read books, and otherwise study alone, without feedback from anyone else. That is not the point of online education.

Critically evaluating your and others' work and objectively broadening perspectives and experiences are what make true online education stand out from online information. Learning communities can help learners discuss and defend their ideas, as well as evaluate and respond to what they learn from others. Although the majority of online education is independent, with learners working on their own for long periods of time, interaction with the group is critical in helping learners put new information into a larger context and critically evaluating new ideas.

The Internet is a wonderful tool for connecting people worldwide and expanding learners' information base. Building a community and creating a growing network of learners who interact with each other on different projects and share different interests is the high point of online education.

Equality in Communities

An important note about learning communities is that learners with different abilities may feel empowered through their participation in these communities. Members are perceived by the way they communicate and the ideas they offer to the group. Online learning communities provide equal playing fields for members who may feel isolated or look different from peers in more traditional work teams or study groups.

Online courses and computerized communication are good ways to build skills and self-esteem, because learners can take their time to craft a message before they send it. The content of the message, not the gender, ethnicity, race, age, religious background, or appearance of the writer, for example, forms the basis of evaluating that message. Until writers disclose personal information or opinions, they are evaluated only by the volume and quality of their messages. Even names may not indicate other background information, as many students have married surnames, adoptive parents' family names, or nicknames that preclude easy categorization. The invisibility of a text-based online communication system allows learners, at least initially the ability to submit their ideas, not themselves, for evaluation by the teacher and other learners. This process allows learners who are shy about participating in a group at least a safe entry point for communicating with other class members.

Even during a chat, all learners are encouraged to participate, and it is difficult to hide in the back of an online room. All learners are expected to volunteer their ideas, and every idea is printed equally on the screen and can be downloaded into print. Learners may feel more at ease by writing their ideas rather than speaking to a group in person. An online forum is ideal for students who may withdraw from face-to-face participation in on-site classes. Being part of an online community frees these learners to share their ideas without fear of censure. They express themselves without seeing other people watch them, and they do not have to worry about negative body language from their peers if they make an unpopular statement.

A learning community should not be used as a way of escaping face-to-face communication, but it can be a method of building self-esteem. Gaining confidence through their participation in an online community can help shy learners become better able to voice their opinions when they participate in in-person meetings.

Online learning communities help make classes enjoyable and effective. These communities allow participants to share more resources, experiences, and insights than one teacher can offer. As well, learning communities may use both asynchronous and synchronous communication, an attractive feature for members who may have very untraditional schedules or who live in widely separated geographic locations.

Problems within Learning Communities

Learning communities need participants. One of the most common complaints about group activities is that online classes, according to many adult learners, are supposed to be independently completed. Students do not have time to work with others, especially if community members live in other time zones or have different job and personal schedules.

As with all collaborative activities, such as those on the job, some learners who are required to participate in a learning community try to take over the group and impose their ideas or will on everyone else. Personality conflicts arise when this situation occurs, and other group members either leave the community or spend collaborative time arguing, instead of discussing ways to work together. Some students do not do their share of the work and are content to let others take over. These personality and work-allocation issues can tear apart a learning community and keep members from accomplishing tasks.

A philosophical issue is that many learners do not see how the Internet can be a wonderful collaborative tool for internal or external learning communities. These students only perceive the Internet as a database, not as a communication tool.

To help alleviate any of these problems, you have to show learners how effective collaboration can take place and guide the learning communities so that members early on realize benefits from participating in them.

Ways to Overcome Problems with Learning Communities

You can do a lot to increase the probability of success in classroom learning communities by following a few guidelines. The community members have to be interested in the subject or activities that pull the group together. You can help generate interest by selecting topics that pertain to learners' career interests or common personal interests that mesh with course objectives. You may have to introduce community members to each other and note these common interests to help the community begin to work together. When learners are interested in the topics of study by the learning communities, they are more likely to find value in participation (Andrews, 2002).

Creating a stable, supportive environment is another step toward success. Andrews (2002) emphasized the need for nonthreatening and friendship-building activities so that new community members have positive initial experiences with a learning community. If learners feel favorably toward class members and collaborative opportunities, they are more likely to participate. You as facilitator also must moderate the community's activities and show your continuing interest in the group (Gunawardena, Plass, & Salisbury, 2001). You should not require group collaboration and then remain aloof from the community that you have created. You must show that you value the communities and keep informed about what is going on within them if students are going to see value in group tasks.

Hilts and Turoff (2002) explained that interactivity is the key to learning communities' viability. Learners must interact with the teacher and each other. The technology also must work easily and make it possible for learners to discuss information, see notes or plan projects, and share resources. For example, the chat room, whiteboard, bulletin board, e-mail, and attachments created with different software, such as PowerPoint or Excel, might be used to help learners create and share information in different formats. Community members may want to exchange presentational slides, .JPG files, PDF documents, and spreadsheets. All technical aspects of facilitating online communities have to function consistently well, or learners will become frustrated and abandon electronic communication for what they perceive as more effective methods of communication, such as phone conversations. Although learners wanting to talk to each other is a positive part of the learning community, they should not use this form of communication only because electronic means will not work reliably.

Hiltz and Turoff (2002) noted that asynchronous learning networks (ALNs), as well as synchronous forms of communication, can help make learners feel like a part of a real class that learns and works together. When you develop collaborative learning activities for your course, and as you plan or redesign a curriculum to include more collaborative work, consider both asynchronous and synchronous methods of pulling learners together.

Emphasizing ALNs can help learners work more easily with group members in different time zones or on different schedules. ALNs give groups the chance to work together, but largely within the individual's time frame. Asynchronous communication can help learning communities overcome barriers of time and space and ensure that all members can participate in group activities.

The Teacher's Role as Facilitator

Facilitating the formation of learning communities is important in the first week of class. Through your group messages, first bulletin board postings, and first weeks' office hours, you make learners feel that they are part of the larger group studying the same materials at the same time. Introductions among all class members are important, as is socializing the group to the "rules of the road" for taking this class.

Then you can work to facilitate smaller communities, made up of personalities you think will work well together on a special project or will discuss concepts at about the same speed in a chat. You may randomly assign some people to work together, or, after you have become familiar with learners' interests and learning styles, you can purposely group people who will create a good mix for discussion or completion of a specific task. Sometimes you become a member of a learning community, but in that situation, your status as teacher is not important; you are just another member of the community.

Smaller communities can range from three to 10 people, but for scheduling and management purposes, four to six is a better number. Each learning community shares information, resources, and experiences, for example, through chat sessions. Some communities also complete a specific project, such as a role-playing exercise, research for a paper, or a series of math problems.

A persistent question about online learning is this: If learners take responsibility for their own education, even if they work in a learning community of other learners new to a subject area, how can educators ensure that learners are correctly interpreting the material? In some courses, learners can memorize data and repeat it for credit; however, that does not indicate mastery of the subject matter. When learners work on their own, they may follow a tangent of particular interest and lose track of the larger perspective. They may research topics that support their own ideas and biases and fail to understand opposing arguments. They may superficially study problems with little understanding of the complexity of situations.

One possible checkpoint for adequate research and interpretation can be provided by mentors. As a facilitator, you may also suggest people outside the classroom (e.g., professionals who can communicate with learners online) who might be good additions to the community. For example, you may suggest that learners contact a professional association's members who expressed an interest in working with learners or who have expertise in a particular subject area. Mixing external and internal communities within a class offers learners the opportunity to work with other professionals who share career interests or specific information useful to a current project.

Professionals from different businesses, countries, levels of experience, career tracks, etc., may be good mentors. Offering different perspectives from those of learners, mentors can provide a framework for discussion and an introduction to new ideas or resources.

Although teachers also should be effective guides who steer learners toward a broader understanding of the subject matter, outside mentors, if they are carefully selected to offer diverse points of view, back up the teacher's influence. They can provide more credibility to the course and the program.

The level of technology is not as important as the quality of the mentorship. Effective learning communities can use low-level technology; the important aspect of a learning community is collaboration. Your class does not have to have streaming audio or video capabilities, two-way audio or video communication, or frequent synchronous communication in order to create an effective community. Working together can be facilitated through e-mail messages, bulletin board postings, online chats, whiteboard sessions, and personal, group, or corporate Web sites.

Chat rooms are often the preferred place for discussion, interviews, Q&A sessions, and group work sessions. Community members may prefer real-time communication instead of asynchronous communication for work sessions, although both synchronous and asynchronous communications are useful. The community members' geographic location, personal and work schedules, and time zones determine which communication methods are used most often and the amount of time they can devote to working with a group.

For example, each member of a class-based community may be required to communicate with group members at least twice a week for the duration of a project. Groups get together to discuss materials, research topics, and share information. It is not unusual for learners to stick around a chat room after the formal session is over, just to compare notes, bond, and plan upcoming work.

Although a few learning communities only last a brief time (e.g., the duration of an assignment or a course), group members may continue to meet informally or formally well beyond the class time. Learning communities even may continue to meet longer than an academic term, grow beyond the initial group, or form an ongoing community based on other mutual interests.

Responsibilities of Community Members

Learning communities thrive when group members feel responsibility toward each other. In Brown's (2001) study of 21 graduate students enrolled in distance learning classes and three faculty from the University of Nebraska at Kearney, participants defined part of their sense of community by this responsibility. Because the group worked together, individuals realized that success depended on the participation of everyone. Learners may often feel a similar sense of loyalty to the group, as well as a fear of letting the group down. Perhaps adult learners who are used to working in teams on the job more easily grasp the concept of working together as a community.

Each community nurtures members who have fewer skills or knowledge. Even members with less knowledge or experience can provide valuable insights, ask important questions, or offer unique perspectives. The emphasis of a successful learning community is mutual cooperation and sharing. Although members may disagree or have different opinions, in a successful learning community, each member feels free to offer an opinion. Discussion is encouraged, and no one person takes the lead all the time. Project responsibilities or group tasks are shared.

The members of a community should police themselves. If one member does not participate as anticipated, that person may receive lots of messages to prompt more participation. Often the messages include offers of assistance or expressions of concern. Group members tend to care about each other, as well as about their success in the course.

Setting Up Smaller Learning Communities

How can you build smaller learning communities while you are busy sending e-mail, evaluating assignments, and holding office hours? Getting the whole class to get to know each other is a big job in itself, but once some larger activities, such as chat sessions, have taken place, smaller communities should be fostered. These groups can deepen learners' educational experiences and create more meaningful interactions. You can break down your regular communication activities and the assignments that you give to learners so that smaller learning groups are formed within the larger class community. Figure 6-1 provides an overview of the way you can build small groups' work into your weekly teaching activities.

Figure 6-1. Schedule of Events for Community Building

Week 1

1. Have learners introduce themselves through group e-mail messages or bulletin board posts.

2. Hold an office hour early in the first week of the course. Get to know as many learners as possible, and encourage learners to chat with each other.

3. Send group messages and create bulletin board folders with important information the entire group needs to know.

Middle Weeks

1. Set up smaller groups for projects. Vary the composition of the groups with each team assignment or project.

2. Hold formal chats with different groupings of learners.

3. Require learners to post bulletin board messages commenting on other learners' posts about a topic. Create a bulletin board discussion of relevant topics, perhaps a new topic each week.

4. Hold Q&A or review sessions in the chat room.

5. Encourage learners to use all media available for working together. Assist learners in scheduling time in the chat room, for example.

Final Week

1. Post information needed to complete the course in a bulletin board folder and group e-mail.

2. Send a group thank you/farewell e-mail message.

3. Encourage all learners to attend the last office hour chat session.

These weekly activities help the group stay on track as a learning community, but allow other, smaller learning communities to form and work on their own. Each day you work online you can plan, or perform, these activities. Working them into your weekly teaching tasks is necessary for a successful class. You can't facilitate all learning activities, but learners working independently and together can tackle projects, analyze materials, and master the concepts contained in the course materials.

Even when learners are not working together on a specific project, they can still talk with each other at least a few times a week. Setting up discussion questions for bulletin board posts, sending e-mail to learners and encouraging students to write to each other, and holding online office hours are just three ways to get class members to share their ideas. These activities, even though they are not highly structured, also help build a sense of togetherness.

Required Group Projects

A typical way to build small, temporary learning communities is to require group projects. These projects can be especially effective if they mirror the tasks that learners will do on the job or in preparation for their career. You never want to require a group project simply to show learners that they can work together effectively online. Each project should have a clear purpose and tasks within the project should be well suited to individual group members' capabilities.

You may create these learning communities, varying group membership for different projects throughout the course, or you may ask learners to determine who will work together. Initially in a course, you may want to set up the groups to match interests and sometimes skill levels.

An important consideration is the location and time zones of the community/group members. Adult learners who take online courses often work late at night or early in the morning, on weekends, and during breaks in the work day. Because learners in one class may work in different time zones from their peers, much less have the same work or personal schedules, group projects may be difficult to manage. If you know that some learners work nights, you may initially put them together for a group project.

Learners in one geographic location or closely related time zones may be good candidates for a successful group. Let group members establish the days and times for required chats so that most, if not all, members can participate.

In some classes, you might group learners who have more difficulty with writing so that the writing/response speed will be about the same for every participant in a chat or every member of a community. You should not label the slower chat as remedial or point out to the class learner differences in typing or writing ability, but after a week or two of e-mail messages and office hours in the chat room, you probably know which learners need more time to craft their messages. You can then assign learners to chat sessions with others who share their skill and speed level. As learners' skill levels improve, you should vary the composition of communities working in different chat sessions or on projects.

Community building is an ongoing process, and it changes with each class you teach, simply because the makeup of each class is different. This overriding task takes up a big part of your daily or weekly teaching responsibilities. You want to make each learner feels included as a part of the larger class as well as smaller learning communities. You may need to send messages to all members involved in a group project to make sure the work is going smoothly. Your communication and teaching style should be inclusive, not exclusive, as you facilitate learning communities. Help students work with each other and outside mentors.

Required group projects should be more than an assignment in one or two online courses within the curriculum. Group projects and collaborative activities should be part of the entire curriculum and involve perhaps not only members of one class, but true across-the-curriculum or shared-course activities that allow students from several courses to work together on a larger project. Students close to completing a degree program also may be asked to mentor learners who are just beginning the program. Any requirements for online collaboration and descriptions of mentoring or group work should be explained in the program's literature. Learners entering an online degree program should be informed that course requirements include such collaborative efforts.

Honesty and Ethics in the Classroom

For any learning community to succeed, members must trust each other and the teacher, and all community/class members must act ethically at all times. Students should be encouraged to collaborate on group projects or even research for individual projects, but assignments made to individuals must be independently completed. Everyone must understand that original work is of paramount importance and that any use of outside sources must be clearly and thoroughly documented.

A thorny problem in all educational programs is honesty. The common focus is plagiarism, although other forms of academic honesty should be spelled out in a syllabus and other institutional literature, like the course catalog. Ethics and honesty are often labeled "academic integrity."

Many academic institutions state their academic honesty, integrity, or ethics statements at a central location on the university's or college's Web site. The statement then might be copied into each individual course site. A good ethics statement should deal with plagiarism.

Summarizing, paraphrasing, and quoting texts or graphics, both online and hardcopy, should be explained. This task may fall to individual teachers, because lengthy examples and instruction are beyond the scope of an ethics or academic honesty statement. In addition to reviewing the mechanics of citing sources appropriately and using a specific citation style, such as Modern Language Association (MLA) or American Psychological Association (APA), teachers may need to explain the rationale behind the process of citing reference information. That plagiarism is cheating by stealing others' ideas and claiming them as one's own should be explained as the serious offence it is. The institutional policies for dealing with plagiarism need to be detailed, and the consequences for plagiarizing information must be spelled out and enforced. As a deterrent, you may encourage or require learners to use plagiarism-checking software before they submit assignments to you for evaluation. The software must be used by learners and monitored by teachers for the system to work effectively.

Honesty is another ethical concern. Dealing with class members and the teacher honestly and fairly should be expected of all learners. Doing one's own work is imperative. Written communication that does not mislead others, by omission of information or deliberately misstating data, should be discouraged, and penalties enforced. "Fairness" also should reflect unbiased dealings with everyone. Discrimination should not be tolerated.

These elements of an academic ethics or integrity statement must be defined and explained effectively. Some examples of good policies can be found in the table of academic institutions' Web sites. The titles of the information indicate the focus of the policy. Although a majority use Academic Honesty, some emphasize the problem of plagiarism and others focus on appropriate conduct.

You can also learn a lot about the institution's emphasis on the policy by how many times a site search for "academic honesty," for example, reveals several Web pages. Some institutions place their statements on the home

Table 6-1. Effective Examples of Academic Honesty Policy Statements

Title of the Statement	Academic Institution	URL of the Statement
Academic Honesty	University of Colorado, USA	www.colorado.edu//policies/acadinteg.html
Academic Honesty	Penn State Smeal, Australia	www.smeal.psu.edu/smeal/integrity/links.html
Academic Honesty/ Plagiarism	University of Leicester, UK	www.le.ac.uk.education/research/ research_student/research_student_ handbook/academic_honesty.html
Academic Honesty	University of Puget Sound, USA	www.ups.edu/dean/Handbook/ Honesty.html
Academic Honesty	University of Chicago, USA	www.uchicago.edu/docs/ studentmanual/academic_honesty .html
Academic Honesty	University of Missouri, USA	Edis.missouri.edu/Policies.htm
Appropriate Conduct and Academic Honesty	McLaughlin College, Canada	www.yorku.ca/mclaughlin/welcome/ academics.html
Statement on Academic Honesty	Columbia Basin College, USA	www.cbc2.org/sserv/honesty/
Academic Dishonesty	College at Oneonta, USA	www.oneonta.edu/library/honesty/ code.html

page, but others link users to student handbooks, groups of policies, and the library (presumably for research policies). As new elements need to be added to academic policies, the statements are updated in the institutional Web pages as well at individual course sites.

Educational concerns about honesty take many forms. The following four issues highlight educators' concerns about online education:

1. Learners must do their own work.

    Whether it is an assignment or a test, learners need to do their own work, without an unreasonable amount of assistance from the teacher, other learners, and people outside the class (e.g., tutors, family members, employers, purchased papers from the Web).

2. Learners must document the sources of information they use in assignments.

    Most institutions suggest a reference style for learners to use in documenting their research, such as MLA or APA style. Learners must be able to document their work accurately and adequately, and they should be penalized for plagiarizing information.

3. Learners must complete all course requirements fairly, from class participation and attendance to academic activities.

    Learners have to participate in the class themselves, even if the activity requires attending an on-site lecture or reviewing materials on a Web site. Although this requirement is difficult to enforce, you can make the use of stand-ins less likely if the course site requires a password. You may not be able to verify identity without being able to see class members face to face, but you can monitor consistency in the way learners express themselves in all formats for written communication.

4. Learners have to abide by confidentiality agreements.

    Some information must remain confidential, whether it is the content of a test for the class or a corporate trade secret. Learners are expected, and sometimes legally bound, to keep confidential information private.

You should assume that your learners are honest, ethical people. They may be unaware of ways to document sources, for example, but they basically want to do their work fairly and correctly. Academic dishonesty is often hard to prove, whether you teach on site or online. How can you be sure that each learner wrote a paper on his or her own? How can you tell if each source in a research assignment is accurately documented or simply made up? How do you know if learners interviewed experts as they said they did, or that the information they provide from their company is OK for anyone to know? These types of questions are difficult to answer in all courses, not just those online.

Of course, online education probably comes under closer scrutiny because most teachers cannot see their learners at all. They rely on printouts in a common font, without the possibility of individual handwriting. Even in a chat room, there is no sure way of telling whether the real John Doe is making an insightful comment, or if it is another learner or someone else. Those teachers who see and hear learners during two-way conversations still cannot watch while learners complete every assignment. The responsibility for honesty is the individual learner's, and teachers should assume the best about their learners.

Nevertheless, there are some spot checks you can make to satisfy any requirements about tests for academic honesty in your classroom. Let us look at the four areas of concern mentioned previously and ways to show that learners are, indeed, being scrupulously honest in your course.

1. Learners must do their own work.

You often encourage learners to work together and collaborate in required or personally created learning communities. Realistically, there is no way you can guarantee that one learner was not heavily influenced by another. That is a risk you take when you invite collaboration. However, once you have read a learner's work for awhile, you get a feel for that person's style and general level of understanding of the material. Anything that deviates wildly from the norm might be questioned to see how much the individual has really learned.

In a group project, one learner might do the whole project for everyone else. Most often, learners tell you if anyone disappears from the project or does not contribute. You may prefer to let the group police other matters, such as letting one person take primary control of a project. All learners' names go on the project, and everyone gets the same grade. Most learners have enough self-interest to want to share in the workload, just to ensure a good grade.

Buying and selling research papers on the Internet is big business, so how can you tell if learners are writing their documents? Internet papers may have glaring errors that may not be obvious to people who have not studied the subject carefully, but will be painfully obvious to teachers. Reading the same paper from different people, perhaps over different classes, is another giveaway. To make it more difficult for learners to buy papers, off the Internet or from other learners who have taken the course previously, you can do these simple tasks:

- Change the topic for written assignments every time the course is offered. You do not have to redesign the course site, but phrase the assignments generally enough when you create a course that you can request a specific topic, certain types of sources, or varying lengths to the assignments.
- Vary the papers from individual to group projects, or vice versa.
- Require some sources that have been created since the last time the course was offered, such as recent news broadcasts, new Web sites, and print periodicals. Make your assignments specific enough that the likelihood of another teacher creating the same assignment would be lessened.

2.   Learners must document the sources of information they use in assignments.

You can help students learn an appropriate citation style by providing them with additional exercises, bulletin board or chat discussions about the correct format, and models posted on the course site. You can add links to free sites that provide additional examples and guidelines for using these documentation styles. Learners who have not had to document research papers for awhile may not remember what kinds of information need to be documented, much less the format for that information. Teaching the proper way to document sources is an important part of any course requiring research.

More importantly, you can discuss with learners what needs to be documented and why. Not everyone understands that information available on the Internet is not free for anyone to use, without citing the source of information. Documenting electronic sources of information is especially important to online learners, because they are in the habit of working with computers and may have little time to track down paper documents. Even their interviews with people may be conducted electronically. You need to take the time to explain plagiarism to learners, so that they know how to avoid it, and the penalties if they do not.

How can you tell that learners did not make up sources? You can run a spot check on references, especially those that just do not look right. You might call someone who was interviewed to verify a quotation, look up (online is faster) a periodical to check on an article, or check with the Library of Congress Web site to see if a book exists. Links to Web sites can be checked the next time you go online; although some sites change daily, you can usually find archived information if it is not on a current site. You can require learners to send you copies of e-mail messages (and to explain to the originator of the message that the message will be shared in confidence with the teacher).

3. Learners must complete all course requirements fairly, from class participation and attendance to academic activities.

Again, you cannot determine who *really* is online with you, unless you know the people and what they look and sound like, and you have that technical capability to work face to face online. Until you have that capability and proximity to online learners, you have to trust that the people enrolled in the class are actually the people with whom you are working.

You also cannot tell how much time learners are spending with the material they are supposed to be reading, or watch them complete a simulation, for example. Some online courses are designed to track learners' logins and logoffs, so you can determine how much time is spent at the course site and how many times a learner entered the site. Whether that time was productive is another matter. Learners learn at different rates, too, so there is no certain way to tell if learning takes place during a given amount of computer time.

You can determine how much the learners in your class understand the material by asking them about specific points or examples from the materials. In a chat session, you do not have to quiz on the most minute detail, but you can request enough detail to know if learners are reading assignments and completing activities. During a chat, you can ask learners to back up their statements with examples, dates, statistics, and so on, to see how much they remember (or have documented to bring with them to the chat session).

4.   Learners have to abide by confidentiality agreements.

Learners sometimes use materials from their workplace as a resource for assignments. You might send e-mail to verify with the learner that the employer allows information to be shared with others.

Also, learners should understand that they should not share their user ID, password, or course code with anyone. Even if another learner cannot get credit for taking the class, letting others into what may be considered a secure class site generally violates an institution's policies.

You can state on the course Web site that information from the class site is for learner use only. It is difficult to track down unauthorized use of course materials, but making learners aware of confidentiality agreements is an important part of any class.

Many institutions promote practices that help curb plagiarism. You may want to save all correspondence from learners, as well as assignments, so you can compare writing samples throughout the course. You are more likely to spot discrepancies in expected style or level of competency when you can view all types of discourse from the same student (Heberling, 2002).

Heberling (2002) also recommended that teachers who question the originality of a written work use a "search in reverse" process. By typing the questionable parts of a sentence or descriptive phrases from a paper into a search engine, such as Yahoo or Google, essays or reports using these phrases are called up. A look at the search results can give you an idea if particularly memorable passages are original gems or simply memorable because they were lifted from another work.

You also might check out sites where term papers are sold. You should search for papers dealing with the subject areas you teach. It's also helpful to discuss assignment topics with your colleagues, so if a familiar paper appears in a different course, you and the teacher of that course can compare notes. To help with this process, keep an electronic file of all major papers submitted by learners. If a question arises about an essay written for one of your classes, you can find the learner's old paper in your electronic files and compare it to the work in question.

The majority of learners are honest and do their own work. To uphold course standards and policies against plagiarism, keep careful records and be familiar with routine checking tools. You should develop and promote the ethical standards you believe are appropriate for your course, and take the steps to enforcing these standards.

If plagiarism, for example, is an increasing problem, talk with administrators about requiring students to use a document-checking site. This type of requirement should be implemented throughout the curriculum, so that learners know how to submit work to online checking sites and understand the institution's policies regarding plagiarism.

Plagiarism Software

Many administrators and teachers are concerned that online and on-site learners use the Web as their primary library and the Internet as the medium for gathering information. Although online learners may have electronic access to academic or public libraries, they still may not take the time or have the interest in looking through the library's acquisitions. Because they are used to working and studying via the Internet, they use the Web as their primary source of information.

This trend bothers educators at several levels. Unless learners are aware of the need to evaluate critically every source they encounter on the Internet, they may select those sources that are listed first during a general search. They may not know about or take the time to work with specialized search engines that can help them find sources especially well suited to their research needs. Internet research can be useful, and in online courses is generally expected, but learners should understand or be taught how to use the Web effectively.

Learners also may need instruction in citing sources correctly, following a standardized style manual. They may need additional practice in quoting, paraphrasing, or summarizing information gathered from a source. Some students may not realize that others' information even needs to be cited. After all, the Web contains lots of information that people voluntarily put there. Why would they not want other Web users to freely take their information? Cultural differences in the ways that information is shared also may have an influence on students, as well as other reasons for plagiarism, including lack of interest in the subject and time pressures to complete an assignment (Williams, 2002). Documenting sources, especially those they found quickly on the Web, may need to be a unit within your course, and you may need to explain carefully exactly what plagiarism is and why it is the focus of so much interest.

No matter how much instruction you provide about Internet research and the careful compilation, evaluation, and citation of source materials, some learners may inadvertently or deliberately plagiarize sources. No matter how familiar you are with the Internet and the sources most likely to be used by learners in your course, you cannot know about everything on the Web. You may be able to conduct spot checks of references and check the URLs/URIs of cited sources, but you probably do not have the time to check every reference cited in every assignment submitted by every learner.

As mentioned earlier, many teachers have begun to use plagiarism-checking software when they grade written assignments, or to require learners to submit their papers to a Web site where the information can be matched against commonly used sources. Some information may be found in literally hundreds of different sources, and tracing the one source a learner used may be impossible.

Although not all sources learners use are part of the database against which assignments are matched, just the process of having learners submit their assignments for a check may make some people more careful about the way they use or cite source information. If you or learners use checking software as a guide, most learners will begin to appreciate the seriousness of plagiarism and understand the practical ways to work with sources for their academic assignments.

You may want to experiment with different varieties of programs before the software is selected for your course. However, as the amount of information available through the Internet continues to increase exponentially, more institutions are recommending or requiring learners to work with plagiarism-identifying software. You should evaluate several programs before deciding which one is best for your curriculum.

Ethics Units

Your course may have a built-in unit on ethics, which is gaining popularity in academia. In addition, you might define ethical behavior as part of the course description. Because many companies and professional associations require employees or members to abide by published codes of conduct, you may want to introduce learners to this concept and show them online examples of such codes. These examples can supplement other readings in an ethics unit, or you may refer learners to these codes if they are preparing to enter a profession requiring adherence to specific ethical guidelines.

Professional associations and business organizations often post their codes of conduct, codes of fair practice, or ethics statements on their Web sites. Although individual businesses may not post their codes on the corporate Web site, they may be indexed elsewhere on the Web.

For example, EthicNet is an index of European Codes of Journalism Ethics, listed by country. Illinois Institute of Technology's Center for the Study of Ethics in the Professions has compiled an Index of Codes, including ethics statements from corporations such as IBM; from this list you find links to reproductions of professional associations' and companies' codes.

Codes of ethics for engineers and scientists are indexed by The Online Ethics Center for Engineering and Science. These and other online indexes can help your students learn about behavioral and attitudinal requirements, as well as legal liability, associated with professional ethics.

Figure 6-2. Codes of Ethics

www.acm.org/constitution/code.html
Association for Computing Machinery (ACM) (professional association's code of ethics)

www.bac.co.uk/members_visitors/members_visitors.htm
British Association for Counselling and Psychotherapy (Code of Ethics and Practice for Counsellors)

www.iwanet.org/about/ethics.html
International Webmasters Association (code of ethics for members)

www.hq.nasa.gov/ogc/general_law/ethics/ethicsrules.html#Description
NASA's Ethics Program (description of ethics programs for NASA employees, contractors, and vendors, with links to legal codes and procedures for ethical business)

www.nea.org/aboutnea/code.html
National Education Association's Code of Ethics of the Education Profession

www.oiaa.com
Ontario Insurance Adjuster Association (provincial code of ethics for the insurance industry)

www.rpnas.com/ETHICS.COD.html
Registered Psychiatric Nurses Association of Saskatchewan (Code of Ethics)

www.econbot.org/ethics.html
Society for Economic Botany Guidelines of Professional Ethics

www.stc.org/policy-principals.html
Society for Technical Communication (code of ethics for members)

www.computer.org/tab/seprof/code.htm
Software Engineering Code of Ethics and Professional practice (code recommended by IEEE-CS/ACM)

ethics.state.wi.us/StandardsofConduct/StandardsConduct.htm
State of Wisconsin Ethics Board (ethics statements for state officials, lobbyists, and lobbying organizations)

www.tiaa.net/ethics.htm
Texas Independent Automotive Association (code of ethics for automotive businesses)

Figure 6-2 provides a representative sampling of organizations' and businesses' Web sites that include a link to a code of ethics. The range of associations illustrates some professional codes for different professions. As part of an ethics unit, you can have learners read several statements, especially those representing their professions, and compare them in a chat or bulletin board discussion. You might ask learners to develop a code of ethics for the current class, following closely the academic honesty standards required by the institution.

Another way to promote discussion of ethical dilemmas and positive solutions is to involve learners in role-playing scenarios depicting academic or business dilemmas that they may encounter. Any of the "honesty" situations described in the preceding sections (e.g., learners caught in a time crunch deciding to buy a project from someone who completed the course a year ago) might become the scenario for a good role play.

Role plays of other ethical situations might also make learners aware of racism, ageism, ethnicism, and other –isms. Through course content, discussions, and activities, you can encourage fair, equal treatment of all learners. Discussions, bulletin board posts, and core content linked to your Web site can also make learners aware of legal and moral issues that pertain to their education.

Summary

Building a community while you present information and evaluate learners' understanding of course content is an important job. Through the amount and types of communication you send to learners, the way you handle yourself professionally in the classroom, and the standards you establish and maintain, you create a secure, nurturing learning environment in which all learners feel they can participate freely. The aesthetics of teaching, including upholding standards of academic honesty and ethical behavior, help build successful learning communities.

An important part of effective group interaction is respect and ethical behavior. In-group communication should be supportive, and a variety of perspectives about a topic should be encouraged. As well, the diversity of group members should be appreciated. Learners should interact ethically with each other in group activities and messages to individuals.

One aspect of ethical behavior that may need to be emphasized throughout your course is academic honesty. You may need to develop units about ethics, use of copyrighted information, and source documentation to help learners understand the responsibilities of using others' information correctly within academic assignments.

References

Andrews, D. C. (2002). Audience-specific online community design. *Communications of the ACM, 45*(4), 64-68.

Brown, R. E. (2001, September). The process of community-building in distance learning classes. *Journal of Asynchronous Learning Networks, 5*(2). Retrieved October 1, 2002, from http://www.aln.org/alnweb/journal/Vol5_issue2/Brown/Brown.htm

Center for the Study of Ethics in the Professions. (2002). Illinois Institute of Technology. Codes of ethics online. Retrieved October 1, 2002, from http://www.iit.edu/departments/csep/ PublicWWW/codes/

EthicNet. (2002). Databank for European codes of journalism ethics. Retrieved October 1, 2002, from http://www.uta.fi/laitokset/tiedotus/ethicnet/

Gunawardena, C., Plass, J., & Salisbury, M. (2001). Do we really need an online discussion group? In D. Murphy, R. Walker, & G. Webb (Eds.), *Online learning and teaching with technology: Case studies, experience, and practice* (pp. 36-43). London: Kogan Page Ltd.

Heberling, M. (2002, Spring). Maintaining academic integrity in online education. *Online Journal of Distance Learning Administration, 5*(1). Retrieved October 1, 2002, from http://www.westga.edu/%7Edistance/ojdla/Spring51/heberling51.html

Hiltz, S. R., & Turoff, M. (2002). What makes learning networks effective? *Communications of the ACM, 45*(4), 56-59.

Jonassen, D. H., Peck, K. C., & Wilson, B. G. (1998). *Creating technology-supported learning communities.* Retrieved October 1, 2002, from http://carbon.cudenver.edu/~bwilson/learncomm.html

The learning community and online instruction. (1999). Retrieved May 20, 2000, from http://dldc-course.ext.missouri.edu/dldcwww/dlplanning/learning.html [No longer available]

Milson, A. J., & Chu, B.-W. (2002). Character education for cyberspace: Developing good netizens. *The Social Studies, 93*(3), 117-119. Retrieved August 18, 2002, from ProQuest database.

The Online Ethics Center for Engineering and Science at Case Western Reserve University. (2002). Codes of ethics and conduct. Retrieved October 1, 2002, from http://www.onlineethics.org/codes/index.html

Williams, J. B. (2002). The plagiarism problem: Are students entirely to blame? In A. Williamson, C. Gunn, A. Young, & T. Clear (Eds.), *Winds of Change in the Sea of Learning: Proceedings for the 19th Annual Conference of the Australasian Society for Computers in Learning in Tertiary Education* (pp. 721-730). Auckland, NZ: UNITEC Institute of Technology.

Part 3.

Maintaining the Curriculum

Of course, you don't teach alone. Even if you never see your colleagues in person, you work with them online and should participate in campus activities. You're part of a network of professionals, including administrators, other faculty, staff, and support personnel. Sharing information with colleagues who share your interests in technology and subject matter and working with those who have backgrounds far different from yours help keep you up to date on educational issues and practices.

As online education changes globally, the changes affect individual courses, the entire curriculum, and the online institution as a whole. Perhaps you don't have as much influence over the entire curriculum-development and –modification processes as you'd like, but you still should be involved in the processes of evaluating courses and determining the direction in which online education should go. Several issues in online education, from tenure and promotion for teachers to institutional or programmatic accreditation to information sharing among educational vendors, will continue to have an impact on further changes within the online courses you teach and develop.

Part 3 describes issues for teachers and administrators. Chapter 7. Developing Support Networks has been designed to help teachers develop internal and external support networks that will assist in professional development and daily teaching activities. Support networks differ from learning communities, although both are important to online educators.

Chapter 8. Managing Programs and Faculty Concerns is directed primarily toward administrators at every level of the institution, although teachers should also be interested in the issues discussed in this chapter. Issues that affect teachers, such as time allocations, courseloads, tenure, promotion, and the hiring process, are discussed in Chapter 8.

Finally, Chapter 9. Planning for the Future includes suggestions for teachers for evaluating their own and others' course sites and documenting changes needed to improve the curriculum, as well as individual courses. Chapter 9 also covers broader issues that should be important to administrators: accreditation, the marketing of online programs, strategic planning, and some trends in online education globally that probably will affect institutions at the local level. Helping programs survive and thrive is the emphasis in Chapter 9.

Maintaining an online curriculum is more than keeping the status quo. "Maintaining" involves planning ahead and implementing not only technological changes but philosophical shifts in the way online education is perceived and presented. As online education changes globally, teachers, administrators, and anyone involved in online education must be forward thinking and anticipate how best to meet learners' needs in a challenging environment.

DEVELOPING SUPPORT NETWORKS

7

Teaching online, as you have read in other chapters, is a collaborative effort, even though when you are teaching, you may feel "home alone" when you work online. When you are sitting in front of a computer screen, intellectually you may realize that you are connected to networks of learners, administrators, other teachers, and members of other support networks. However, those people often seem remote when you are working at home around midnight. You and your institution need to develop a series of support networks so that any learner or teacher working online at any time knows that she or he is not alone.

Support networks also provide other types of non-technical support, such as career assistance, general background information, directions for further research, and emotional support. Each is equally important at some point in an online class. These support networks are not ongoing learning communities, but places to go when you need immediate help. Having that support, and also making it available to learners, is important for your success in an online educational environment.

Types of Support Networks

Support networks differ from learning communities in their primary purpose. A support network provides many types of assistance in addition to the possibility of learning about a topic. For example, a support network may provide technical assistance, whether through a FAQ or in-person answers to your questions.

Support networks may be comprised of experts who share their expertise with individuals, institutions, or companies. They may offer special activities, such as workshops, meetings, and conferences. They may publish newsletters, magazines, journals, monographs, reports, or other educational/professional documents. They may create training materials to assist professional development. The types and amount of support vary by the composition of the network, but the network is usually permanent.

You use this information or support system when you need to solve a problem. Usually you are a passive participant initially, a user instead of a creator or sharer of information. Instead of regularly meeting with a learning community and participating in ongoing educational activities, you turn to a support network to receive assistance to solve a particular problem. Later, you also may volunteer to offer assistance based on your experience, but initially when you use a support network, you truly are the user. That is not to say that learning communities are not supportive—they are, and they provide valuable sources of information. In fact, the professionals who answer your initial questions may become a member of a learning community that you form or in which you participate. A support network, however, has a more immediate use and helps you solve a problem right away.

The amount of time you spend with a support network is probably less than you spend working with a learning community. You tend to use support networks infrequently—only when you have a problem or an immediate need—and then work on your own once the problem is solved or the need met. Unlike a learning community, in which you actively participate on a regular basis or to meet an ongoing educational need, a support network gives you whatever type of support you need until you can work effectively on your own.

Support networks may be internal or external. Many internal support networks are made up of colleagues at an institution who develop and disseminate online information and work with a common curriculum. These internal support networks of course designers, administrators, and technical support staff are critical to your ability to function in a computerized environment and to teach or train others successfully online.

Although these networks are valuable, you also find some external support networks to keep your teaching up to date and to help you find appropriate resources for learners studying specific subject areas. You need support networks to help you develop more effective online education designs and course materials and to provide technical assistance. External support networks help you validate your teaching methods and strategies and indicate what needs to be updated. They also allow you to share your expertise and become a resource for other professionals.

Internal Technical Support Networks

Technical support is an important type of support network. The institution should have a reliable, efficient technical staff that can do the following:

- Answer questions through e-mail, phone, or other media quickly and accurately
- Be available as much as possible, especially during hours when learners and faculty are more likely to be working online
- Provide non-technical answers and solutions to inquiries and problems
- Demonstrate software and hardware

- Troubleshoot courseware, e-mail, and Web site problems
- Advise faculty about future software, hardware, or network upgrades

Some technical support teams also train faculty, install and maintain software and hardware, maintain the local network, plan upgrades and changes, and generally guide the institution in computerization. They may also develop documentation, such as training guides or manuals, instruction sheets, and FAQ lists. Technical support is a crucial part of a successful online educational program, and your institution should have the adequate technical support to offer online courses.

Technical help should always be available, and real people should be online or available by phone or in person, as necessary. Just as online education never really ends and is "always open for business," so should support networks be available 24/7/365. In an online, international environment, it is always a typical work day somewhere. Even if your institution's buildings close, its Web presence is still open and active.

If maintenance or server downtimes are scheduled, they usually take place when the university's on-campus faculty and staff are less likely to be around. Weekends and nights are common times for the system to go down. However, if you are teaching online, the convenient downtimes for people working online may not be so convenient. Online learners often work at atypical times for a "normal" work week, and international learners may find the scheduled downtimes take place in the middle of their business day.

Of course, no schedule can please everyone, and equipment does require service and maintenance. In addition to knowing the traditional technical support people for the university or college, you also need to develop a technical support hotline or backup plans for your class.

Official Technical Support for Students

On your course site or the bulletin board, and possibly in an early e-mail message, you should publish all important technical support information provided by the university or college. The times and days of technical support's operation, the type of assistance (e.g., by phone or e-mail, through a Web site), the type of information learners need to provide, and the types of available assistance should be explained. This boilerplated information should be kept current and given in several forms to each learner who takes your course.

If your institution lacks a formal technical support network, you have to develop one yourself from colleagues who know more than you do about hardware, software, and networks. You also need to work closely with course designers (if you were not involved in the initial design process) so that you can understand why and how the Web site and course materials were developed as they were—and what to do if the course site does not operate as expected.

At the least you need a list of e-mail addresses and phone numbers, plus some bookmarks to sites that provide useful, easily accessed technical information. Your list should note people resources—those colleagues on whom you can call for a quick response to your question—as well as documentation resources—such as FAQ lists, online Help, and instruction sheets.

In-Class Technical Support

In a well-designed course, instructions for using classroom tools and how-to information for specific assignments should be included at the course site. However, learners new to the online environment may need additional guidance with logging into a chat room, posting messages in a new or an existing thread or discussion folder, or accessing a whiteboard, for example.

Learners across the class may use a variety of browsers or different versions of a browser, which may not be compatible with the course design. Not all browsers treat Web-based information the same way, and individual class members may need to know if their difficulty is related to the course site, their browser, or another factor. These are typical problems facing online teachers, especially early in a course.

Although a Help Desk or Technology Hotline also should be able to solve these problems, some new class members may be shy about asking formally for help. They usually prefer to ask the teacher or each other first. Using the course bulletin board as an in-class source of help can help learners as a group solve their own problems, and often common interests or friendships developed by helping one another can lead to an ongoing learning community.

Learners may want to keep track of problems and solutions to their common problems in a separate bulletin board folder. Helping each other or just reading through the list of problems and solutions—or multiple approaches to solving the same problem—can be very helpful and provide effective, casual technical support. Usually at least a few students taking an online course are majoring in computer science, information technology, systems design, software development, or another computer-oriented technical area. These students may be able to offer some helpful tips or general troubleshooting guidelines to solve an immediate problem. However, once the crisis has been averted, the university's or college's Help staff should be consulted to prevent further problems and to ensure that learners are using the university's/college's established computer network as they should.

You may want to develop a technical FAQ list and post it on the bulletin board or elsewhere at the course site. A list of common technical problems and the ways the official Help staff suggest to prevent or correct them can make learners feel less intimidated because of the glitch and give them readily available, private technical assistance.

Of course, if someone cannot get into the course site, the information located there is not very helpful. You also should keep a copy of the FAQ list handy so you can answer questions by e-mail, fax, or phone. The institution's official Help staff also should be available by phone to help learners who cannot work online at that time.

Finally, give learners a backup or emergency e-mail address so they can contact you electronically if the class-based e-mail system is not working. A Web-based e-mail system may be helpful as your backup so that you can access your e-mail from any public or private computer without forwarding mail through a POP mail account. Having a backup e-mail address is worth the hassle of receiving duplicate messages from class members or having learners send e-mail to the backup instead of the primary account.

The university or college may have a strict policy about the e-mail address that must be used for submitting assignments to teachers or for other class issues. The backup address should be reserved for emergency use only, and you may need to remind learners of that if they send non-emergency messages to a non-university/college e-mail account. As a last resort, you can refuse to reply to non-emergency messages sent to your backup address, if learners persistently avoid using your official address for tasks like submitting assignments. You want to be accessible but still follow the institutional policies for class activities. Offering an emergency e-mail address is a good backup plan, but it should supplement, not contradict, institutional policies.

If you want class members to contact you by other than electronic means, you may want to give them a phone number and/or a fax number so they can call you or send you information in a technical emergency. However, you may want to establish times and reasons why learners use these forms of communication if the class is supposed to operate only online. You or your institution's flexibility in the types of acceptable communication with online learners should dictate the number of communication backups you offer.

Technical Support Networks for Teachers

Administrators must plan ways for teachers to receive the technical support they need, not only in course development or redesign, but also with daily teaching activities. Links to the Help staff should be readily available to you, as much as to your students.

Technical support should be advertised to prospective teachers through the institution's Web site, too. Prospective employees often check out the university's or college's Web site as they decide whether to apply for a teaching position. If technical support is not mentioned or highlighted in some way from the institution's faculty resources, home, or technical assistance pages, potential teachers may get the idea that technical support is not a high priority for the administration.

To indicate the institution's ongoing support of faculty and students, administrators should make sure that descriptive information about the level and availability of technical support is easy to find. The University of Phoenix Online, for example, describes "complete technical support" that is available to faculty and learners 24 hours each day. This statement is located after the Software and Hardware Standards list and is clearly displayed on the site's How It Works page. Stating the institution's commitment to ongoing technical support is a selling point for both teachers and learners.

External Technical Support Networks

Manufacturers of hardware and software may provide you with additional documentation that can be used to solve learners' technical problems or provide them with user-friendly guidance on making the most of their computer systems. Free documentation linked to a company's Web site and tips provided by online user groups may give you and other class members better ideas about how to troubleshoot problems or find new shortcuts to common tasks.

Before a course begins, you may want to browse the Internet to locate appropriate external Web sites, newsgroups, bulletin boards, or other places where learners can gather more technical information about the software needed in the course or the typical types of hardware learners need to operate in order to use the course Web site. In addition, you may want to subscribe to online newsletters or read technical publications to keep up to date with changes in the technology. The more you know, the more you can help learners troubleshoot typical problems they may have with the course site, networks, browsers, hardware, and software.

Non-Technical Internal Support Networks for Faculty

Other types of internal support networks should be formed within your institution, not only for teachers, but also for anyone who is taking or plans to take online courses. Administrators often play the initial role in setting up internal support networks, although individual teachers may also develop their own networks of colleagues who provide assistance and information. Internal support networks can include university or college committees at the departmental or institutional levels, faculty bulletin boards, and faculty chat rooms.

Committees

Academic or programmatic support also may be provided by ad hoc or standing committees within the institution. If you work only online, you may need to conduct research to find out which committees have been formed on the campus and how these groups function.

You also need to keep up to date about new policies and procedures being discussed or implemented by the institution. Changes on site regarding technology probably will have an impact on your online classes. It pays off to know about on-site, institutional committees. You might find technology issues debated in committees dealing with the following:

- Computer purchasing and leasing
- Computer training
- Computer users' groups
- Continuing education
- Educational technology
- Human Resources training or policy creation
- Information technology
- Tenure and promotion

Try to find a schedule of meetings held throughout the academic year. As well, locate a list of faculty and administrators who participate in these and similar types of policy-making bodies that may have an effect on the amount and types of computer technology used in your classes; the structure, growth, and maintenance of online programs; and assistance to faculty who teach in those programs.

You should keep in touch with on-site and online program coordinators to keep abreast of business decisions about everything from hardware, software, and network purchases to future directions for technology use to expansion/reduction plans for online education to faculty issues like training and salaries. Keep a list of departmental committee members, and discuss current curricular issues with faculty who teach online.

Unfortunately, online faculty often have to take the initiative for volunteering for committees or at least keeping up with technology-related groups on site. Adjunct faculty often are not contractually obligated or encouraged to serve on institutional committees, but if you are an adjunct, you still can contact committee representatives to see what is going on and to voice your comments.

This type of institutional information network can be a lifeline. You need to know what is going on within the institution and have a list of contact people who can answer your questions or voice your ideas in committees.

To help develop a strong internal support network (or several such networks), try the following:

- Attend at least one on-site or online meeting or conference each term—more if you can.
- Join or create a mailing list of online teachers at your institution.
- Participate in technology-related in-service programs or online workshops.
- Participate in bulletin board discussions.
- Document your ideas for online curriculum development, back them up with additional research, and present them to your supervisors or committee representatives.
- Keep up with information technology and educational technology news and developments.
- Be proactive in your academic involvement. Volunteer. Report. Document. Question. Discuss.
- Keep in touch with your mentor. Seek advice.

Be as actively involved with online educational policies and practices, not only so that you can develop curricula and courses that are up to date and relevant, but also so you can influence, not just be influenced by, the decisionmakers in your institution.

Faculty Bulletin Boards and Chat Rooms

Program coordinators or supervisors of online faculty, as well as higher-level administrators, should encourage faculty to participate in discussions about their courses, the curriculum, and the institution's policies for online education. Administrators must develop several venues, at different levels in the institutional hierarchy, for faculty to discuss online teaching issues and share information that can help support course and curriculum development. A university-wide bulletin board or series of scheduled and publicized chat sessions among upper-level administrators and faculty can be used to discuss curriculum planning, technology changes, and strategic planning, for example.

At the program level, bulletin boards just for faculty teaching in that program are a good place to make announcements, share teaching tips, and troubleshoot technical problems. An informal chat room that is always open can be a place for faculty to drop in to see who is there and to talk casually. Scheduled chats, such as online program faculty meetings, more formally address concerns and successes offered by faculty members.

The flow of information across the institution regarding immediate and future issues must be shared among all administrators and faculty, and bulletin boards and chat sessions are just two ways to begin that sharing of information.

External Support Networks for Faculty

External support networks are links outside the immediate university or college, although they may be affiliated with individual faculty or administrators, organizations with a chapter housed at the institution, departments, or programs. These external networks may provide contacts for membership and collaborative opportunities within groups. However, they may also be more passive but highly effective sources of information, such as professional publications.

Lynch (2002) reminded educators and administrators that faculty who are new to online teaching need access to lots of resources as they make the transition to online work. Best practices, examples, models, research, and teaching tips are especially important to new online educators. Administrators must plan ways for all faculty, although new or untenured faculty especially may need these resources, to learn about external support networks and the types of resources they make available to online teachers. Information about faculty resources should be prominently displayed at the university's or college's Web site, and there are many effective ways to include this information in the institution's Web design.

Kentucky Virtual University (2002) highlights a link to Faculty Resources, which is a well-developed series of helpfully linked list items to many different types of internal and external resources. The Course Development section links teachers to articles about best educational practices, seminars and conferences, and checklists for developing teaching materials.

The California Virtual Campus (2002) directly links its Professional Development Center to the institutional home page. The Center's tabbed sections guide teachers to more information and links regarding communities, conferences, and training, among other resources. The Communities section provides links to academic communities, technical support, and institutional support. If prospective teachers browse this site, they will probably be impressed with the number and variety of available resources.

If the university or college is part of an online educational consortium, consisting of several institutions that share resources, the professional development, technical support, and faculty resources information un-doubtedly will be more developed and include links to many external entities that share information with all the member institutions. For example, the American Distance Education Consortium's home page (2002a) highlights menu links to many topics of interest to online educators. Courseware, online resources, Internet trends, conferences, workshops, standards, accessibility, and security are just some issues highlighted on the home page. When teachers click the Online Resources button from the home page, they find multiple screens/pages of links to articles, application forms, presentations, and organizations that can provide detailed information about a wide range of topics. Everything from digital libraries to American Indian resources to research projects to newsletters to articles debating privacy policies can be found in the lists of links. Administrators whose institutions have created a consortium to share resources should make faculty in the affiliated universities and colleges aware of the array of resources available to them. Part of the benefit of participating in a consortium is information sharing, and developing faculty support net-works through links with institutions in the consortia is a valuable result of this information sharing.

These three examples illustrate how administrators can help develop and promote faculty support networks. Of course, the networks are only effective if teachers take advantage of the resources available to them. If your institution provides lists of faculty resources or links to external support networks, visit these networks and share information with your colleagues about which resources have been most helpful to your teaching and professional development.

Professional Associations

Outside of your classes and collaboration with colleagues, you are probably part of several groups. Within your community, you may be a soccer parent, Shriner, zoo volunteer, Democrat, etc. You have a life outside of your employment, and your other interests and networks can provide you with valuable resources that may be appropriate for use in the online classroom. Your associations and affiliations may pertain directly to what you teach, or they may be more general. You may be interested in becoming a member of professional associations involved with distance education, or you may prefer that your memberships focus on a specific subject area that you teach. The wider your interests, the greater the number of possible learning communities and support networks you may join or create.

The people whom you meet through a professional association may become mentors for your students: They may participate in an online chat session, work with learners through a mailing list, and provide documents, Web sites, and interviews that can become part of the class' Web-site information. Most professional associations publish information that might be helpful to your students and maintain a Web site to which you might refer learners.

Print and electronic resources are an important support service. They indicate in which content areas you are up to date and where you can go to develop new skills and gain new information when your knowledge or skills base is out of date. They are impersonal resources in that you can access them in print or through a Web site; you do not have to talk to anyone to gain valuable links to new sources of information. The support network provides information that you can access at any time, from just about anywhere.

Your affiliation with a professional association provides you with more personal resources for your online courses, too. Through meetings and conferences, you learn what other people are doing in online education, so you can begin to update (or suggest changes to) the classes that you teach. Through your discussions, in person and online, with other educators, you learn how they have solved technical and logistical problems in their Internet-based courses.

As a support network, a professional association likely offers personal assistance through an office of friendly people who are available by phone, fax, e-mail, and mail to answer questions, link members to resources, or accept information to share with other members. Office staff balances the need for electronic, Internet-based resources with a human connection.

If you are specifically interested in associations that study and promote distance learning, including online education, you might check into these (as well as many other) associations internationally: the American Distance Education Consortium (ADEC, 2002b), the Open and Distance Learning Association of Australia (ODLAA), Canadian Association for Distance Education (CADE), the American Center for the Study of Distance Education (ACSDE), the European Distance Education Network (EDEN), the United States Distance Learning Association (USDLA), or the World Association for Online Education (WAOE). As well, universities and colleges worldwide host distance education centers and consortia; in the United States, several states, including California, Texas, and Florida, have regional associations to promote distance learning.

The Commonwealth of Learning, a Canadian organization, may provide additional resources through their Web site (www.col.org). The Learning Technology Task Force (LTTF) of the Institute of Electrical and Electronic Engineers (IEEE) lists links to the International Forum of Educational Technology and Society, which offers online discussions and a mailing list through Distancelearn.about.com. You should check out local and regional, as well as national and international associations, to determine which groups are best for your professional growth.

Bookmark the sites that interest you now, but conduct monthly searches to find new sources or update these bookmarks. Because many sites are offered, you may want to experiment with several resources to see which are going to be most valuable to you, or which networks allow you to get answers to your questions most easily.

Many professional associations offer similar benefits and services. If you are teaching a course in your area of expertise, see if your local chapter or national/international headquarters can provide you with information or contacts that may be useful as you develop new materials and assignments for your classes.

If you are a member of several professional associations, you expand your networks that much more. Usually you find several associations that share interest in a general subject area. These sub-interests of your general interest areas may lead you to different associations whose members specialize in a related discipline. By becoming a member of several learning communities, you add to your list of contacts to work with students or to provide core information for courses. You also learn about many different aspects of a single profession or subject area.

Here are a few ways you can become a part of or work with support networks:

- Join one or more professional associations.
- Join a special interest group (SIG) or two within a professional association.
- Read the literature produced by these associations to learn more about the subject and what is new, as well as to see if any materials may be useful to learners. Some journals and newsletters are found in print and at a Web site; others are purely electronic or print publications. Check them all. (Remember to get permission before you link the class site to another site or reproduce information.)
- Attend meetings, virtual or on site, to learn more about specific subjects and make contacts with other members.
- Participate in a mailing list, bulletin board, or chat.
- Bookmark the association's Web site, and check the site frequently for updates, announcements, and possible links of interest to your students.
- Create an e-mail or group list of people you have met who share similar interests and can share information that may be useful to you or your students.

Of course, not only professional associations can provide you with information that might be useful in your professional development or course design. Friendships that you develop with other parents whose children go to the same school, play in the band, run a fundraiser, and so on might become part of your support network or learning community. People with whom you work on a civic committee, neighbors on your block, and people in your yoga class may surprise you with the common interests you share or the useful tidbits they know and are willing to discuss. Use the many learning communities of which you are a part to help you expand your knowledge of current topics, as well as specific interests. Branching outward with your learning communities can help you filter information that can help students in many unexpected ways.

Educational Networks and Publications

A computer search through an often-used search engine like Yahoo, Excite, Webcrawler or a megasearch engine like Dogpile or AskJeeves can give you links to thousands of sites involving some aspect of distance education. However, you need to remember that not all distance education is online education. You have to sort through many sites to find the most useful ones for the type of course you teach, the venue and technology you use, and the age and experience level of learners in your classes.

Because online education is a booming business, you will find lots of sites promoting a vendor's products and services. Although commercial sites are designed to market a company's programs and the technology to support them, you still can get some good ideas about what is current and upcoming in online education by visiting vendor sites.

As well, many companies also provide newsletters about online education or technology, hoping that you will join their mailing list not only to receive e-mailed newsletters, but also advertisements or announcements. You may not want to join every newsletter mailing list you find on the Web, but a look at archived issues may give you an idea if a particular newsletter is worth a subscription.

In addition to commercial sites, particularly higher education is involved with many distance-learning sites. Some may promote only their courses, but you will also find research information and notices about conferences and publications at many Web sites. Again, you need to browse through academic sites to see which ones are valuable enough to bookmark and peruse at length.

As a starting point, Table 7-1 lists sites that deal with information ranging from distance education in general (although they provide information about online education specifically) to sites designed for teachers of K-12 in the U.S. to university courses internationally. The sites, including links to newsletters, journals, and associations, give you an overview of a vast, rapidly growing segment of the Web universe.

Web-site information changes rapidly, and any URLs/URIs listed here may change by the time you want to use them. However, these sites have been viable for a long time, and the associations of which they are a part may change their address, but they are likely to be around for a lot longer. If a particular URL/URI does not work, you can conduct a search to find the latest address.

Because so much information explodes onto the Internet each week, additional networks and sites are bound to be added to your personal list of favorite Web sites. However, the following list should provide you with a starting place for finding an online network that can assist you in learning more about online education or in developing specific materials for your courses.

In addition to the professional associations listed in the previous section, you might find newsletters and journals from these or similar associations useful as resources or links in a support network. Table 7-1 describes some example publications from an ever-increasing number of online newsletters and e-journals.

A master list of international newsletters and journals is maintained by The International Centre for Distance Learning (ICDL). Many universities and libraries have similar lists that you may want to compare. The ICDL list is useful because it provides a brief description of the newsletter, in print and online, and the contact information for finding the newsletter or journal or subscribing by mail.

Other sites also provide lists of associations, consortia, academic sites, commercial sites, publications, and conferences dealing with various aspects of distance learning. A few others are listed in Table 7-2.

Table 7-1. Online Newsletters and E-journals

	Title	URL/Listserv	Description
Newsletters	Virtual University Gazette	www.geteducated.com or www.geteducated.com/vugaz.htm	This free monthly electronic newsletter is sent to more than 30,000 e-mail subscribers. If you want to learn more about consulting services, online courses, and other topics of interest, check www.geteducated.com, the general Web site. If you are only interested in the newsletter, go to www.geteducated.com/vugaz.htm. There you can subscribe to the newsletter, which you will receive each month in your e-mail. You also can read previous issues archived at the Web site. Subjects range from corporate and academic courses to hot topics of concern.
	Networking	www.thenode.org/networking	This bulletin offers information about what is happening in distance education within Canadian schools.
	World Link	www.cyberbee.com	K-12 teachers may find the curriculum ideas, research tools, links, articles, and conference notes at this site useful. The home page has a link to newsletters. Although the focus is on integrating Internet use in a traditional classroom, many curriculum ideas can be applied to purely online classes. Ideas used in lower grades can be upgraded for use in adult-level courses.
Journals	The American Journal of Distance Education (AJDE)	www.ed.psu.edu/acsde	Documentation, monographs, articles, and other research tools are featured in this publication.
	Bulla Gymnasia Virtuales	www.cybercorp.net/gymv/bulla or by e-mail at majordomo@cybercorp.net	You can receive this newsletter either through the Web site or by e-mail.
	The Chronicle of Higher Education, Distance Education	chronicle.com/distance	Although articles from the print version are also found online, the distance education section is updated frequently online with news.
	Distance Education Journal	www.usq.edu.au/dec/decjourn/demain.htm	A refereed journal, this publication from the University of Southern Queensland includes research articles and book reviews. Volume 22, Number 2 is the last issue at this site.
	Distance Education Journal, Open and Distance Learning Association of Australia	www.odlaa.org/publications.htm	This refereed journal is now available by subscription (as well as with membership) through links at this site. The publisher, beginning with Volume 23, Number 1 (2002), can be contacted at www.tandf.co.uk/journals/carfax/01587919.htm.
	e-Journal of Instructional Science and Technology	www.usq.edu.au/electpub/e-jist/	Also from the University of Southern Queensland's Distance Education Centre, the journal describes technology trends.
	ED, Education at a Distance	www.usdla.org/html/membership/publications.htm	The United States Distance Learning Association produces this monthly e-journal. Current and past issues are linked to the ED site.
	EDPOLYAR (Educational Policy Analysis Archive)	epaa.asu.edu	This journal is an outgrowth of the Edpolyar peer-reviewed list providing articles about educational policy analysis.

Table 7-1. Online Newsletters and E-journals (continued)

Journals	Vanderbilt University's Journal of Asynchronous Learning Networks	www.aln.org/alnweb/journal/jaln.htm	Models of online learning are featured in this journal.
	WWW Journal of Online Education (JOE)	www.nyu.edu/classes/keefer/waoe/waoej.html	This journal emphasizes online education specifically and highlights creative approaches to online course design. Global communication and the Internet culture are covered in some articles.
	West Georgia University, Journal of Library Services for Distance Education	www.westga.edu/library/jlsde	Although this refereed electronic journal focuses on university-level library services for students in distance education programs, the articles may be useful to university teachers in general.
	West Georgia State University Online Journal of Distance Learning Administration	www.westga.edu/~distance/jmain11.html	A related e-journal to the previous entry may be helpful to course designers and administrators. Although the scope of these U.S. journals is narrower than some other sites and publications listed in this chapter, the quality of the information is high, and you may find specific articles especially of use for professional development.
	Distance Educator	www.distance-educator.com	The commercial site gives something to everyone interested in electronic education. You can sign up to receive international daily news highlights from the world of distance education. Other links allow you to chat with a learning community of educators. Another link provides you with the latest issues of *DE* (www.distance-educator.com/de_ezine). Much information in this e-zine is about higher technology as it is used in the classroom or training center; videoconferencing and streaming video are described. You find lots of product information at this site, but if you are looking for commercial trends in technology, you probably want to read a few issues of the e-zine.
	On the Horizon	www.emeraldinsight.com	This journal offers a strategic planning resource for educational professionals. Submissions can be sent by e-mail.
	Journal of Computer Assisted Learning	www.blackwell-synergy.com	The online journal is available by subscription through Blackwell publications.
	Campus-Wide Information Systems	www.emeraldinsight.com/cwis.htm	Higher education professionals can submit articles by e-mail to this e-journal.
	British Journal of Educational Technology	www.blackwellpublishers.co.uk/journals/bjet	Subscriptions to this UK-based journal for educators can be made through Blackwell.
	Education, Communication & Information	www.tandf.co.uk/journals	This journal is one of several e-journals provided through Taylor & Francis. It is focused on the interaction of innovations in educational theory, practice, and technologies.
	Educational Media International	www.tandf.co.uk/journals	This journal is one of several e-journals provided through Taylor & Francis. This one emphasizes new developments in educational and mass media.
	Innovations in Education and Teaching International	www.tandf.co.uk/journals	This journal is one of several e-journals provided through Taylor & Francis. New developments in educational technology are featured.

Table 7-1. Online Newsletters and E-journals (continued)

Journals			
	Open Learning	www.tandf.co.uk/journals	This journal is one of several e-journals provided through Taylor & Francis. The journal covers international education and training, theory and practice.
	Educational Technology & Society	ifets.ieee.org/periodical	This journal is published by the International Forum of Educational Technology and Society and the IEEE Learning Technology Task Force. It has been designed for developers of educational systems, educators, and AI researchers.
	Polish Online Journal	lttf.ieee.org/we/	This bimonthly distance education journal provides articles both in Polish and English.

Table 7-2. Sources of Online Lists

Open Directory, Distance Learning Journals	dmoz.org/Reference/Education/ Distance_Learning/Journals	This site provides a list of journals.
Oak Ridge Research	www.oak-ridge.com/ierdrep1. html	The site lists journals, mailing lists, and discussion groups related to distance education and provides links to other newsletters and research tools. This site is especially useful to university-level teachers and researchers. Adult and continuing education information also is provided.
Central Missouri State University	library.cmsu.edu/disted/dis/ DISTEDII.html#Journals	A good list of library references is provided by the university. The site gives you links to listservs, books, journals, and newsletters that you may want students to review.
Distance Learn.About	distancelearn.about.com/ education/distancelearn	This commercial site offers links to newsletters, other Web sites with general information about distance education, and organiza- tions. The site is designed to appeal to all levels of educators, K-university.
Learning Technology Task Force (IEEE)	lttf.ieee.org	This group with IEEE provides lists of information and maintains an e-journal, among other tasks.
Online Collaborative Learning in Higher Education	musgrave.cqu.edu.au/clp	This Australian Web site offers links and information about best practices.

As you can tell from these selected publications, sites, and lists, just about every aspect of distance education is covered, and much information relates specifically to online education. The type of information varies from theoretical to practical, high tech to low tech, refereed to volunteered. Commercial sites and academic forums are well represented on the Internet.

You can add to these starting points with your own research. Online education is a hot topic, and lots of information is available in print and on the Internet. As the number of academic and commercial vendors increases, so does the amount of information about online education. The trick is to monitor sites that are most useful to you and periodically conduct additional searches to find new sources of information.

In addition to learning from these sites and organizations, you also have something to offer them. Forming support networks is not just a one-way activity in which you receive the benefits of learning from others' experience and having places to go for and people who will help you with information about education- or your specialization-related topics. You also may offer expertise based on your increasing number of experiences and knowledge.

Electronic or print newsletters, journals, and magazines may solicit articles, helpful tips, or research from teachers and trainers. Researching, writing, and submitting articles to publications is not only a way to help support a network of professionals with similar interests, but also a way to let others know about you specifically. Your circle of connections and support can only grow as you share your ideas and expertise with others.

If writing for print publications is not your favorite sharing activity, you might want to participate in meetings, conferences, or workshops where you can deliver information in person and interact with others (face to face or electronically) to collaborate on projects or discuss current issues. These meetings help you expand your support network and allow the network to grow stronger, as more people participate.

Based on your knowledge of specific groups and publications, you might encourage administrators or managers to enter a consortium with other like-minded institutions or businesses. You may want to suggest a new publication or the formation of a professional group founded by your institution or company. Expanding the professional network, at the individual as well as the institutional or corporate level, is crucial for the growth and effectiveness of support networks.

Newsgroups and Mailing Lists

You can create a newsgroup or mailing list made up of participants from your other learning communities or contacts from internal or external support networks. Groupware programs are an easy way to make sure everyone gets the same information. Group e-mail, chat sessions, and mailing lists are great ways to make sure everyone receives notices, news, and announcements of events. A support network can grow into a learning community, as news and announcements are shared and archived.

Several mailing lists and newsgroups for people specifically interested in distance education already exist. You may want to visit them and decide if you want to join one or more groups. As with the lists of links and e-publications, the following lists are representative of a wide range of groups and lists available through the Internet. These are meant to provide a starting point for your research and participation.

Table 7-3 highlights some commonly referenced distance education discussion groups and mailing lists.

Other lists encourage participants to discuss higher education, adult education, information technology, learning styles, and educational policies, for example. Numerous discussion groups, newsgroups, chat rooms, and mailing lists allow educators to discuss hot topics. You should check for lists and groups pertaining to your particular subject areas of interest, as well as the levels of technology in which you are interested.

Table 7-3. Newsgroups and Mailing Lists

Information about newsgroups and mailing lists can be found through these links and associations or academic institutions that house these groups and lists.

Newsgroup for Distance Education	news:alt.education.distance
Online Education Interest Group, Melbourne University	www.edfac.unimelb.edu.au/online-ed
ADLTED-L, Canadian Adult Education Network	majordomo@oise.utoronto.ca
ADLTMETH-L, Adult Education Teaching Methods List	listserv@TAMUK.EDU
AEDNET, Adult Education Network	listserv@alpha.acast.nova.edu or Listproc@pulsar.acast.nova.edu
DEOS-L, International Discussion Forum For Distance Learning	listserv@LISTS.PSU.EDU
DISTED	listserv@psu.edu or listserv@uwavm.bitnet
EDTECH-L, Educational Technology	listserv@VM.CC.PURDUE.EDU
OCC-L, Online College Classroom	listproc@hawaii.edu
ONLINE-ED	graeme.hart@whirligig.com.au
RESODLAA, Research Special Interest Group of the Open and Distance Learning Association of Australia	majordomo@usq.edu.au
STLHE-L, Forum for Teaching and Learning in Higher Education	listserv@listserv.unb.ca

Summary

Implementing curricular changes and keeping your courses up to date require you to work with support networks. You cannot possibly know all that you need to plan curriculum changes, participate in a university's or college's strategic planning, or simply answer all the content and technical questions learners may ask in each class. Internal support networks can help you solve immediate problems faced by class members and keep you up to date on the institution's policies and plans regarding online education. External support networks can help you see the bigger picture of online education outside the institution where you teach and give you information to provide to administrators and faculty when decisions about online education need to be made.

It is easy to log off and feel removed from the action when you work only online. To ensure you can give or get assistance with your courses and changing technologies, you need actively to seek out or create new support networks. Working online means that you have access to many electronic resources; however, you also need to connect with people who, just like you, teach online and face the same challenges, problems, and opportunities to succeed.

In addition to support networks for your peace of mind and practical application, learners taking your classes also need support from you and the institution. It is often up to you to develop support networks for members of your classes. Create FAQs, and send messages that provide professional and technical support for learners.

Keep involved with your institution and its policies and procedures. Develop contacts who can answer your questions or relay your helpful suggestions or advice to others. That sounds like an easy process, but, if anything, you probably have too many Internet resources available to you. Information overload is a problem with Web use today, and you simply have to browse when you can. The lists and links in this chapter give you a starting point for your online research, but you will need to expand or narrow your research, depending upon your interests and experiences with online education.

In addition to seeing what others have done in their programs, you may want to take a free course offered through a vendor, just to see how others structure their courses and use technology. Free classes are available through the Web, and most are non-credit. Pick an interest area you want to explore in more detail, and experiment as an online student. Experience is a valuable online resource.

Internal and external support networks can only support you if you seek them out. Work with a variety of resources, not only when you are hurriedly trying to find an answer to an immediate problem, but later, when you have more time to see what else is available to you to make your teaching more effective and pleasurable.

References

The American Distance Education Consortium. (2002a). ADEC Distance Education Consortium home page. Retrieved October 1, 2002, from http://www.adec.edu

The American Distance Education Consortium. (2002b). Online resources. Retrieved October 1, 2002, from http://www.adec.edu/online-resources.html

California Virtual Campus. (2002). CVC Professional Development Center. Retrieved October 1, 2002, from http://pdc.cvc.edu/common/home

IEEE Computer Society, Learning Technology Task Force (LTTF). (2002). Institute of Electrical and Electronic Engineers (IEEE). Retrieved October 1, 2002, from http://lttf.ieee.org

The International Centre for Distance Learning (ICDL). (2002). Literature. Retrieved October 1, 2002, from http://www-icdl.open.ac.uk/lit2k/

Kentucky Virtual University. (2002). Faculty resources. Retrieved October 1, 2002, from http://www.kcvu.org/partners/f-resources.asp

Lynch, M. M. (2002). *The online educator: A guide to creating the virtual classroom.* London: RoutledgeFalmer.

University of Phoenix. (2002). How it works. Retrieved October 1, 2002, from http://www.uoponline.com/how.asp

MANAGING PROGRAMS AND FACULTY CONCERNS

As online education moved from being a fad to a money-maker, many institutions, businesses, and individuals jumped at the chance to offer online courses. As mentioned in previous chapters, not all courses are created equally, and not all curricula have been designed to work well online.

Perhaps because of the way online education has been introduced on many university campuses, faculty who have not taught online may be suspicious of colleagues who do. Fear about the quality of an online curriculum may deter faculty from participating in its development. As well, those who have had a bad experience in developing a course for their institution may be negative toward online education as a whole. How can administrators and faculty make sure that online education is considered equally important (but not more or less so) than on-site classes in an institution that offers both?

Rahman (2001) emphasized that leaders among faculty and administrators must support online programs if they are going to survive, much less thrive. As well, the faculty in general must support and participate in online education at their institution for the programs to be successful. It takes the entire university/college community working together to make sure that online programs are worthwhile and receive the support at all levels needed for program development and implementation.

Sometimes that support is difficult to get, as many faculty familiar with teaching on site and leery of technology do not see the need for online education and do not want to teach an online course, much less participate in a fully online curriculum. Johannesen and Eide (2000) described teachers feeling threatened by new technology and fearing that in the push for online experience they might become superfluous. Although Johannesen and Eide pointed out that teachers will not be made redundant by computer technology, many teachers worry that automated academic programs will take over not only online education, but hybrid on-site classes as well. There is concern about the continuing importance of teachers to guide learners or help them make meaning from diverse sources of information. If the Internet becomes the key provider of information, and learners can access it on their own to complete predetermined assignments, there is a fear that teachers may not be necessary. Even feedback and grading can be automated functions of an online system.   The changing nature of education naturally involves changes in academic structures and the expectations of teachers and administrators, as well as learners. However, fears and concerns about changes within academia must be faced and alleviated before more faculty agree to support, in principle if not in their personal practice, online education.

Hagner and Schneebeck (2001) categorized university faculty based on a modification of Everett Rogers' 1995 adopter classifications. Entrepreneurs who bask in technology and enjoy risk-taking activities form one group; these innovators are comfortable working on their own. Risk aversive types are unsure of how to use technology and wonder if they will be successful teaching online. They need training and other assistance before they will take the leap into online education. Reward seekers look at online education as a means to an end—greater rewards from the institution. They are pragmatic about their careers and teach online because the experience will help them gain tenure or promotion. Reluctants, or computer illiterates, do not see any benefits of working online and believe that online teaching methods are not as effective as face-to-face, on-site teaching activities.

Probably every institution has a mix of faculty fitting these categories. Getting them to work for a common goal may be next to impossible, especially if a large number of reluctants or risk aversives make up the current faculty. If enough preparation time, training, and support can be provided to members of the risk-aversive and reward-seeking groups, in time they may become valuable online teachers. Entrepreneurs need to be brought into the larger faculty as problem solvers, as they are not typically team players. Their solutions to course-based problems may be helpful to other faculty who follow them online, even if entrepreneurs initially did not solve problems just to help other teachers. Administrators need to analyze the faculty and develop training and other incentives that will motivate a divergent faculty.

Age does not seem to be a factor in determining who supports online education. Many younger colleagues, who are members of the so-called computer generation, do not use computers in their teaching and see only pitfalls in online education. These educators value paper books and in-person discussions, and they wholeheartedly believe that true learning takes place among people face to face, not across the Internet. They also face practical problems in using computers in education in general—plagiarized research papers bought and downloaded from the Web, selection of biased and questionable Web sites as key sources for student papers, rote recitation instead of discussion when students send e-mail to the instructor instead of being in class to participate, et cetera. Understandably, these teachers have valid concerns about Internet misuse in education and changing perceptions about authoritative sources of information, for example. These concerns have been voiced by faculty of all ages.

Those who embrace the Internet and online education for its possibilities in bringing together a diverse group of learners and making courses and degree programs available to more people than those who can work on site need to work with faculty members who see little value in online education. Of course, there are problems at many levels, from issues of idea ownership, copyright, and privacy to computer accessibility to pedagogical designs to promotion and tenure issues. The situation is complex. However, unless those who feel positively toward online education, from the highest levels of administration to the newest teacher, start discussions and work to begin resolving some of these issues and concerns, online education will continue to be a point of contention among faculty and between faculty and administration.

King, McCausland, and Nunan (2001) described the process of converting on-site to online programs at the University of South Australia as an opportunity to explore and reconsider teaching and learning strategies. This opportunity requires organizational changes, which are always fear-inducing and difficult to make. Getting faculty and administrators to agree on structural changes is often a long process, and the debate whether to go partially or all the way online for new programs is a hot topic in many institutions. The environment of change—filled with problems and possibilities—is being faced by many institutions as they develop online courses or a complete curriculum.

Five Principles for Developing an Online Curriculum

Perhaps the following list can provide suggestions for implementing successful online programs within an academic institution, while lessening the fears (or the downright animosity) among faculty and administrators. The following five suggestions may pave the way for better relationships among all faculty and administrators and help those who plan future online curricula:

1. Recognize that the ways courses or programs may be created can differ, but the resulting "product" should be equally high quality.

All educational offerings should be high quality, whether they were designed to be used in an on-site classroom or on a Web site. Educators (primarily teachers) should be actively involved in the creation of course materials, and these materials should be evaluated frequently to ensure their continued accuracy and importance to a study of the subject matter.

Online classes in reality may be more difficult for learners to complete, not because of the course content or the technology used in the flow of information among teachers and learners, but because online education requires students to take more responsibility for learning the information and completing course activities. The concept that online classes are "easy A's" should not be true or promulgated, by administrators, faculty, or learners.

Peterson and Savenye (2001), in an editorial preface to a special issue of *Computers and Composition,* pinpointed a key ingredient for online curriculum development. They emphasized the need for an entire discipline to rethink its purpose, commitment, and priorities in light of online education. The process of writing online, as one example, has been changed by the introduction of computerized forms of communication. Computerized processes and products are being researched to see how they differ from non-computerized communication, and how that affects the implications for teaching. The Internet has added another dimension for research, as collaborative and individual communication processes and products have changed even from those completed with a stand-alone computer. Because of the Internet element of communication, further changes to teaching are being debated. The entire nature of communication, and therefore the disciplines relating to communication, must be rethought.

The way a discipline is perceived, and the way that its practitioners define themselves and their work, have a direct bearing on whether that discipline considers online course or curriculum development as suitable. The content needed for adequate understanding of an entire discipline must be able to be delivered well online, using a variety of media. Activities that help learners practice skills, discover and test ideas, and synthesize knowledge must be completed electronically. If a curriculum is to be fully realized online, every course, every link in the knowledge-development and -acquisition process must be delivered online in such a way that learners who may never see teachers or touch lab materials can become an expert within that discipline. No wonder so many academics argue against online education. Distilling a discipline into electronic units that may be explored without the watchful guidance of teachers in labs and classrooms, workshops and libraries seems difficult. However, in practice, academic degree programs have been successfully delivered online, and the paradigm within a discipline expanded to include the presence of electronic information and the ways it has an impact on that discipline.

Not every discipline may be well defined through an online curriculum, and although some topics may be well suited for an online course or two, an entire curriculum might not be a good match to be transferred to online instruction. The successful implementation of an online curriculum relies on that discipline's experts (including but not limited to educators) determining that the body of knowledge and skills that make up a particular discipline are a good match for the current state of online education. Conversely, those who study and participate in a discipline must analyze how electronic communication and information may create changes within that discipline, and how that in turn will affect teaching practices.

2. Value on-site and online faculty equally.

Faculty, whether they teach primarily online or on site or they work both online and on site, should be valued equally. Electronic work should be evaluated and regarded as highly as on-site work, and the faculty who teach online classes should be able to achieve the same respect and recognition for their online work as faculty members do for their on-site work. For example, faculty members who develop educational software, create online materials or courses, assist in the development of an online curriculum, and participate in online professional development activities (e.g., workshops, conferences) should receive full credit for this time-intensive work. Electronic examples of scholarly activities and professional development should be encouraged in tenure packets and materials submitted for evaluation for promotion. CDs, zip and floppy disks, Web sites, and online demonstrations of educational materials should be considered equally effective measures of professional involvement as the more traditionally evaluated print books, conference papers, research proposals, and other paper documents.

All faculty members should have access to resources provided by the institution. Online faculty should be able to use research facilities and receive benefits such as funding of professional development activities. The quality of the faculty member's contribution, and the opportunities to make further contributions, should not be determined by how much or little that person works online.

All faculty should be allowed to participate in the institution's activities and policy-making bodies. Because many online faculty members live far from the university's or college's physical campus, they usually cannot attend meetings held on that campus. Allowing online faculty to participate in meetings through conference calls or videoconferences is important to make online faculty be perceived as part of the "real" faculty. All faculty should be alerted to possible changes in the institution's policies and invited to share their ideas. For online faculty, this might mean participation in online bulletin boards or e-mail discussions, and administrators consider ideas discussed or submitted in person, on paper, or by computer. The venue of participation should not matter as much as the opportunity to participate, and the merit of the discussion based on the quality of the ideas, not on the forum through which they were submitted.

All teachers/facilitators who work at an institution should be valued equally and considered appropriately for compensation, course loads and work schedules, access to resources, professional development activities, and tenure and promotion. These issues often divide faculty members, and administrators must be sensitive to the concerns of all faculty members, whether part-time or full-time faculty, tenured or non-tenured, online or on site.

3. Avoid playing off on-site classes against online classes.

Because online programs are newer, even within institutions with a successful distance learning program using other technologies (e.g., video "correspondence" courses, television broadcast classes), they may be perceived in very different ways. At one extreme, they may be seen as a necessary economic evil to compete with other universities or colleges now offering online programs. At the other extreme, they may be considered a savior of a traditionally campus-based institution, propelling the university or college into the Internet Age. However, one educational format should not be favored over another to the latter's detriment. Both on-site and online programs need administrative support to allocate the appropriate, necessary resources for success.

Online classes should not be discounted, either philosophically or financially. Online courses and on-site courses should not have to compete for the same group of learners. The cost of classes, as well as the frequency they are offered, the quality of the course, and the amount of credit offered, should be established so that the same course is consistent, whether offered online or on site.

Fee structures, for example, should be comparable for on-site and online classes. If learners discover that they can receive credit for the same course but pay a different fee structure for an online course, the value of the online course is perceived as different from its on-site version. For example, if learners need to take Composition 101 as part of their general education requirements and have the option of taking the class online or on site, the fee structure may be a determining factor in which format is selected. If the online class costs less, learners probably will take the class, regardless of their suitability to take online courses. The online class is thus perceived as "cheaper" than the on-site version, when in reality the quality of the course is equal to that of the on-site course.

Scheduling classes so that they compete with each other is another problem with perception. Many online courses are offered in several configurations: a six-week, 10-week, or 12-week online version of a course that regularly runs 15 or 16 weeks on campus. The shorter online version may be perceived as easier or less rigorous, simply because the time frame for completing the course is compressed. Again, the online course may simply require learners to do more in a shorter period of time, but the perception is that the course is simpler.

Therefore, information about degree programs should clearly state if learners can take both online and on-site courses toward their degree, or if they must take only on-site courses or only online courses. If both types are allowed within a degree program, any limitations to the number of hours of online or on-site courses must be clearly noted. If the online courses truly are interchangeable with the on-site courses, then administrators may want to consider how they should market their programs to different target groups, once again, so that on-site and online courses do not compete for the same niche market.

Online courses usually are offered on demand or more frequently than on-site courses. The sheer number of online sections may make the courses seem like assembly-line education. The institution needs to ensure that the way online courses are promoted leaves no doubt among potential learners or teachers that online courses are not simply educational fast food but are an integral part of a well-designed curriculum.

Technology needs to be equally dispersed throughout the institution. Online classes require technological improvements on a regular basis, as well as effective technical support. However, on-site classes should not be ignored in favor of technical support only for online classes. On-site labs, Web-enhanced courses taught on campus, and computer resources in faculty offices, for example, are equally important. The institution should not pit "haves" against "have nots" by treating online courses and on-site courses differently. Administrators need to ensure that faculty and learners have the level of technology needed for a high-quality education, no matter where the learning takes place.

Online and on-site classes should follow the same rules within an institution, too. The academic standards for course design and the required credentials for teachers should be similar, allowing for any practical differences (e.g., on-site teachers should live within the geographic region where they teach, online teachers should be able to work easily with the course site and any related hardware or software). Performance standards for learners and any entry-level requirements or prerequisites also should be similar. One type of program should not be considered better, easier, or of a different quality.

Teachers and administrators need to work closely together to ensure that the perceptions of online courses are accurate for teachers and learners, and that fee structures, course schedules, use of technology, and catalog descriptions of individual courses reflect the high quality of online courses. On-site courses should not have to compete for learners (and the courses' survival) against the same courses taught online, and vice versa. There should be a niche for both types of courses within a well-designed curriculum or curricula.

4. Create equally credible online and on-site courses and degree programs.

The institution should develop a good reputation for the quality of its individual courses and degree programs. The structure of all curricula should be pedagogically sound and technically usable and innovative. Teachers should be well trained and prepared to work closely with learners. Administrators should work with faculty and learners to plan curriculum changes and develop an effective strategy for maintaining high-quality programs. All these statements should be givens, whether the courses and programs are delivered on campus or via the Internet.

5. Set up a dialogue between on-site and online faculty—if they are different groups of faculty.

Faculty who teach online and those who teach on site may involve very different groups who have different perceptions about online education. To help faculty across the institution work well together, administrators must create ways for faculty to discuss their differences, explore positive ways of working together, and use newer technologies to enhance all courses. Faculty who live and work far from the physical campus must be brought into the campus community. If the first few principles, especially the second, are followed, this final principle may already be taken care of. However, discussions to plan online curricula may require bringing specific faculty members together to collaborate on potential new courses or programs and to address concerns of all faculty members.

Although setting up a dialogue among all faculty certainly will not solve all problems or eliminate biases for or against online education, the process may successfully bring together faculty, instead of separating them. Making on-site and online faculty aware of what others do, and showing faculty with less technical expertise how they might use the Internet, for example, to enhance their courses, can be a positive step forward.

Administrators must take care not to isolate faculty. They should find ways for them to work together or communicate and create a "family" of all people teaching together. To help establish this sense of belonging to a unified faculty, administrators must be sure that online faculty receive notices, get invited to the same events, participate in discussions, et cetera.

Success in each of these five areas involves dealing with faculty issues and course issues. Throughout the rest of this chapter, the focus shifts to faculty issues that are important for administrators to understand and deal with. Managing an online curriculum involves not only developing and maintaining courses and programs, but working closely with the teachers and learners involved in those courses and programs. Listening to faculty concerns and planning ways to move the institution forward as educational issues change are crucial parts of managing a successful online program. As the educational workplace changes, so must policies and practices involving faculty.

Faculty Issues

Faculty issues include time allocations for course development and curriculum modifications, compensation, course loads and work schedules, access to resources, training, tenure and promotion, hiring, and freelance teaching. Administrators need to work with faculty on these issues to develop clear institutional policies that cover not only the current state of online education, but can also be modified to reflect further changes in the way online teachers work.

Time Allocation

Teachers everywhere value time. There never seems to be enough for educational activities. Three areas per course that require teachers' time and attention are course preparation, course development/curriculum development, and in-class time spent on synchronous or asynchronous activities.

Course Prep Time

Online teachers need time to prepare for each course, even if the Web site already provides the information that learners need to be able to complete each module or lesson. Starting bulletin board folders or threads, posting messages, sending group e-mail, finding and presenting supplementary information, and developing questions or information for chat sessions are some class prep activities that most online teachers face at least weekly. The type of course and the online structure for the course help determine how much course preparation is needed.

Of course, all teachers need prep time, whether they work online or on campus. On-site courses often use computer technology to deliver course content and provide learners with work-related experiences, especially in Web-based or Web-enhanced on-site courses.

However, many on-site courses also rely on more traditional delivery methods, such as teacher lectures and printed textbooks. Learners may rely on hands-on experiences in a lab or workshop setting to gather important information and skills needed to succeed in the course. Teachers and course designers who are developing purely online courses (or Web-based on-site courses that in effect are online courses overseen by a teacher meeting students face to face) may need more development time to create materials that are technically effective and operational, as well as pedagogically sound.

On-site teachers, of course, also need time to develop and reproduce effective course materials. However, those teachers who use photocopiers or the university's print shop to produce paper copies, transparencies, and slides, for example, may not need the same lead time for producing (not creating) new assignments or course content.

Course Development/Curriculum Development Time

Online classes require technical development and startup time, as well as content development. Teachers who are developing multimedia materials for on-site classes (e.g., videos, PowerPoint presentations, slide shows) or setting up in-class events (e.g., videoconferences) also need more development time. They may create materials on their own, but they also may work with IT specialists or new media experts as they collaboratively develop computer- or Web-enhanced materials. These activities must be integrated into the course framework.

Although computer- or Web-enhanced classes may rely on technology for specific learning modules, the teacher is usually present to oversee the use of the modules or to explain what to do to use the technology correctly. Unlike online courses in which the user interface must be clear and self-evident, on-site, teacher-led courses may require the use of technology, but learners have other means to gather information and get answers to their questions.

Curriculum changes also require ongoing commitments of time and energy. Teachers must be aware of institutional policies that affect courses within the curriculum, as well as the need to modify the current curriculum. As changes need to be made from outside the course, such as directives by upper-level administrators to add a new course, teachers must be involved in the curriculum-change process.

However, teachers also modify the curriculum or individual courses within it to reflect changes in subject matter and technology. The need for ongoing curriculum evaluation and modification requires ongoing allocations of time dedicated to the evaluation, modification, and creation processes.

Rahman (2001) described the need for new criteria to be used when online courses and programs are evaluated. Online education can be innovative, and therefore new criteria should be established to analyze and evaluate its innovations within a discipline and education. Perhaps the criteria for allotting course preparation, curriculum development, and lead time should not be based on the type of class, or even whether it is offered on site or online, but on the variety of media and the required technical expertise needed to develop the course materials.

Rahman (2001) also suggested that educators first must identify the unique characteristics of online courses and programs. Academic communities then need to be made aware of these characteristics and become convinced that online education does a good job of delivering high-quality instruction. If all faculty and administrators understand the place that effective online education has in the institution, strategic planning for new courses or an online curriculum may be easier.

Administrators who think that once an online course is developed it is set forever—or at least for several years—are sadly mistaken. Just as on-site teachers routinely update their materials and provide new copies of documents or assign new readings based on recent periodicals or textbooks, so must online teachers (and those working with Web-enhanced courses) be able to update their course materials in multimedia formats to keep the course site and materials relevant.

Administrators also need to recognize that teachers working in on-site classes with noncomputerized resources may be able to work on their own, with little technical collaboration with staff members. Online teachers, on the other hand, may be required to work with course designers, IT staff, and administrators who are developing a unified appearance and structure, and common technology, for all online courses.

Teachers who develop Web-enhanced learning materials may fall between these endpoints on the curriculum-development continuum. Course development and delivery require a great investment of time and energy, and the ongoing evaluation and modification processes therefore require additional, ongoing investments of time (Rahman, 2001).

Perhaps administrators should consider the types of materials and the medium/media required for presenting course information when they determine how much lead time—and the compensation and assistance required for this work—is needed to create a high-quality course. The designation of online or on site may have little meaning when determining an appropriate amount of lead time and course preparation before teachers are ready to deliver instruction.

In-Class Time

As noted in my informal survey of faculty colleagues, in-class work through e-mail, chat or whiteboard sessions, as well as grading and feedback, involves a great deal of time each week. A National Education Association (NEA) (2000) survey of faculty at universities and colleges found that two-thirds of faculty members think it is highly likely that faculty members who teach in distance learning programs will have more students and will work more hours for the same pay.

The issues of teaching more students per class and doing more work for the same amount of money are primary concerns for faculty. Theoretically, because an online classroom does not have physical space or time limitations, and learners can work with an established course structure through the Web, any number of learners can be enrolled in a class. In practice, class sizes need to be limited because collaborative activities and teacher-learner discussions need to be kept small enough to be manageable and to allow the teacher/facilitator to participate with collaborating groups of learners.

As class sizes grow, more in-class time is needed for chat sessions and other synchronous activities. The numbers in a chat group, for example, should be kept small so that everyone can participate effectively and the teacher can easily facilitate the session. Increased numbers of learners also means increased numbers of e-mail messages to be sent to individuals. Although group messages and bulletin board posts can provide information to many learners at the same time, feedback about assignments, responses to individuals' e-mail, and help provided to learners requiring additional assistance take up much more time with a larger number of learners per class.

A criticism of online education is that learners do not receive the personal touch from teachers; they only learn on their own, with minimal guidance. The quality of instruction, because there is little or no face-to-face communication, is necessarily poor. Teachers also are perceived as "cheated" in the learning situation because they cannot see the spark of understanding and learning in students' eyes as they make important connections among ideas.

In well-designed online courses, these criticisms can be largely avoided because teachers can spend time with the group and individual class members. Frequent communication, chat sessions and other synchronous activities, and personal attention are hallmarks of good online teaching. However, online teachers can only create personal relationships with learners when the class sizes are small and there is time designed just for interpersonal communication.

Administrators need to allow online faculty adequate in-class and course prep time, as well as figure this time commitment into course load allocations and other faculty responsibilities. Workload adjustments may need to be made for online faculty so that they have the time they need to work effectively with learners and to keep designing worthwhile curricula.

Compensation

Teachers who work primarily on site and teachers who work only online need to be valued equally on the pay scale, too. When online education was more of a novelty, and few teachers had the experience or expertise to work well online, higher pay just for agreeing to teach online provided an incentive for some administrators to find high-quality faculty to teach courses. Now, however, as more online courses and experienced teachers are available, the problem is often reversed. Because online courses are considered by many administrators to require little work other than answering e-mail or posting a few bulletin board messages, the pay for online teachers is falling at some institutions.

Compensation is a major issue among all faculty, tenured or non-tenured, adjunct or full time. The issue is further complicated by several different compensation practices based on different categories of teaching. On-site, full-time teachers who occasionally teach online are usually classified one way, whereas adjuncts who teach both online and on-site courses for the same institution are considered differently. Tenured faculty at one institution who occasionally teach online for another university usually fall under the "guest lecturer" or "adjunct" categories at the second institution. Teachers who pick up one online class as an overload to their regular course load may be paid one amount for teaching that course, but the pay scale for an adjunct teaching the same course usually is different. A salaried teacher who regularly teaches an online course may have no distinction between the amount of pay received for an on-site or an online course—they are all considered the same as part of a salaried faculty member's regular course load. Each faculty classification may have a different compensation schedule for the same type of work.

Some institutions pay faculty by the online course or per X number of students enrolled in a class. The amounts may differ depending on whether the course is taught on site or online.

Administrators need to realize that teaching online often requires more daily work than teaching on site—although both types of teaching require a great deal of time and effort. Some administrators and on-site faculty may perceive online teachers as lazy—simply because they are not seen in a classroom on campus. This perception is not only wrong, but also it is unfair. The amount and type of work (which can be measured) and not the teaching venue should be the foundation of the pay scale.

Course Loads and Work Schedules

As noted previously, course-development activities, for on-site and online teaching, should be recognized as time-consuming professional activities that require additional time (and presumably compensation) than using all predetermined materials for teaching a course. When teachers develop new course materials for an existing class or create an entirely new course, they need to be given release time that is the equivalent of extra pay or need to be paid for their additional work.

Professional development or curriculum-development grants also may provide incentives for teachers to invest more time in online education.

According to Lau (2000), universities and colleges also have inconsistent policies regarding release time and course load for online faculty members. Although some institutions provide some release time so that teachers new to online education can be trained and adequately prepare for teaching a course, not all universities or colleges have such policies. If online education is perceived as a chore, with no benefits for faculty members, few faculty members will volunteer to learn new skills and develop new course materials to work in Web-based classes.

Administrators need to plan annual schedules for full-time and part-time online teachers. Balancing the anticipated need for teachers to facilitate specific courses with the planned growth of online programs can allow adequate staffing for online courses. Both faculty and administrators should look at the need for additional faculty if current teachers will receive release time from their regular course load. Planning ahead allows faculty to plan their course loads and allocate time for course- and curriculum-development activities, as well as teaching load. It also helps administrators anticipate hiring needs as the number of online courses changes.

Access to Resources

Online teachers need to be given consideration for technical and office improvements. Although teachers who live far from campus may not need an on-campus office, they do need access to university or college facilities. Online teachers are often expected to own, maintain, and upgrade their computer equipment and to pay for any connection charges for dial-up, wireless, or hardwired Internet access. On-site teachers usually do not have the responsibility for maintaining office or lab computers they use in their course-development activities or teaching. Helping online teachers have adequate access to the hardware and software needed to teach via the Internet is an important component of retaining effective online teachers.

Support for other professional development activities are needed for online as well as on-site teachers. Online teachers must keep up with new research in curriculum design and technological innovations. Attending conferences or participating in workshops is a good way to keep online educators involved in their profession. Providing the time to participate in conferences and workshops and reimbursing teachers for their expenses also are critical if teachers are to be encouraged to participate in these types of professional development activities.

Training

Online teachers need training in several areas: 1) teaching strategies and methods suitable for the subject matter and delivery formats, 2) subject matter, 3) online resources, and 4) tools. Learning how to be an effective online teacher should be a top priority. Knowing where to point and click to achieve the desired result is necessary, but it has a lower priority than understanding the principles of effective online teaching. Hativa, Barak, and Simhi (2001) concluded from their research to determine what makes effective teachers (not specifically online teachers) that effective teachers must be prepared for their role as educators. Crucial components of this preparation are knowledge of many teaching strategies, from which teachers select those best suited to their personal style, learners' needs, and the subject matter. Teachers also need to learn skills in how to teach, such as organizing ideas and materials and clearly expressing themselves, often in many different ways, so that students understand the subject and the tasks they need to complete. Too often training focuses on button pushing and clicking, when it also should emphasize high-quality teaching methods first and tool use later. Training must be ongoing, and it must cover many areas of online education, theoretical and pragmatic.

One of the best investments an institution can make is to train faculty. Anyone who plans to teach an online course for the first time, is going to teach an updated course or a new course, or is working with new tools or technology needs to be trained. Training may take place at conferences, but other types of training should be ongoing for online faculty. The home institution should offer on-site and online versions of the same in-service activities and make them accessible at convenient times. These activities may include discussions of effective teaching methods and ways to implement new technologies in the classroom, wherever it is.

On-site training can be provided in a three-hour workshop or a series of mini-courses—whatever is appropriate to the amount of information that needs to be covered and the amount of time it typically takes to work with new equipment. Online teachers who live far from the physical campus may not be able to attend on-site workshops offered at convenient times and locations for on-site teachers. Therefore, online sessions, such as conference calls, videoconferences, or chats, may need to be offered in the evenings or on weekends to accommodate the needs of online educators.

Online tutorials should also be a part of the training materials, not only to supplement on-site activities, but also to provide guidance and practice for teachers working on the virtual campus. The important consideration is that *all* teachers be given professional development opportunities.

Training activities need to be planned so that the quality of the materials is high, the trainers are qualified and have time to devote to faculty education, and time and space are reserved specifically for training sessions. These activities need to be offered regularly; for example, each online term a new training program can be offered for first-time online teachers. As well, additional sessions should be offered on an as-needed basis when new tools, hardware, software, or course designs are going to be introduced. Training needs to take place before, not at the same time as teachers begin a course using new elements.

Although most institutions offer some type of professional development through training activities, not all employers ensure that teachers have the time or support to take advantage of these events. Training activities should be scheduled at a variety of convenient times. Monetary incentives may be a part of the institution's training strategy, to ensure that teachers are not only encouraged to attend, but also that their dedication and time are appreciated.

Simply tacking on another job to a teacher's workload is not a good training incentive. Bower (2001) suggested that administrators provide appropriate incentives that ease the way for faculty members and IT specialists to move into online education. Providing well-planned, effective training sessions and giving teachers release time and other benefits to take advantage of training help create a better trained, contented faculty and help faculty members work more closely with IT experts.

That means, of course, that training activities need to be a budget item, not an afterthought. Investing in faculty competency and security is important, and it requires an institutional commitment. Administrators may have to document "before" and "after" statistics to measure the effectiveness of faculty training and students' evaluations of courses. Showing that training is beneficial to the programs overall, as well as to teachers, is a selling point in favor of investing in training.

Trippe (2000) recommended four approaches to faculty training: 1) training prior to the first online class, 2) support during the first online course, 3) ongoing workshops to cover practical topics (e.g., writing assignments, grading, evaluation, critical thinking, copyright information, Web pages, syllabus preparation), and 4) faculty evaluation and feedback mechanisms. These venues for training not only prepare new online faculty but also help experienced faculty keep up with new technologies and educational methods.

After all, Trippe concluded, confident, highly trained, and knowledgeable faculty members create a successful learning environment. They know how to interact with learners and encourage such interaction. They develop effective educational techniques that help learners achieve course objectives. Learners ultimately meet their objectives and are satisfied with their educational experience. Developing such a faculty requires administrators to be committed to the idea of ongoing training opportunities for all teachers.

Tenure and Promotion

The number of full-time and part-time (adjunct) faculty teaching online also should be addressed. Not all online faculty should be adjuncts, although the option of teaching online for part-time teachers is usually appealing both to the teachers and to administrators. Teaching online in the evenings, at odd times throughout the traditional work week, and on weekends allows more professionals (teachers and other subject experts who are not primarily teachers) to facilitate online classes. However, online faculty should also include full-time faculty as well as adjuncts, just as on-site faculties usually consist of a mix of full-time and part-time personnel. As well, tenured and non-tenured faculty should be involved in both online and on-site programs.

Some part-time faculty work as adjuncts until full-time, usually tenurable, positions are available, and then they apply for these jobs. Adjunct faculty who have worked exclusively online, and who have equally good track records in their classrooms and have the appropriate credentials, should be considered equally with adjunct faculty who have taught on site or new applicants who have not previously taught for the institution.

The individuals' credentials and experience, not just the medium in which they have worked, should be used to determine who should be hired for a tenure-track position. If part-time online faculty geographically distant from the university or college are willing to relocate to be able to teach both on site and online, they should be considered for permanent teaching jobs.

Tenure-track, tenured, or otherwise full-time faculty who teach both online and on site should be evaluated equally with their colleagues who teach exclusively on site. For example, in annual reviews and course evaluations, the quality of the teacher's work should be evaluated fairly and equally. If more effort was put into developing a new online course, that activity should be rewarded, just as if a teacher devoted a great deal of energy into developing an on-site course. The medium should not be considered as much as the quality of the teacher's work and the amount of time devoted to various teaching and professional development activities.

Unfortunately, because online activities often are less visible to all faculty and administrators, teachers who work primarily online must prove that their electronic work is just as valuable and just as effective as the more traditional methods of publishing information and teaching courses. Many academic departments are only now wrestling with the way to evaluate a course Web site as opposed to hardcopy course materials such as syllabi, assignment sheets, and workshop handouts. Chatroom office hours and time spent writing and responding to e-mail often have not been compared to the number of hours teachers advise students in their offices or are seen with an open door to their campus office. The means of evaluating and respecting work done online as well as in person on site must be comparable so that teachers' work is fairly reviewed for pay raises, tenure, and promotion.

In a study of online teachers conducted by Bonk (2001), co-sponsored by JonesKnowledge.com and CourseShare.com, nearly seven out of 10 college educators listed Web use in their tenure, promotion, and salary evaluations as one of their major concerns. Faculty recognize the need for including Web-based work in their portfolios for administrative review and are concerned that either such work is not evaluated properly or is not even considered. Administrators and purely on-site faculty need to be made aware of all activities that online teachers complete. However, with this awareness must come professional recognition that these online activities are just as valuable and should be weighted just as heavily in faculty evaluations. Administrators who evaluate online work must know how to conduct these evaluations fairly and be able to determine the quality of the electronic resources being reviewed.

Lau (2000) noted that some faculty and administrators consider separate tenure tracks for faculty who teach online and for faculty who teach using more traditional methods. Teachers who work with new technologies and have to develop new materials and methods for courses may have different criteria for evaluating their work.

Having separate tracks may not be feasible for many departments or institutions that rely on online faculty from several sources: tenure-track on-site faculty, adjuncts, and guest lecturers. Because tenure-track faculty may teach a combination of online or on-site classes, depending upon faculty interests and program-scheduling needs, the university or college may not be able to identify teachers for a separate online tenure track. However, the amount and quality of Web-based work must be evaluated appropriately so that online teachers get respect and professional advancement for their online work.

Somewhere full-time, tenured or tenure-track teachers (not program coordinators or course developers) work exclusively online. However, most online teachers are still full-time educators who teach both online and on-site courses for the same institution or are online teachers who work part-time for an institution (and usually have another full-time job, in or out of academia). More online, tenure-track positions need to open up as online education becomes more common.

Of course, administrators and colleagues need to "see" that online teachers are doing just as much for the institution as their on-site counterparts do. Attendance via videoconference or chat session at departmental meetings, for example, might be required of full-time faculty. Management of committees might be part of a full-time faculty member's workload, but the way that committee meets or works may have to involve some electronic meetings.

As departmental and university or college administrators plan for the changing roles of faculty members, the issues involving reasonable course loads, faculty evaluations, and institutional service must be designed to include both on-site and online faculty members. Helping all faculty members work to the best of their abilities and receive fair and equal consideration is a key in achieving positive working relationships among all faculty.

Hiring Faculty

A crucial management decision involves hiring faculty for online programs, and the way institutions have handled hiring varies widely. Here are some popular choices:

- Full-time on-site faculty also teach online courses as part of a regular course load.
- Full-time on-site faculty also teach online courses, as an overload to their regular teaching requirements.
- Part-time faculty who have a background (e.g., degree, experience) in teaching teach online courses as adjuncts.
- Part-time faculty who have specific experience in a subject area, but little prior teaching experience, are hired to teach online courses occasionally.

Online courses are often thought of as secondary by administrators, often because they are newer programs, and their long-term viability has yet to be proven. On-site teachers, as well, may not have the incentives or personal motivation to learn new technologies and develop new course materials to be used in online courses. A common response to these situations is that on-site teachers who want to take on an online course or two are encouraged to do so, but only in addition to their regular course load. Overload pay, and perhaps additional time, training, or monetary incentives, encourage teachers to take the plunge into online education.

As the number of online courses grows, waiting for volunteers to staff the courses becomes riskier. At that point, many institutions hire adjuncts to teach online sections. This option frees up full-time faculty to teach on site only (if they wish) and ensures that numerous sections can be staffed. Because adjuncts seldom receive benefits and are paid based on the number of learners in a course, the number of course hours, or a formula using these and other factors, administrators may be able to save money by hiring adjunct instructors as the need arises. Adjuncts are not guaranteed that they will teach courses; if a class does not receive enough enrollment, the adjunct's contract is voided.

Adjuncts who are experienced teachers, especially in an online format, are often a good solution to staffing online courses. Some institutions bring in adjuncts who have few teaching credentials but who have lots of experience with the subject matter. For example, someone who manages a local company agrees to teach a business course.

Currently, most institutions do not hire full-time faculty to teach only online. Perhaps they will be a welcome addition to full-time on-site faculty in the future, but the use of adjuncts or faculty teaching overloads is much more common.

If an institution's online programs are to remain credible (as well as accredited), the credentials of online faculty, full-time or adjunct, should be high quality. Familiarity with educational processes and methods, the ability to develop an effective curriculum, interest in teaching online, and ease in working with learners in a purely online environment are important factors when administrators select faculty for online classes. Learners need to feel assured that the quality of an online degree is just as high as that of a degree program completed on site.

Investing in faculty should be a high priority for the institution. Adjuncts who work only online should be given the same benefits as on-site adjunct faculty. For example, if on-site faculty receive travel stipends for attending a conference, the same benefit should be offered to online faculty who meet the same requirements for attending a conference. Full-time faculty who want to teach online should have an online course count at least as much as an on-site course. The venue, on site or online, should have no special impact on a teacher's evaluations or pay; the quality of the work and the quantity of teacher involvement with learners and the curriculum should be the deciding factors in faculty evaluations.

Administrators must believe that online education is as valuable as on-site education. The quality of the course is what matters, not where it is taught. In the same way, administrators need to ensure that online faculty and on-site faculty are treated similarly. Innovative work, new curriculum development, and extra time spent on enhancing courses should be rewarded across the board.

The administration has to take the lead in developing effective faculty evaluation forms that account for all the types of courses and media educators may use in a classroom and the types of research, training, and personal development activities that are appropriate for online and on-site adjunct and full-time faculty.

Freelance Faculty

Online teachers today are limited only by their areas of expertise and teaching effectiveness when it comes to hiring. Many on-site, tenured or tenure-track teachers also teach online for one or more institutions at the same time. As well, adjunct faculty may teach online or on site for several institutions. Add to this mix professionals in business and industry who have specialized expertise in one or more subject areas. All these people may work as freelance online teachers.

Administrators need to hire carefully from this pool of potential online educators. Everyone who plans to teach online should have the proper credentials and teaching experience, as well as familiarity with the required technology.

In some online programs, only experts from business and industry are encouraged to develop and teach "real world" courses. However, all personnel who facilitate online courses (or on-site courses, for that matter) should be familiar with effective teaching practices. If businesspeople who are experts in their profession are hired to develop or facilitate online courses, they must be trained to use effective instructional designs, if they do not already have that expertise.

Teachers who work for multiple institutions may need to make sure they are not creating a conflict of interest with their primary employer by teaching the same courses for many institutions. Administrators may need to work with teachers to establish guidelines about the number of employers that can be adequately served at one time, or the total number of courses that can be taught across institutions at one time.

The growth in the freelance education market should continue as more online teaching opportunities arise. Teachers are no longer limited to jobs in a geographic area. With online access, they can work for institutions worldwide, limited only by their access to the required technology and the amount of time they need to be effective teachers in each class.

Bonk (2001) described this group of freelancers as faculty members who come to online education for widely divergent reasons. They may be new Ph.D.s looking for a tenure-track position but not yet able to find one. Tenured faculty on a summer break may take on additional classes. Professionals who are not primarily teachers may try their hand at teaching. Graduate students who plan to become full-time, tenured faculty one day gain experience by teaching online. These and other groups of subject experts work as freelancers.

Because freelancers are not part of a tenure-track process, administrators may be tempted to use a variety of part-time teachers instead of creating tenure-track positions for purely online teachers. Keeping quality of instruction high and offering benefits to experienced online teachers are important considerations. Hiring well-qualified freelancers should be only one option for online faculty positions. Developing tenurable online faculty for permanent online positions should also be encouraged. Online education should not be a "freelancers only" type of teaching, although freelancing is an attractive option for many full-time teachers.

Summary

Online educators, wherever they teach and however far they live from the on-site campus, must be given equal respect and opportunities for professional growth and advancement. Pleasant working conditions and the potential for career advancement should be priorities for administrators, as well as faculty.

Managing online courses and programs involves working closely with faculty and dealing with the important issues and concerns described in this chapter. Changing institutional policies as the definition of *education* expands is a critical process for administrators. As the nature of online teaching changes, so must the institution's plans for helping faculty work most effectively with students and keeping up with the state of the profession.

References

Bonk, C. J. (2001). *Online teaching in an online world.* Retrieved October 3, 2002, from http://publicationshare.com/docs/faculty_survey_report.pdf

Bower, B. L. (2001). Distance education: Facing the faculty challenge. *Online Journal of Distance Learning Administration, IV*(II). State University of West Georgia. Retrieved October 3, 2002, from http://www.westga.edu/~distance/ojdla/summer42/bower42.html

Hagner, P. R., & Schneebeck, C. A. (2001). Engaging the faculty. In C. A. Barone & P. R. Hagner (Eds.), *Technology-enhanced teaching and learning: Leading and supporting the transformation on your campus. EDUCAUSE leadership strategies no. 5* (pp.1-24). San Francisco: Jossey-Bass.

Hativa, N., Barak, R., & Simhi, E. (2001). Exemplary university teachers. Knowledge and benefits regarding effective teaching dimensions and strategies. *The Journal of Higher Education, 72*(6), 699-729.

Johannesen, T., & Eide, E. M. (2000). The role of the teacher in the age of technology: Will the role change with the use of information- and communication technology in education? *European Journal of Open and Distance Learning.* Retrieved October 3, 2002, from http://www.eurodl.org/eurodlen/index.html

King, B., McCausland, H., & Nunan, T. (2001). Converting to online course and program delivery: The University of South Australia case study. *International Review of Research in Open and Distance Learning, 1*(2). Retrieved October 3, 2002, from http://www.irrodl.org/content/v1.2/unisa.pdf

Lau, L. (2000). *Distance learning technologies: Issues, trends and opportunities*. Hershey, PA: Idea Group Publishing.

National Education Association. (2000). *A survey of traditional and distance learning higher education members*. Washington, DC: NEA. Retrieved March 20, 2002, from http://www.nea.org/hc.pdf

Peterson, P. W., & Savenye, W. (2001). Editorial. Letter from the guest editors. Distance education: Promises and perils of teaching and learning online. *Computers and Composition, 18*, 319-320.

Rahman, M. (2001). Faculty recruitment strategies for online programs. *Online Journal of Distance Learning Administration, 4*(4). State University of West Georgia. Retrieved October 3, 2002, from http://www.westga.edu/~distance/ojdla/winter44/rahman44.html

Trippe, A. P. (2000). Training for distance learning faculty. *DEOSNEWS, 12*(3). Retrieved October 3, 2002, from http://www.ed.psu.edu/acsde/deos/deosnews/deosnews12_3.asp

PLANNING FOR THE FUTURE

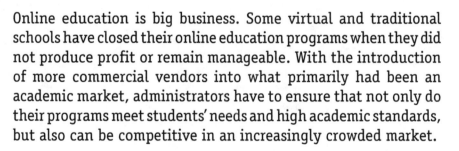

Online education is big business. Some virtual and traditional schools have closed their online education programs when they did not produce profit or remain manageable. With the introduction of more commercial vendors into what primarily had been an academic market, administrators have to ensure that not only do their programs meet students' needs and high academic standards, but also can be competitive in an increasingly crowded market.

Offering online education programs is not for everyone. If your programs are going to remain useful and marketable, you have to be committed to upgrading your course content, teaching methods, curriculum, and technology to keep pace with learners' needs and expectations. Online education is not a fad, and its future involves some important potential changes in the way teachers develop and present information, the independent nature of academic institutions, and the marketability of specific programs.

Unfortunately, like every other business endeavor, online education is a business. It has to be profitable as well as high quality, or it will not survive. However, education should be more than just a business. Having the power to influence learners, and, you hope, to improve their lives, is a serious responsibility. For online education to have a purpose, beyond making money, the programs have to be well designed, accurate, timely, and well taught. Sound educational design should be the first priority. Only when there is an excellent product and a plan for an effective learning process should marketing take place.

Let us say that your institution has developed a wonderful educational program and has been successfully marketing it. Learners take the courses and eventually complete degrees, or they take courses that enhance their personal and professional development, even though they are not getting credit toward a degree. How often should you upgrade courses? When should the entire curriculum be overhauled? How much should be invested in training? What policies may need to be updated or revamped to keep pace with the direction in which online education is headed? In short, how will the curriculum remain competitive in the current market, much less the future? How will online courses keep up with or surpass your competitors' courses?

Individual teachers can keep courses high quality by keeping teaching methods up to date, developing new course materials, and maintaining a reputation for effective teaching. Administrators can do their part by monitoring courses within a program, checking on the success of other institutions' and commercial vendors' programs, training faculty, having programs accredited, and assisting with marketing. Everyone should play a role in keeping online education effective and successful.

The Teacher's Responsibilities

As a teacher, you are one of the front line who works daily with the course design and materials and reads the problems and complaints from students having problems with course content or the technology. By keeping up to date with what is going on in other institutions and with online education in general, you are more likely to keep your teaching skills updated and to offer valuable guidance when a course is modified. Courses are generally evaluated and modified at least once a year, more often if technical changes need to be made. Throughout the year, then, you can analyze what is working well and what can be improved.

Learning from Others' Sites

Collaborating with colleagues is an important part of your job. You may not see them in person if you are working off site, especially far away from the physical institution, but you can keep up with what is going on in other classes. You should participate in the bulletin board postings and chat sessions held for online teachers. Share your ideas, and try what others are doing differently in their classes. Find out if you can visit another teacher's course site, to view the types of feedback from students and the amount and types of communication between teacher and students.

Of course, that means that you should be open to having other teachers or administrators look at your online work, too. Being part of an active learning community of teachers working within the same institution is important to trying out new ideas and assignments and solving problems.

Broadening your perspective about what is useful and what designs are best means that you also should visit sites hosted by others outside your institution. For example, teachers you meet at a conference may be able to share the URLs/URIs and passwords for demonstration sites. The demonstrations may have been created with different courseware, and you may prefer one to another. You may learn how other systems deal with downloadable text or graphics files, links to internal and external Web sites, e-mail to individuals and groups, chat rooms, whiteboards, calendars, gradebooks, and so on.

What should you look for when you visit another site or work with a demonstration of courseware? As much as you can ascertain, either from the site itself or the teacher, look at these elements. You might create a similar notesheet to evaluate other sites you visit.

You can take notes about the categories listed in Figure 9-1 as you work with the information at the site. For example, by reading the assignment descriptions, you know if the assignments are designed for an individual or a group, if they are to be completed in real time or at the learner's leisure, and what type of interaction with the material or others is required. Looking at a course syllabus or assignment due date list gives you information about the number of assignments and the breakdown of assignments per learning segment.

Figure 9-1. Notesheet for Checking Out a Course Site

When you check out a course site, note these items:

1. Hardware

__ Special equipment is required to access the site.

__ Learners can enter the site using different types of computers, with different operating systems.

__ A dial-up connection is fast enough to work well with the site.

__ A direct or dedicated line is required to work well with the site.

__ A wireless connection is stable enough to work well with the site.

__ The computer requires additional devices, such as sound or graphics cards, a CD player, or more memory, to access all materials.

__ The computer does not require any special devices in order to access and play all materials.

__ An older PC can be used by learners to complete this course.

__ A brand-new PC can be used by learners to complete this course.

Additional comments about hardware:

2. Software

__ Specific browsers are recommended or required.

__ Specific versions of one or more browsers are recommended or required.

__ Any browser can be used to access course information.

__ Required software is provided to learners online, on a floppy disk, or on a CD.

__ Learners must provide their own software.

__ Common versions of popular software are required for completing assignments or using materials.

Additional comments about software:

Figure 9-1. Notesheet for Checking Out a Course Site (continued)

3. Networks and policies regarding their operation

__ Course or institutional networks seem secure.

__ Course or institutional networks are easy to access and work well.

__ Course sites include privacy and security statements.

__ The institution's privacy and security policies are documented online.

Additional comments about networks and policies:

4. Educational tools

__ Tools are easy to use, because they are intuitive or allow transfer of skills from learners using similar Web sites.

__ New tools are explained and demonstrated at the site.

__ Several tools are available for use with asynchronous learning or communication.

__ Several tools are available for use with synchronous learning or communication.

__ All tools work.

Additional comments about educational tools:

5. Types of materials and media

__ Different learning styles or preferences are incorporated into the course design.

__ Multimedia are used frequently.

__ Course materials are text or print based.

__ Streaming information (audio and/or video) is available.

__ Audio, video, graphic, and text files are available.

Figure 9-1. Notesheet for Checking Out a Course Site (continued)

__ Materials can be downloaded quickly.

__ If text files are printed, the average printout is a manageable size.

__ The amount of linked material seems appropriate for the length of the course and the subject matter.

__ The quality of the materials is high.

__ (It seems that) most materials have been created by the teacher or the course designer.

__ (It seems that) most materials have been taken from other sources.

__ Sources of information are documented or attributed properly.

__ The sources seem current and accurate and represent a variety of viewpoints.

__ The information seems timely.

__ The materials can be reused.

__ The materials can be used only in this course or only one time.

__ The online materials stand alone, without the need for a textbook, CD, or other supplementary materials.

__ Supplementary information is found in a textbook, CD, or other format.

Additional comments about types of materials and media:

6. Number and types of assignments

__ Assignments are listed in a course syllabus or schedule.

__ Point values, due dates, and descriptions are listed for each assignment.

__ The number of assignments seems reasonable for the length and depth of the course.

__ The number and type of assignments per week or learning module seems practical and reasonable.

__ The types of assignments reflect different learning styles or preferences.

__ Assignments are appropriate for studying the subject matter.

Figure 9-1. Notesheet for Checking Out a Course Site (continued)

__ Assignments are appropriate for this educational level (e.g., an undergraduate university class, a post-graduate class, a non-credit professional development class).

__ Real-time and asynchronous assignments are required.

__ Instructions are provided so that learners know in what format the assignments should be completed.

__ Instructions are provided so that learners know how to submit the assignments.

__ Instructions are provided so that learners know how to use plagiarism-checking software or tools.

__ From the course site, learners know when they will receive feedback about the assignments and what type of responses they will receive (e.g., an e-mail message, a posted grade).

__ Policies about academic honesty, grade scales, and expectations for performance are listed on the course site.

Additional comments about number and types of assignments:

7. Amount of required interaction with the material

__ Learners are required to complete journals, workbooks, essays, research papers, or questionnaires.

__ Learners are required to participate in chat sessions, conference calls, or videoconferences.

__ Learners are required to send a certain number of e-mail messages or post so many comments on a bulletin board.

__ Learners are required to participate in lab sessions.

__ Learners demonstrate their mastery of the subject matter or a skill in several ways throughout the course. (These ways, not previously listed on the notesheet, include _____ _____.)

Additional comments about required interaction with the material:

Figure 9-1. Notesheet for Checking Out a Course Site (continued)

8. Amount of required interaction with others in the class

__ Learners are required or encouraged to participate in group activities or projects.

__ Learners are required or encouraged to work alone on some or all assignments.

__ Outside assistance from mentors, colleagues, teachers, or other students is allowed or encouraged.

__ Learners are required to interview people outside the class.

__ Interpersonal contact is suggested or required between a learner and others inside and outside the class.

__ A specified amount of communication is required between the teacher and learners, and between the learner and others in the class.

__ The teacher's response time is reasonable and consistent.

__ Communication seems to be primarily asynchronous.

__ Communication seems to be primarily synchronous.

__ More than one communication method is used in the course. (Communication methods include _____.)

Additional comments about required interaction with others:

9. Evaluations

__ Learners evaluate the course and teaching effectiveness at the end of the class.

__ Evaluations are confidential (according to privacy or security policies).

__ Evaluations are completed and submitted online.

__ Evaluations are completed and submitted other than online.

__ Evaluations require learners to select from multiple choice or other listed selections.

__ Evaluations allow learners to submit written comments.

__ Teachers see the evaluations. (You may not be able to learn this from the Web site, unless it is documented in a privacy or security statement.)

Figure 9-1. Notesheet for Checking Out a Course Site (continued)

__ Others (e.g., administrators) see the evaluations. (You may not be able to learn this from the Web site, unless it is documented in a privacy or security statement.)

__ Evaluations are used to improve the course or curriculum. (You may not be able to learn this from the Web site, unless it is documented in a privacy or security statement.)

Additional comments about evaluations:

10. Length of course and number of learners

__ The length of the course seems appropriate for the amount and depth of information covered.

__ The class size seems appropriate for effective communication among learners and the teacher.

__ The class size seems manageable for the teacher, who has to read assignments, grade projects, et cetera.

__ The class size seems manageable for learners, who need to develop one or more learning communities as they study the subject matter.

__ The length of the course seems appropriate for the amount of credit given for the work.

__ The time frame seems appropriate for an online course.

Additional comments about length of course and number of learners:

When you look at another educator's class site as a model, you probably have to ask the teacher for some information. For example, you should not be able to see the online gradebook that tells you how many students are completing the course. If you can, you want to get the teacher's impressions of the course and students, and the strengths and weaknesses of the technology and the course design.

Documenting what you have learned is useful not only for your own teaching, but for administrators, who need to justify changes in course design or teaching methods. It may also be useful during accreditation processes.

Documentation also helps you more easily compare your course with others. This or a similar checklist helps you look at your course site more objectively. You can also track changes to the course by keeping print records of your evaluations. Using this type of checklist each time you teach a course is a good way to remind yourself (and others) of what is good about the course and what still could be improved. It provides documentation that you can use when your work is evaluated, too.

Submitting Your Ideas and Documentation

As you develop and teach online courses, you should be browsing the Web to find new materials, using your networks and contacts to find new information or bring new resources to learners, and testing new technology to see what might improve your course site. As well, through course evaluations and your interactions with learners, you have a good idea about what works well and what needs to be updated in each course.

At the end of a course or a natural time break, such as the end of a term or a fiscal year, submit a list of your suggestions and ideas for improving the course or curriculum to your supervisor. Any documentation that supports your suggestions should be included. It is part of your teaching responsibility to work with administrators and technical specialists to keep improving courses and to modify the curriculum as necessary. Get in the habit of submitting your ideas to administrators, beginning with your immediate supervisor or program coordinator, so that you can be more actively involved in the evaluation and curriculum-enhancement process.

Administrative Responsibilities

The majority of accreditation, marketing, and strategic planning tasks fall to someone in the administration, although everyone—course designers, IT specialists, teachers, even students—should be involved in some way in these processes. As well, strategic plans should be reviewed and updated annually, to ensure that the institution's curriculum and courses remain effective, well designed, technically relevant, and competitive.

First, administrators need to listen to teachers and take seriously their suggestions for change. Administrators at every managerial level in the institution need to be made aware of the current state of online programs and developments that will affect the curriculum. As well, administrators need to be familiar with the bigger picture of online education globally. Because administrators have more power (i.e., they determine the budget for and direction of online education more than teachers can), they should deal with some of these bigger issues responsibly. A strategic plan, based on data from teachers as well as trends within the institution and outside academic and business communities, must reflect not only what is happening today at the local level, but also what probably will occur in the next few years globally.

Accreditation, the marketing of online programs, and strategic planning go beyond the daily or annual business of administering programs, hiring faculty, and updating the curriculum; they will affect the ability of online programs and courses to survive in a changing, challenging global marketplace.

Accreditation

Accreditation for online educational programs works a little differently than traditional accreditation for on-site courses and programs. However, the need for accreditation is the same. Learners, as well as other educational institutions and commercial vendors, must know that your institution's programs provide high-quality instruction that has been evaluated by an impartial, outside agency that works regularly with online education.

Because so many courses are offered by so many different businesses and institutions, it is often difficult for potential students to determine which courses are the best for them to take. Several academic and commercial vendors may offer seemingly similar course content. Particularly learners who need or want recognized credit for their online coursework need to feel confident that the courses they take have been held accountable to some agency other than the institution offering courses. Accreditation is one way to give students this confidence.

Of course, accreditation is important to faculty and administrators, too. Being affiliated with accredited programs makes good professional sense. If you want people to take your online courses seriously, accreditation is an important step in developing credibility.

Regional accrediting agencies evaluate and approve traditional on-site academic institutions and their programs. In the United States, non-governmental agencies monitor and review distance learning institutions based in one of six geographic regions. The agency within that region oversees a particular institution.

The six agencies in the U.S. are the Middle States Association, the Northwest Association of Schools and Colleges, the North Central Association of Colleges and Schools, the New England Association of Schools and Colleges, the Southern Association of Colleges and Schools, and the Western Association of Schools and Colleges. The standards across the regions are uniform; degrees and courses from one accredited school in one region can be transferred to another accredited institution in another region. Regionally accredited schools may accept courses from accredited distance learning programs, or they may not recognize this accreditation. Distance learning courses and programs are usually evaluated separately from on-site institutions' programs.

These standards are made available online or in print. For example, The Higher Learning Commission of the North Central Association of Colleges and Schools provides an extensive PDF document to help educators prepare for accreditation reviews. This overview will be updated with the results of a new accreditation survey. The Commission started reviewing requirements in 2001, with the results of Restructuring Expectations: Accreditation 2004 becoming the product of this review (Higher Learning Commission, 2001). Administrators should keep an eye on new developments in accreditation and updates from their institution's accrediting body.

Accreditation offers quality assurance regarding the curriculum and course design. Areas that may be assessed during accreditation include curriculum, instructional methods, course and program evaluation processes, the availability of library resources and other learning materials, and institutional services, such as student services. Facilities and financial soundness are also considered (Yeung, 2001).

The program's or institution's quality might also be evaluated by the number and types of activities that help socialize learners. Experiences that benefit learners' lives by helping students work well with others should be reviewed, and the institution should actively plan ways for bringing learners together for meaningful social/learning experiences (Bower, 2001). Showing how learners interact with each other, faculty, and administrators may be especially important for online programs, because the lack of face-to-face interaction is often a criticism levied against online education.

The accreditation process also can illustrate the institution's credibility. Rahman (2001) described five areas for a successful program to be able to recruit and retain high-quality faculty (and presumably learners as well). These areas—program, faculty, process (i.e., there are established, fair policies followed by the institution), platform, and leadership credibility—must be carefully developed. These seem to be effective checkpoints for accreditation, too.

Online education falls under distance learning, which is accredited in the United States by the Distance Education and Training Council (DETC). The DETC is nationally recognized as the accreditation agency for institutions that sponsor home-study programs; the Council does not just accredit online educational programs, but any type of home study.

An institution's online programs can be evaluated if the institution is recognized as a "real" academic institution and has operated online programs for at least two years. The DETC does not check programs and invite institutions to apply for accreditation; it is up to the school to apply by sending an Application for Accreditation to the DETC. Schools are not automatically accredited; they must meet the DETC's published standards. Even if a school is accredited, it must comply with DETC regulations and file annual reports, for example. A school is then reviewed every five years to see if it will keep its accreditation.

According to information provided at the DETC Web site, this online accreditation process is unique in the U.S. The basis of accreditation is the instructional method, not the educational level of the subject matter. Unlike regional accrediting agencies that do evaluate subject matter, educational level of courses, and instructional methods, the DETC is the only body that accredits online programs and courses, whether they are degree, non-degree, vocational, or avocational. If it is online education, the DETC accreditation is the one to seek.

Educational sites provide a great deal of information about the latest in accreditation of online programs. A good place to read about the latest in distance education is *The Chronicle of Higher Education* (2002), in print and online; you can also search for information about accreditation. The *Virtual University's Gazette* (2002) provides basic information about accreditation. Although the site is primarily geared toward students, the FAQ list cites information about accreditation and why it is important for online educational institutions.

Of course, you should check the DETC's Web site for explanations of accreditation and the process of receiving it. These and other useful Web sites, as well as print information from regional accrediting bodies and the DETC, can help you determine how best to prepare for accreditation and why it benefits your institution and your students to have accredited online programs.

Once accreditation has taken place, information about the accrediting body and exactly what has received accreditation should be posted prominently on the program's or university's Web site. Potential and current faculty and students are interested in accreditation and want to belong to an accredited educational body. Prospective students look for a measure of quality when they decide to which institutions they want to apply. Displaying accreditation information at the course and program Web sites is a good way of showing that online education at this institution is highly regarded.

The University of Phoenix Online (2002), for example, provides a link to information about its accreditation and lists its affiliation as a member of the North Central Association. American Intercontinental University (2002) lists the address and phone number of the Commission on Colleges of the Southern Association of Colleges and Schools. This university also notes on its About AIU Online pages that its degrees at all levels—associate, bachelor, and master—have been accredited. Designing similar links to accrediting bodies and highlighting accreditation status are good ways to promote your programs.

Marketing

Knowing your niche market in an important part of a course's, program's, or institution's success. You can have the most wonderful online courses in the world, but if they do not meet a specific group of learners' needs, no one will take the courses and know how wonderful they are. Online learners may be different from students who want a traditional venue. If they are taking classes only online, they probably are adults with a busy schedule and many competing responsibilities. They may be interested in a degree program or a series of courses. They may be computer literate, but not yet have the latest, fastest equipment.

That still describes a large number of potential learners. You need to determine who needs *online* education, not just distance learning. For example, Michael Fragale, United States' Public Broadcasting Service's Adult Learning Service, explained in a July 6, 2001 *Chronicle of Higher Education* article that the number of students taking PBS' telecourses rose from 55,000 students in 1980 to an expected 450,000 in 2001 (Carr, 2001). Although Internet-based classes are growing, there is still a large audience for telecourses in distance education.

Even within distance education, segments of the learner population prefer courses using different instructional media: correspondence with print, CD, video, or audio components; broadcast telecourses; interactive TV; or Internet. You need to know the format that is best for learners studying the subject areas covered in your courses and the level of technology they can access. Just because online information is available to some people does not mean that older distance learning technologies are not viable for a large market.

Joining the online revolution does not mean that institutions have to eliminate any other distance learning programs currently in place. Some courses are better suited to other presentation methods than those available through the Internet. Some learners prefer other instructional methods, and lots of people still do not have daily access to computers. Administrators and teachers need to know what online education can offer the institution's niche market that other distance education programs cannot.

Unique features that make a program stand out from that of a competitor should also be identified and played up. One selling point may be that the online institution and its programs are accredited, by the DETC and/or specific professions' accreditation agencies. Other selling points may be that the program or courses offer different instructional methods or specialized subject matter. If courses or the institution has been recognized by professional associations or educational groups for an award, this information can be made part of the marketing program. If faculty members have received federal or private sector grants for researching or improving practices in online education, the program's target market should be made aware that faculty are on the cutting edge of online education and continually striving to improve the quality of the curriculum and individual courses.

A preliminary market analysis should take place before courses are developed. However, as courses and the curriculum are upgraded, it is time to revisit this issue. The institution should note any special awards, grants, or accreditation received since the courses were first offered or curriculum first implemented. The current course offerings must still (most importantly) be meeting learners' needs and be competitive in the present market.

Administrators and teachers should meet to discuss questions like these: Are online courses providing information to meet the audience's learning styles and preferences? Is the level of technology too low, too high? Are the acceptable types of hardware and software too broad for adequate troubleshooting and learner assistance? Are hardware and software too specific, so that not everyone can take the classes being offered? Do institutional requirements for hardware and software need to be updated? These are not just design questions; they have an impact on the marketing strategy and the number and type of potential learners you want to reach.

If other institutions in the area are marketing the latest technology as part of their online programs, administrators have some choices: try to keep up with or surpass competitors' technology, go lower tech to reach a market that cannot meet higher-tech requirements, or develop programs using technology that no one else is offering. Technology and subject matter are two big issues in marketing courses. You have to ensure that learners can get the information they need easily and provide courses that are necessary to improve learners' skills, provide new experiences, and add to their knowledge.

Educators often debate whether online education is creating more of a "have/have not" society. As technology advances, and items like streaming video and interactive computer conferencing become the norm in online courses, will more or fewer people be able to take online courses? Will high-tech requirements allow only the computer savvy or learners with the capability of buying the latest equipment to take courses online? Will companies and institutions subsidize education by providing suitable hardware and software for learners, or will that drive up the price again? If only low-tech educational solutions are used, will highly computer literate learners be turned off by slower, older methods of communication and information retrieval? Will the use of lower levels of technology and primarily print media for information dissemination and communication be the most effective means of getting across subject matter? You have to understand where learners are now—technologically and economically—and which groups you want to target that are different from this current audience.

For example, public access computers are allowing people who do not own computers more access to the Web. Although these computer systems are not the fastest or latest technology, they are opening the Internet to more potential learners. Lower-tech courses that can be accessed easily from public terminals, such as those in libraries or community centers, may reach a new group of learners who would benefit from some online courses. They may not be able to afford both a computer at home and online courses toward a degree, but they may be able to take courses if they do not have to outlay large sums of money for a computer system.

Whatever is decided about the levels of technology and which courses are best suited to be online, the educational strategy has to be consistent and lead to an effective marketing strategy. You cannot offer everything to everyone. So to whom do you want to continue to market your programs? Which new markets for your programs have arisen since the last time the marketing strategy was updated? Answers to these questions drive everything else, from course updates to curriculum development to faculty training to program promotion. A sound educational strategy needs to be in place, so that you can continue to market, or assist those who market your programs.

Use university resources to help market degree programs in particular. Most institutions have a public relations office that can assist with the creation of brochures, Web-site promotions, broadcast advertisements, and press releases. Although costs associated with these promotional materials need to be budgeted, professional help from university staff who can work with teachers and administrators is a good investment. These professionals understand the institution and can talk with the people in different departments who are responsible for various aspects of an online degree program.

However, other avenues for letting people know about your program should not be overlooked. Links within the university's Web site can guide people to information about your program. Linking approved program information to Internet search engines like Excite, Google, and Yahoo can bring hits to your site (Lynch, 2002). Linking your program with the appropriate professional associations can help spread the word.

Campus professional associations, including chapters of national organizations and alumni groups (Lynch, 2002), may assist in promoting your programs. You might see if you can get a feature about the online degree published in print and electronic campus newspapers, magazines, and alumni publications. Using all of the university's resources can help make your marketing more effective and reasonably priced.

Strategic Planning and Trends in Online Education

Strategic planning should illustrate how the curriculum should grow—which courses need to be added or removed, which courses need to be updated immediately or on a regular schedule of updates. However, strategic planning as technology changes also includes more than pedagogical changes based on course content. It also includes anticipated developments in technology and a realization of how quickly or slowly those innovations will reach the majority of prospective learners. Then the institution needs to upgrade hardware, software, and networks to accommodate the changes as incrementally as possible, to avoid techno- logical culture shock for teachers and learners. As the need for specific courses is determined, the number of highly qualified and trained faculty must be in place to facilitate these courses. Strategic planning must account for the curriculum, the people involved in presenting and learning it, and the technology used to implement the curriculum.

Strategic planning is important for every curriculum, but the plan cannot be put away and forgotten until it is time to develop the next required plan. A strategic plan should be a vibrant document that is checked frequently. If a deviation from the plan is necessary, the modification should be documented and a rationale provided for the change. At times, the modification may indicate the need for a whole new strategic plan, which is then developed and discussed right away. Strategic plans must reflect the institution's mission and the direction for online education. They must be workable plans that have the faculty's and administration's support. Following and updating an online program's strategic plan is an important managerial activity.

A strategic plan should emphasize not only the immediate institutional needs and priorities—such as developing and updating programs, imple- menting a curriculum or curricular changes, marketing programs, and preparing for accreditation. It also should acknowledge and help educators plan for changes within the larger "outside" world of online education. As society and technology change, new issues arise that demand administra- tive policies that protect and assist teachers and learners. Some current issues include privacy, ownership of information, plagiarism, and general security of online information. As changes occur, new issues must be considered by faculty and administrators, and new initiatives added to the strategic plan.

The concept of using shared learning objects or multimedia teaching objects requires administrators to envision their courses as part of a larger educational effort that raises questions about the independent structure of one institution's online programs. Usability testing and the development of standards of online courses and programs may require the institution more formally to evaluate its online courses and development processes. Privacy policies and security are ongoing concerns that must be part of a strategic plan. These areas must be revisited as new social, legal, and technological changes take place within a country as well as globally.

These and other issues are facing everyone who helps develop and deliver online curricula. Those who work with a strategic plan need to be made aware of changes within online education and begin to plan now for their responses through possible changes in policies and practices.

Shared Learning Objects

Administrators and teachers should consider the implications of using shared learning objects for their courses and programs. A learning object is a shared piece of information that could be used by learners taking the same kind of course at any institution. The teachers or course designers would not have to develop their own information if a high-quality version is readily accessible online. Downes (2001) reminded educators that if a common document is available online in general, it is available worldwide. If teachers create even one educational document and make it accessible on the Internet, then educational institutions that teach the same subject matter could use that Web-stored educational document.

Engelhardt, Kárpát, Rack and Schmidt (2001) referred to this information as *multimedia teaching objects*, but their purpose is the same: to share well-designed, commonly used information among teachers and institutions. Shared multimedia information can enhance online courses by providing tested, usable, engaging materials without requiring individual teachers or course designers to produce such technically advanced applications.

Why should institutions consider sharing information or teaching objects? Cost is one factor (Downes, 2001). High-quality interactive materials are expensive and time consuming to produce. Technical design sophistication is another reason; many online teachers or course designers do not have the equipment or know-how to produce extensive multimedia presentations (Engelhardt et al., 2001). A third reason may become program survival. If institutions do not share information and try to go at it alone in the marketplace, they may not be able to compete with universities or colleges that are part of a collaborative agreement. Individual institutions may not be able to keep pace with competitors who offer flashy multimedia that offer learners multisensory, highly interactive course materials (Downes, 2001).

The use of shared learning objects raises some questions that administrators and teachers have to consider about the future of their online programs: Who owns the information? Who is the owner of this intellectual property? Who is responsible for creating the objects or information to be shared? How credible are the objects—or their creators? How well do the objects fit into current courses? How can courses incorporate the learning objects instead of being built around available objects? How does the use of shared learning objects enhance each course and the curriculum as a whole?

Sharing information that is increasingly expensive to produce seems like a good idea. However, each institution should base the creation and use of learning objects not solely on economic factors. Of course, it is helpful if costs can be cut in materials production and if the availability of more multimedia presentations attracts more learners. The quality of the curriculum should be enhanced, not sacrificed, by the use of learning objects. Educators should still be responsible for creating or sharing appropriate information and selecting which objects are useful to learners enrolled in specific courses.

Usability Testing of Academic Courses

Usability testing seems like a good idea, even if in its formal stages it can be a costly budget item. After all, each course site must work if learners are going to locate information and, you hope, learn from it. However, usability testing does more than answer the question Does it work?

Usability testing also involves beta testing several elements. For example, these areas might be the focus of one or several tests: how users really find information within the design, if the design is readable and attractive, if the information is easily understood, how effective the site-navigation devices actually are, and whether learners with different styles and preferences work equally well with online materials, for example. All components of usability—including readability, functionality, comprehension, and design features—can be studied to see if the course materials, site structure, and individual course sites are indeed "learnable" for an appropriate variety of users. In fact, if educators want online information to invite more than just "users" of a site, usability testing should be involved so that the people who work with the course information truly are "learners" through the site.

Few teachers work with the human factors research enough to be able to test a course site adequately. However, you can alpha test your own site before it is launched for others to use. In addition, the institution can set up some less formal beta tests with current learners and faculty, just to see if the interface is as transparent as you think it is or if the use of the navigation tools really is intuitive.

These useful tests should be conducted as the course design is being developed. More substantive usability tests can provide course designers, administrators, and teachers with data to enhance future modifications to the course site and development of additional courses. These tests also can identify potential problems that typical learners may have with the site. Right now most institutions emphasize the functionality of course sites, and that may be enough for the time being. However, the need for further formal usability testing may not be so far away, and administrators should start planning for it now.

In an April 2002 *eLearn Magazine* article, Quigley explained that the standards and usability tests that are appropriate for e-business might need to be modified before they can be applied to online education. However, standards for e-commerce have been proven worthy; setting standards for online education may require different standards that are appropriate to education, but the process is important. Making sure a course site is designed not only to be attractive and workable, but geared to promoting learning is the key to effective testing of educational sites. One direction for further research is to test the usability of each course design to supplement ongoing research in human-computer interfaces and cognitive studies.

The educational market currently does not demand formal usability testing, but administrators may want to begin planning and budgeting for future in-depth tests. Quigley (2002) noted that administrators need to realize the importance of usability testing. Because as yet there are no requirements or outcry for time- and cost-intensive training, administrators may not feel a sense of urgency to impose standards on course designers at their institutions. Planning ahead for future testing and standards, however, would be valuable.

Developing usability standards may yet be on the horizon, but administrators and teachers should receive a heads-up notice now. Beginning to test course designs more fully and working with human factors experts to develop some preliminary quantitative and qualitative tests can only help enhance course and curriculum design.

Privacy and Security

Creating a safe learning environment, in which teachers are fairly certain that students are who they say they are, only authorized learners and academic community members have access to online information, and electronic information is protected, requires the technical specialists, faculty members, and administrators to have a plan in place. Most often, the technical security of a system is the domain of IT specialists, who receive input from other members of the institution. Other policies, such as those involving privacy, tend to be established by the administration in response to legal or social initiatives. However, at whatever level is appropriate, these concerns must be addressed before learners and teachers can feel that their online classroom is a secure, supportive environment that promotes learning and collaboration.

Privacy

Who has access to view files? What kinds of information are being gathered by the institution? How is personal information used? These are just a few questions surrounding online privacy, especially as it relates to learners' and faculty members' use of institutional Web sites.

Information about site users may be gathered from group e-mail, bulletin board posts, chat transcripts, newsgroup listings, and whiteboard files, for example. Whenever people use a public forum for their information, they should be aware that others will read, and may use in a different context, their information.

Personal information submitted through online forms, evaluations, or questionnaires may be stored and evaluated by a host of administrators, faculty, or even outside audiences. Although site visitors or students who are asked to fill out these interactive documents can choose not to participate, they may not realize how their information can be used, or who ultimately may view their comments or personal information if they do participate.

Online courses may be monitored, so interactions among the learners and teacher can be documented or evaluated by administrators or other teachers. Cookies may store information about passwords or system preferences. Tracking the way learners and teachers use institutional course and other Web sites also may take place, so that the computer used to access the site is noted. The duration of the visit, type of browser, and paths taken among pages can be recorded.

All these examples involve privacy issues, and novice teachers or learners may have no idea how much information has been compiled about them and their computing practices. An equally serious concern is the way that information will be used and the people who will have access to it.

Administrators, in collaboration with faculty, staff, and learners, need to develop policies regarding the types and amounts of information being collected and acceptable ways for data to be used. Everyone who accesses the institution's Web site or databases or uses institutional computers must be made aware of how, when, and especially why information is being gathered.

The University of Arizona's Electronic Privacy Statement (2002) does an effective job of describing the type of information collected by the University: e-mail and forms, system generated, monitoring, and cookies. The policy details how this information is to be used and indicates an alternative to online submission of personal information. Throughout the multipage site, the University emphasizes that information gathered electronically is kept in house and is not sold or distributed to outside parties. Cautions about public electronic information, such as messages posted on bulletin boards, are made to users, who are also notified that the University does not keep transcripts or logs of public information. Confidential information, such as student records, is protected by law. The types of electronic data and their possible uses and safeguards are well delineated in this document.

Many universities and colleges emphasize their privacy policies at the institutional Web site. Online courses then should provide a link to the institution's privacy statement (and security information) so that learners understand the approach being taken to create a safe learning environment. The flavor of the statement reflects each institution's special concerns about such a broad issue.

The Industrial Centre's site at The Hong Kong Polytechnic University (2002) assures users that it not only complies with the Personal Data (Privacy) Ordinance, but that it will try to exceed global standards.

The Robert Gordon University (2002) in the United Kingdom explains all situations in which certain types of information are used for practical projects or ongoing research. Data may be gathered through click-stream, HTTP protocol elements, and searches, and site users are alerted to these possibilities. Contact information and detailed descriptions of data types are prominently displayed in this privacy policy.

Canada's Athabasca University (2002) assures site visitors that the university does not sell or rent information gathered from its Web site. The data-collection process is described in reader-friendly language, which provides definitions of basic terms like *cookies*. All use of information complies with the relevant sections of the Alberta Freedom of Information and Protection of Privacy Act. E-mail, phone, and fax contact information conclude the privacy statement. The language used in this statement is easy to understand, and the style can help allay readers' fears about privacy violations.

In the U.S., the University of Alabama (2002) states up front that site users' privacy is respected and no data are collected unless visitors participate in online research. The University further explains how responses to electronic questionnaires are used. Privacy practices are in compliance with the Family Educational Rights and Privacy Act (FERPA). The University of Alabama's statement is thorough, highly readable, and concise—one page.

Niagara University (2002) takes a stylistically different approach by first listing ways that their Web site notifies users of information being collected. In greater detail, the University explains how information may be gathered and used by cookies, log files, newsletters, surveys, and referrals from friends. Opt-out mechanisms that give visitors the right to refuse providing personal information are in place throughout the site. This multipage document thoroughly details the University's practices.

WebCT courses offered through the University of Tasmania (2002) are password protected. The current privacy policy statement describes how server logs accumulate data about class members' access to the course site. This information is used to help designers improve the course. The data also allow teachers and university staff who have academic reasons for using the information to assist learners and to monitor their progress. All information gathered through the course site helps improve the online educational experience. The statement also cautions learners about posting messages in public places, such as bulletin boards and chat rooms, where other students can read them. Posting only information that you are comfortable with anyone knowing is a good rule of thumb. Phrasing the policy statement to address online course concerns is important. Individual courses may need privacy statements in addition to those written for the institution at large.

These examples illustrate the variety of approaches that institutions can take in presenting their privacy statements. The particular concerns of their students, faculty, staff, and target market influence how much information is presented and which issues are covered in greater detail. By understanding the concerns and interests of the majority of visitors to and users of your site, you can craft a well-organized, friendly statement that helps allay fears about interacting with Web-site information. In addition to describing policies affecting the entire institution, you may want to develop privacy policies that refer to situations specific to online courses or programs.

You may want to review several privacy policies before you develop your own, for an online course or program or the entire institution. Effective privacy policies should include descriptions of the following:

- Types of information gathered
- Situations in which information is gathered
- Ways the information is used
- Who can access the information
- Where information will be sold or rented, if applicable
- The length of time that information is kept

- Security measures in place to protect site visitors' or users' personal information
- Opt-out procedures and alternatives to sending personal information electronically
- Contact information to personnel who can answer questions about policies and procedures
- Applicable laws about privacy and security

You also may want to monitor sites that deal with privacy in general, just to keep up with trends in national and international privacy and security. Whether you are a teacher or an administrator, it is important to keep up with international trends and requirements if you are working with online education. Some organizations with sites that may be helpful include Privacy.org, Privacy International, Privacy.net, and the Online Privacy Alliance. These few examples are representative of a growing number of sites dealing with privacy and security issues.

Security

Another ongoing debate involves computer security not only for online programs, but also for the entire campus. Security measures should be included in the institutional policies relating to campus-wide computer use. Although these policies should be in place for on-site as well as online faculty, staff, and learners, they are especially important to those who work completely online and receive and submit electronic information.

Online security may involve something as simple as requiring updated virus-protection software and then making it available (preferably free) to all learners and teachers. The university or college may require teachers to accept assignments only through the course bulletin board or e-mail accounts, so that they can be automatically tracked and scanned for viruses.

Larger security measures may involve the distribution of passwords and login information created by IT personnel. Administrative policies then set standards for providing passwords to faculty and students and setting penalties for permitting unauthorized users to have these codes. The periodic changing of passwords also should be encouraged, if not monitored for compliance.

Files can be encrypted, and institutional policies established to keep Web sites, including course sites, and administrative databases as secure as possible. Students want to know, for example, that their records and payments are secure and that no unauthorized person may gain access to academic or personal information, such as credit card numbers. Servers can be made more secure for faculty files or databases (Lynch, 2002).

Many institutions have set up departmental groups or university/college committees to develop new policies as security measures change. Technological changes and shifts in the political climate may require security policies to evolve in response. Concerns about technoterrorism, for example, can provide the impetus for more stringent security measures.

A good example of a university-wide security statement is one created by Oxford University (2002). The Web site offers links for those needing more information about security issues or wanting to discuss new developments or concerns. The Computer Security Web pages link readers to virus-protection information, news about possible problem areas, and FAQ lists. The site links users to local and outside newsgroups, such as ox.sig.security, alt.comp.virus,   sci.crypt,   comp.os.netware.security,   and comp.security.firewalls. As you can tell from the names of these newsgroups, individual groups may emphasize a specific security topic. Contact information helps faculty in particular alert officials to possible problems or vulnerabilities with the current system.

Administrators at your university or college should establish a similar center for providing information and troubleshooting. This body also should advise administrators and faculty about the best way to protect electronic information.

Reports may be issued by faculty committees. For example, the University of Wisconsin-Madison's Web site offers a report compiled by the Ad Hoc Electronic Data Advisory Committee way back in 1991. This report provides information about similar security measures at other universities' IT Web sites. However, the policies put in place as long ago (in online educational terms) as the early 1990s are still an effective example of ways to emphasize information for faculty and administrators. Warnings about file confidentiality, comments about U.S. federal acts referring to privacy and security, definitions, security procedures, and recommendations are detailed in the committee's report. Promoting institutional policies and explaining the rationale for them go a long way in helping all faculty members be aware of and participate in the decision-making processes regarding security. Although this type of document should be updated when committee members or policies change, the level of detail in the University of Wisconsin-Madison's report makes it a useful model for developing your own policies and procedures.

As with privacy policies, you should review what other institutions are providing in their security statements. These examples will help your institution draft and electronically publish effective security standards.

Summary

Teachers, course designers, IT specialists, human factors experts, and administrators have important roles in the success of online education, and their roles should expand as online education becomes a more complex academic and business endeavor. As students', teachers', and administrators' expectations for online courses rise, so must the institutional commitment for updating programs and improving instructional design and technology used in courses.

Online courses must be marketed to those who need and want them, and learners must receive a high-quality education from their online classes. That means that everyone involved in online education must keep evaluating the subject matter and ways it is presented to students to ensure that each course is current, appropriate to the learners' needs, and accurate.

Accreditation is one step in documenting the effectiveness of your online programs, but that alone is not enough. Keeping up with what the competition is doing and developing programs specifically designed for online education marketed toward a specific group of learners are keys to program success.

Upcoming issues, including the use of shared learning objects and the need for formal usability testing, are just some concerns and interests of educators involved with online learning. The nature of teaching online is changing. As new issues arise, the academic community must work together to develop newer, more flexible policies regarding education, without sacrificing the quality of the learning or working environment.

The online learning/teaching environment must be a secure, protected place where students and educators feel safe working together. Building security measures to protect information from being accessed by those without authorization is critical to the ongoing success of online education. Teachers and learners should not fear possible misuses of information gathered by institutions or lack of privacy. All sorts of privacy and security concerns need to be dealt with, not only in the planning stages of a course or curriculum, but throughout the growth and continuing management of online education.

Teachers have special concerns about the ways that their online work is perceived by others inside and outside of their institution, and administrators need to find creative and supportive ways to bring all faculty members together. Helping the university or college community to understand online education and its place within the institution is a required task for both administrators and teachers.

Online education can be profitable for commercial vendors and academic institutions, but the aim should be high-quality education, presented in the best online formats available for the targeted learners, and taught by well-trained, confident faculty. The infrastructure for supporting online education needs to be carefully planned and maintained, today and with strategic plans for the future. Policies and strategic plans must be responsive to changes in technology and global trends. Teachers, administrators, and learners must work together to achieve success in online programs.

References

American Intercontinental University. (2002). About AIU online. Retrieved October 2, 2002, from http://aiudegreeonline.com/2/about.jsp

Athabasca University. (2002). Web site privacy statement. Retrieved October 16, 2002, from http://athabasca.ca/misc/privacy.htm

Bower, B. L. (2001). Distance education: Facing the faculty challenge. *Online Journal of Distance Learning Administration, IV*(II). State University of West Georgia. Retrieved October 3, 2002, from http://www.westga.edu/~distance/ojdla/summer42/bower42.html

Carr, S. (2001, July 6). PBS sticks to its strategy for telecourses, unafraid of competition from the Internet. *The Chronicle of Higher Education*. Retrieved July 15, 2001, from http://chronicle.com/free/2001/07/200107060Iu.htm

The Chronicle of Higher Education. (2002). Retrieved October 8, 2002, from http://chronicle.com/distance

Distance Education and Training Council. (2001). What does accreditation mean? Retrieved October 8, 2002, from http://www.detc.org/content/whatdo.html

Downes, S. (2001, July). Learning objects: Resources for distance education worldwide. *The International Review of Research in Open and Distance Learning*. Retrieved March 12, 2003, from http://www.irrodl.org/content/v2.1/downes.html

Englehardt, M., Kárpát, A., Rack, T., & Schmidt, T.C. (2001). A virtual knowledge marketplace. *European Journal of Open and Distance Learning*. Retrieved May 1, 2002, from http://www1.nks.no/eurodl/shoen/icl01/schmidt/ICL2001_paper.html

The Higher Learning Commission. (2001). *Accreditation of higher education institutions: An overview*. Chicago: North Central Association of Colleges and Schools. Retrieved October 2, 2002, from http://www.ncacihe.org/overview/200/HLCOverview.pdf

Industrial Centre. The Hong Kong Polytechnic University. (2002). Privacy policy statements. Retrieved October 16, 2002, from http://www.ic.polyu.edu.hk/privacy.htm

Lynch, M. M. (2002). *The online educator: A guide to creating the virtual classroom*. London: Routledge/Falmer.

Niagara University. (2002). Privacy statement. Retrieved October 16 2002, from http://www.niagara.edu/privacy.htm

Oxford University. (2002). Information technology security. Retrieved October 17, 2002, from http://www.ox.ac.uk/it/compsecurity/

Quigley, A. (2002, April 4). Usability-tested e-learning? Not until the market requires it. *eLearn Magazine*. Retrieved April 10, 2002, from http://www.elearnmag.org/

Rahman, M. (2001, Winter). Faculty recruitment strategies for online programs. *Online Journal of Distance Learning Administration, IV*(IV). State University of West Georgia. Retrieved July 20, 2002, from http://www.westga.edu/~distance/ojdla/ winter44/rahman44.html

The Robert Gordon University. (2002). Privacy policy. Retrieved October 16, 2002, from http://www.rgu.ac.uk/policy/privacy.cfm

University of Alabama. (2002). Privacy policy. Retrieved October 16, 2002, from http://www.rolltide.com/Home/5253.asp

University of Arizona. (2002). University of Arizona electronic privacy statement. Revision 5/16/2002. Retrieved October 16, 2002, from http;//info-center.ccit.arizona.edu/ ~security/uaelectprivstmt.htm

University of Phoenix Online. (2002). Accreditation. Retrieved October 1, 2002, from http://www.uoponline.com/accred.asp

University of Tasmania. (2002). University of Tasmania WebCT interim privacy policy statement. Retrieved October 16, 2002, from http://www.utas.edu.au/coursesonline/privacy/

University of Wisconsin-Madison. (1991). Report of the University of Wisconsin—Madison Ad Hoc Electronic Data Advisory Committee. Policies and procedures governing access to electronic files. Retrieved October 17, 2002, from http://www.doit.wise.edu/security/ policies/uwaccess.htm

Virtual University's Gazette. (2002). Retrieved October 8, 2002, from http://www.geteducated.com/articles/d/faq.htm

Yeung, D. (2001, Winter). Quality assurance of Web-based learning in distance education institution. *Online Journal of Distance Learning Administration, IV*(IV). State University of West Georgia. Retrieved May 1, 2002, from http://www.westga.edu/~distance/ojdla/ winter44/yeung44.html

GLOSSARY

ALN	Asynchronous Learning Network; a network of learners that collaborate asynchronously to complete learning activities or share information
asynchronous	not in real time; completed at the user's convenience; e.g., e-mail is asynchronous
bandwidth	the amount of information that can be sent across an Internet connection; often measured in bits per second (bps); e.g., when you check the current bandwidth for your dial-up Internet connection, you see 52999 bps, which means that 52999 bits of information per second are being sent through the current dial-up connection
behaviorism	a teaching strategy or method that allows a teacher to impart information to students, such as through lectures or notes; more passive method of acquiring information
constructivism	a teaching strategy or method that allows students to apply concepts they have learned and to make meaning from more abstract concepts; often involves activities such as workshops, problem-

	solving activities, or other ways of applying what has been learned to practical situations
cookie	information from a server to a browser that the browser then saves and sends back to the server on request; user information and preferences are often stored in cookies
courseware	software to help you create an online course; software that allows you to structure an online course
external link	hypertext link that leads outside your Web site
external support network	a group of people and available resources found outside the university or college to assist faculty and staff
for-credit course	course taken for hourly credit toward a specific degree; course taken to meet requirements of a program or degree
FTP	File Transfer Protocol; a way to retrieve or send files through the Internet; a method of file retrieval or submission in use before the Web
GIF	Graphic Interchange Format; usually smaller graphics files than JPEG/JPG files; useful graphics format when the graphic has large areas of the same color, such as line art or logos
HTML	Hypertext Markup Language; a system of codes used to format information for viewing on the Web
hybrid class	a course involving regularly scheduled face-to-face sessions and required

	Internet interaction; a course that is a blend of online and on-site course methods and technologies
internal link	a hypertext link to information within your Web site
internal support network	a group of people and available resources within the university or college to assist faculty and staff
JPG	sometimes seen as JPEG; Joint Photographic Experts Group; a graphics format that is best for photographic files; a format generally with larger file sizes that GIF files
mailing list	a group of subscribers sharing similar interests to which e-mail is sent and then copied and distributed to all subscribers
multimedia	media providing multisensory experiences, such as sound, visuals, animation, and interaction with the media
non-credit course	course not taken for hourly credit toward a specific degree; course taken for personal interest or retraining, but not toward completion of a degree
peripheral	an extra piece of hardware or software needed to operate resources or to provide information; e.g., a CD with information to supplement the course Web site's resources
plug-in	usually small software that adds features to a larger program
PNG	Portable Network Graphics; a graphics format specifically for use on the Web

	that can compress images without losing their quality
shared learning objects	information that can be used by several different courses, institutions, instructors, students, etc., and is made available on the Web for more people to use
streaming audio	real-time or asynchronous audio information that can be played online; e.g., real-time audio such as a radio broadcast, or asynchronous audio such as a prerecorded speech
streaming video	real-time or asynchronous video information that can be played online; e.g., real-time video such as a news broadcast, or asynchronous video such as a previously taped lecture
URL	Uniform Resource Locator; the address of an Internet resource; now often replaced with the term Uniform Resource Identifier (URI)
XHTML	Extensible Hypertext Markup Language; a language combining features of Extensible Markup Language (XML) and Hypertext Markup Language (HTML); requires more precision in coding but allows more flexibility in Web design
XML	Extensible Markup Language; a language that defines data formats for complex documents; offers a broader scope of formatting options than Hypertext Markup Language (HTML)

INDEX

A

academic curriculum 31
academic integrity 51, 190
academic socialization 34
academic standards 256
accreditation 68, 98, 285
activities 5, 77, 162, 191
activity fees 15
adjunct 262
adjunct faculty 110, 231
administrators 31, 77, 117, 222, 248, 276
aesthetics 189
alpha 97
alpha test 297
American Center for the Study of Distance Education 235
American Distance Education Consortium (ADEC) 233, 235
American Psychological Association (APA) 169, 206
animation 10, 56
announcements 141, 167, 232
assignment 5, 40, 78, 118, 162, 190, 226, 261, 278
assignment sheets 8, 91, 171, 268
asynchronous 7, 41, 89, 121, 170, 192, 258
Asynchronous Learning Networks (ALNs) 199
attachment 148
auditory learner 72

B

bandwidth 51
behaviorism 12
behaviorist approach 12, 40
beta test 97, 296
broadcast 56
browser 226, 299
bulletin board 7, 34, 85, 118, 162, 194, 225, 254, 278

C

Canadian Association for Distance Education (CADE) 235
CDs 88
chat 226, 278
chat room 34, 85
chat sessions 10, 118, 162, 191
checklists 71
class sizes 261
codes of conduct 215
codes of fair practice 215
committees 229
Commonwealth of Learning 235
compensation 254
compressed multimedia files 58
conference 223, 253
conference call 108, 122, 191, 254
confidentiality agreements 208
conforming learners 71
constructivism 12
constructivist approach 12, 40
cookies 299
copyright 51, 89, 156, 250
course activities 252
course design 31, 118, 172, 256, 277
course designer 5, 79, 118, 224, 258, 286
course development 258
course evaluations 81
course loads 254
course materials 40, 80, 251, 277
course objectives 21
course readings 123
course registration 33

About The Author

Lynnette R. Porter is a writer and teacher who has taught online, Web-enhanced, and on-site classes at several universities in the United States. She earned an M.A. in English and technical writing and a Ph.D. in English, with specializations in rhetoric, composition, and technical communication. Her research interests are varied, but since the mid-1990s have emphasized online education. She has presented papers or participated in conferences held by the Society for Technical Communication, Association of Teachers of Technical Writing, Asia-Pacific Chapter of the Association for the Advancement of Computing in Education, Australasian Society for Computers in Learning in Tertiary Education, National Business and Career Education Association, Popular Culture Association, American Businesswomen's Association, and Association for Business Communication. She is a fellow in and a former board member of the Society for Technical Communication.

International Journal of Distance Education Technologies (JDET)

NEW! **NEW!**

The International Source for Technological Advances in Distance Education

ISSN:	1539-3100
eISSN:	1539-3119
Subscription:	Annual fee per volume (4 issues): Individual US $85 Institutional US $185
Editors:	Shi Kuo Chang University of Pittsburgh, USA
	Timothy K. Shih Tamkang University, Taiwan

Mission

The *International Journal of Distance Education Technologies* (**JDET**) publishes original research articles of distance education four issues per year. **JDET** is a primary forum for researchers and practitioners to disseminate practical solutions to the automation of open and distance learning. The journal is targeted to academic researchers and engineers who work with distance learning programs and software systems, as well as general participants of distance education.

Coverage

Discussions of computational methods, algorithms, implemented prototype systems, and applications of open and distance learning are the focuses of this publication. Practical experiences and surveys of using distance learning systems are also welcome. Distance education technologies published in **JDET** will be divided into three categories, **Communication Technologies, Intelligent Technologies, and Educational Technologies**: new network infrastructures, real-time protocols, broadband and wireless communication tools, quality-of-services issues, multimedia streaming technology, distributed systems, mobile systems, multimedia synchronization controls, intelligent tutoring, individualized distance learning, neural network or statistical approaches to behavior analysis, automatic FAQ reply methods, copyright protection and authentification mechanisms, practical and new learning models, automatic assessment methods, effective and efficient authoring systems, and other issues of distance education.

For subscription information, contact:

Idea Group Publishing
701 E Chocolate Ave., Suite 200
Hershey PA 17033-1240, USA
cust@idea-group.com
URL: www.idea-group.com

For paper submission information:

Dr. Timothy Shih
Tamkang University, Taiwan
tshih@cs.tku.edu.tw

Just Released!

Web-Based Education:
Learning from Experience

Anil Aggarwal
University of Baltimore, USA

During the past two decades, tele-communication and Web-enabled technologies have combined to create a new field of knowledge known as "Web-Based Learning and Teaching Technologies." The main objective of *Web-Based Education: Learning From Experience* is to analyze the experiences gained while implementing and utilizing these technologies. The book addresses many issues associated with Web-based education, and explores the opportunities and problems faced by colleges and universities to effectively develop and manage Web-based education programs and environments.

WEB-BASED EDUCATION: Learning From Experience — Anil Aggarwal — Information Science Publishing

ISBN 1-59140-102-X(h/c); eISBN 1-59140-110-0 • Price: US $74.95 • 350 pages • © 2003